HELLO, THANK YOU,

GOOD-BYE!

Modern Adventures in
an Ancient World

iUniverse, Inc.
New York Bloomington

Hello, Thank You, Good-Bye!

Modern Adventures in an Ancient World

iUniverse books may be ordered through booksellers or by contacting:

iUniverse
1663 Liberty Drive
Bloomington, IN 47403
www.iuniverse.com
1-800-Authors (1-800-288-4677)

ISBN: 978-1-4401-3655-9 (pbk)
ISBN: 978-1-4401-3654-2 (ebk)

Printed in the United States of America

iUniverse rev. date: 5/14/2010

HELLO, THANK YOU
GOOD-BYE!

Modern Adventures in an Ancient World

Written and Illustrated by

Aloha Williams

For Stephen
my travelling companion

&

For Mom
who nudged the idea into reality

Table of Contents

Introduction..1

Adjusting to Germany...3

Great Britain August 1998 8

Italian Blitz September 1998 24

Holland Fall 1998 36

Viva La France February 1999..43

Republic of Georgia May 1999 56

Russia June 1999..73

The Baltics States July 1999..89

Ode to Poland August 1999 102

Austria, Hungary, Slovakia & the Czech Republic September 1999...112

Our Pilgrimage to Israel November 1999 126

Egypt February 2000..145

Tunisia April 2000 164

Scandinavia June 2000 174

Kiev Ukraine July 2000...183

The Emerald Isle-Ireland August 2000.............................196

Greece September 2000...212

Swirling Dervishes of Turkey October 2000 224

Mad Dashes Through Germany November 2000 237

Morocco November 2000 246

Belgium December 2000...258

Andalucía Spain 2001 266

Paris in Spring May 2001 279

Souda Bay, Crete, June 2001 289

Iceland September 2003..295

The Azores September 2004 305

Afterword...314

Travel List 319

Introduction

"I don't want to go!"

"It's only for three years," my husband argued.

"That's an eternity! Why couldn't we stay here longer?"

We were comfortable in Texas living in a three-bedroom home nestled on an acre of land with a large swimming pool. Our neighbors brought us produce from their garden, raising the finest okra I've ever eaten. I had a fun part-time job teaching prospective teachers at a nearby university. Austin was a short haul down the highway where there was live music and water skiing. Even if I were the daughter of a geography professor, this was my home and I didn't want to leave.

As the wife of a military dentist I had followed my husband whenever and wherever his job took him moving like clockwork every three or four years. But we had never had a foreign assignment. When the orders came for Germany, it was a shock! I thought of everything that could possibly go wrong, mentally preparing for the worst. What if something happened to my parents while I was so far away? What about our single son? I had done some traveling before but always knew I could return home. Moving was an entirely different matter. Forget about exotic destinations, I wanted to stay planted on American soil.

Mixed emotions filled my heart and I moaned and groaned. Perhaps it was a cover for my fears. After a month of feeling sorry for myself, I began to reconcile to the inevitable move. I wasn't happy, but at least I didn't oppose it.

Now the question was what were we going to do about the relocation? I began asking anyone and everyone who had lived in Germany for advice. One experienced military wife said, "Don't try buying your way across Europe. You'll have to haul it home and it will get damaged." It was good advice. I tried to absorb all suggestions and began shuffling our possessions. Two shipments would go to Germany and one would stay in storage.

To make the most of our three impending years in Europe, our dinner conversations centered on what we really wanted from this move. Stephen is not a shopper. We didn't want to buy more stuff that we had to haul around until we retired. We weren't golfers, wine connoisseurs, or avid sports people. However, we did have in common a keen interest in foreign languages, and loved learning about new cultures. It didn't take us long to decide on travel. We could meet interesting people and have cultural adventures at the same time. From then on, our choices were made with travel in mind.

My enthusiasm began to grow. We started German language lessons. We pared down so that we would have money for trips. We elected to live on base, since it would be easier to leave for vacations. We sold our newer car and kept the older, smaller Nissan Sentra. We took only our living room furnishings, storing everything else.

We made a dream list of the sights we wanted to see. *Each of our thirty-six months had a destination.* Factors such as weather were considered when listing places like Scandinavia, (not in winter), and Egypt (not in summer). It was an ambitious plan, but was a starting point. As we expanded our list, we became more aware of possibilities.

Packed, and shipped, we headed to Germany, little guessing what great adventures lay in store.

Adjusting To Germany

June 1998

Bleary-eyed from the all-night flight from the States, I handed the immigration agent my passport. He stamped it and waved us on to claim our baggage. As we cleared customs we heard a voice.

"Stephen! Stephen!"

"Over here!" my husband shouted back.

"Welcome to Germany! I'm Dr. Perkins!" My husband's co-worker had come to pick us up. Introductions were made and I returned a few niceties. He drove us to our new home, an hour away from Frankfurt Airport. Our first glimpses were of tall dark forests and rolling grass-covered hills. Suddenly a car appeared from nowhere. It quickly roared past so fast that the van shook in its wake, our first experience with "No Speed Limits" on the autobahn!

As we pulled into the village of Landstuhl we were struck with the cleanliness of the town. Dr. Perkins announced that every Saturday morning folks were required to sweep the gutters in front of their houses. I thought he was joking but later found out it was true. I was tickled to see medieval half-timbered cottages and noticeably feel the tempo slowing down. Dr. Perkins pulled up to the headquarters on the hill and we piled out. He walked us through the entire building and introduced us to all the staff. I was in a fatigue-induced catatonic state, but Dr. Perkins reminded us to stay awake that we would adjust faster to the time difference. Somehow we managed to keep our eyelids open, but we were grateful to find our pillows that night.

We stayed on base our first two weeks, enabling us to function in English. When we stepped outside the gate, though, it was all German. The radio played familiar American music, but as soon as the announcer started talking in German I was lost.

Signs were in German. Fortunately the German language uses romanized letters, unlike the swirling letters in Asian countries, so you could at least attempt some understanding.

We had shipped our car out six weeks early, so it would be ready for us when we arrived. The car plan worked out well and we had transportation within a day of landing.

We quickly learned that the right lane on the autobahn is for slow traffic and trucks going around 55 mph. The left lane was for the fast autos. We learned to check our rearview mirror often since speeding cars sneaked up on us. Several times I checked my empty rearview mirror only a second later to see lights flashing from an oncoming car doing over 120 mph. The flashing meant for me to move over to the "slow lane." Getting a driver's license in Germany is expensive and challenging, so Germans handle the wheel better than Americans. However, because of high speeds when there is an accident, it is usually fatal.

Our experience with German telephones was more frustrating. In the United States all phone number are ten digits including the area code. In Germany phone numbers are not uniform. One phone number may have only seven digits, while another has eleven. The first few numbers change depending on whether you are calling within the country or long distance. I frequently got wrong numbers and every time heard: *Kein an schluss fuer diese telefon nummer*, which meant that you got the wrong number! If you were lucky you could sometimes request an English speaking operator. I don't remember how many times I slammed down the receiver in frustration.

The German money was easy to use. As the value of the bill increased so did the size of the bill and each denomination was printed in a different color. I wish that the United States would adopt this practice, since I have heard many international visitors struggle with our same-size, same-colored money.

After two weeks our apartment in a four-plex on Landstuhl post came available and we could order our furniture to be unpacked. Until our shipment arrived we used loaner furniture, a bed, a kitchen table and a couch. We were pleased that our apartment was spacious and had large windows.

We quickly learned to love the German window system. The windows open sideways into the house making them easy to clean. There is an outside cover called a *latten* that rolls down over the glass, not only protecting it, but also closing out any light at night. Because the window ledges were a foot wide I could place plants on the sill without fear of them falling. The curtains could be washed easily without removing the little plastic hangars. I appreciated not poking myself with a sharp metal clip each time I cleaned the curtains.

Germans built their houses to last centuries, not generations. So the walls were very sturdy, made of concrete with no drywall. When we accidentally hit our heads there was no buffer and it hurt! I quickly learned to gauge the distance of the solid walls.

Our other neighbors across the hallway, Peter and Suzanne, gave us a warm welcome! The wife was the military soldier and her husband was the spouse who followed her around the world. Their two daughters, Kristine and Charlene, were smart and vivacious. Our hallway conversations yielded lots of good information. It was nice to have someone who was already familiar with the way things were done. Our upstairs neighbors were Pat and Mike with two daughters. They were also cordial. One holiday they arranged for our entire unit to share Christmas dinner. The fourth unit was unoccupied.

We didn't want to have an American experience in Germany. We wanted a German experience. So Stephen and I decided to attend the German church even though there were two huge English speaking congregations nearby. It was a good choice, but it wasn't always easy to sit through services I didn't understand. Stephen became adept at speaking German and was able to pass a basic proficiency examination. I survived through sign language and broken phrases. Some of the younger church members spoke fluent English and were able to interpret in tight spots when needed.

Are the Germans, friendly? Yes, once you got well acquainted. Otherwise they are reserved. Part of that comes from respecting personal space. Getting well acquainted, though, might take a long time. One woman at church told me that until someone invites you to use their first name, you call them Mrs. So and So. After knowing one woman for 20 years, she was finally invited to use the first name.

I read that one-third of all Americans could trace their ancestry to Germany. My parents' neighbor, George Rohbock, was a German American. During World War II he fought for the Allies, and was captured. The Germans couldn't figure out how a man with the last name of Rohbock could be fighting for the Americans. I guess it was no different than my father a Horiuchi fighting against the Japanese.

The Germans were careful how they used their resources. There were 82 million people living in a limited land mass smaller than the State of Texas, but they were wise conservationists. They recycled their garbage and carefully monitored the use of water, gas and electricity, partly because of high prices. We rarely saw polluted air. The forest master or *meister* had great jurisdiction telling people if they could hunt, what trees to cut down and how the forests would be taken care of. We have no equivalent position in the States.

Stephen loved the orderliness of the country. The fields were neatly tended and even a simple farm contained few weeds. I loved how many drove Mercedes Benzes, not as status symbols but as utility vehicles hitching a wagon to their car for farming. There was no need to buy a separate truck. My favorite taxi ride was in a yellow Mercedes Benz.

Germans are punctual, no I take that back. They are early. Our church started at 11 a.m. but many people arrived 20 minutes before the meeting. Once I hosted a tea. I was running a bit behind when the doorbell rang 25 minutes before the start. I was still in my bathrobe and was so embarrassed when my first German guest arrived. I learned to be ready at least 30 minutes before any event in that country.

I never got skilled at converting metric measurements into our archaic pounds and feet. Grocery shopping, using a dictionary to figure out ingredients, proved challenging at times. Often I didn't recognize products but would occasionally try them. I loved lamb's lettuce, a small round leaf that had the best nutty flavor topped by an equally yummy yogurt dressing.

One practice I loved was filling up tables at a restaurant. When an eatery was crowded and two chairs sat empty at your table, the owners would place other customers there. Those folks generally ignored you, but we usually initiated a conversation. Today nothing irks me more than to see two people at a four-person table when I am waiting a half hour for seating. Not letting a seat go empty increased the restaurant's revenue and cut down on customer waiting time.

I still laugh at the memory of my first ice cream cone purchase. The man behind the counter spoke to me in German and held his hand perpendicular to his body with the pointer finger upward. I didn't catch what he said, but agreed it was one cone. He put scoops on two cones and charged me for two. I paid somewhat puzzled until I realized that the Germans begin to count "one" with the thumb and that the pointer finger meant "two," unlike Americans who begin counting with the pointer finger.

Nothing was hugely different, but there were little things we had to learn to do the German way. An international banker's wife who had dragged ten children around the world once shared it takes the first year in a new place to find out how things work. She advised the reader not to get frustrated, but to take it all in stride. It was sagacious advice.

Great Britain

August 1998

OUR FIRST JOURNEY

Great Britain was a good choice for our first serious travel as newly uprooted Americans in Europe. It was the land of my husband's ancestry--Stephen is both Welsh and Scotch. We took comfort that English was spoken although there were times I questioned if British and American English had the same origins. George Bernard Shaw once said England and America are two countries separated by a common language.

Being a typical American, my husband thought we could cover all of Great Britain by car in a week. After all, Americans say how small Europe is. We soon found our itinerary too ambitious. We did one thing right, though--we skipped London on this tour. We could easily fly to the big city, but we couldn't always drive to the smaller hamlets.

We began our early morning departure by car blitzing across Germany, Belgium, and France. We had to decide how to cross the English Channel, whether to take the three-hour ferry from Calais, or the newly opened underground tunnel, the Chunnel, a half hour plus loading and unloading. The Chunnel or Eurotunnel was a 31 miles undersea rail with passenger service and vehicle shuttle between France and Britain. It had just opened after years of delay.

We opted for the Chunnel, since it would shave several hours off our long drive. The only thing I regretted was not seeing the chalky White Cliffs of Dover, long romanticized by writers.

The Chunnel train debarked at Folkestone, England. A lengthy three-hour drive to Stonehenge, our destination, still lay ahead of us. Even though the historic site was several hours out of our way, we were determined to see it.

I had a funny experience peripherally associated with the Stonehenge. When I first arrived in Europe, I asked a local librarian for a good novel on Germany trying to orient myself to the region.

"I am looking for a book to introduce me to the area. Can you recommend any?" I asked.

He paused, "Let me think. Ah, here's a good book to read." He produced a small tome. "It's about the Stonehenge and England."

"England? Isn't there anything on Germany?"

He shrugged his shoulders. I did read the book and learned about the Stonehenge and Druids!

I had long pictured Stonehenge on the top of a hill since most photographs show it against a clear sky. I was surprised that the Stonehenge was located in a wide flat valley. A Brit told us he could formerly walk right up to the stones. We could not touch the stones because an ugly wire fence cordoned off the perimeter. An admission fee was being levied, too. Had we paid and gotten inside the first wire fence, there was a second fence still keeping people at bay. We traipsed obediently around the outer fence with other tourists.

Still there is nothing quite like being there in person. We were amazed at the massive sizes and wondered how the stones were transported the 250 miles from Wales. The vertical rectangular stones stand approximately 13 feet high forming a circle about 108 feet in diameter. Originally comprised of 30 upright sandstone blocks, the 17 remaining stones are evenly spaced one to one and half yards apart. Balanced on top of them are horizontal lintels. No written record exists so scientists can only speculate on the purpose of the rocks. There is more and more conjecture that the site is associated with the early Druids. A simple monument of rough-hewn stones continues to baffle the experts, and keeps the tourists coming.

Driving on the left side of the road wasn't really that difficult but took some time to become accustomed to it. I will confess that there were several unnerving incidences when I looked at the car in front of me and it appeared to have no driver. I had to remind myself that the driver in England sits on the right side. Also sitting on the left side of the car in the left lane was a bit stressful when there were only inches between the car and the stone wall that often buttressed the road.

Another disorienting experience was driving roundabouts, or traffic circles. On the continent the circle is common although rather small and we could usually see the other side tracking where we were going. In England, full grown forests marked the center circle so we could not see across. If we lost count of the number of exits, we had to go around again and again. This happened more times than I'd like to admit.

COTSWOLD AND OXFORD

Our first day's final destination was a British air base billet near Fairford located in the Cotswold Region. The cluster of towns in the area appeared to be lifted off the pages of Beatrix Potter's *Peter Rabbit*. Thatched roofs cut to follow the contour of the houses were held up by whitewashed walls or stone masonry. Window baskets overflowed with colorful flowers, making every bend in the road a tantalizing surprise. I expected to find a tea party where the Mad Hatter and his friends would be in attendance. Or some furry creature would be imparting his wisdom to us mortals.

The spell was cast and I wanted to remain my entire week exploring every single thatched cottage and reveling in my findings. Towns were honey-colored limestone remnants from the medieval era offering no big tourist attraction other than being picturesque. It has stood for 300 years. I've often thought about the region and how hiking or bicycling would be the proper way to absorb the full enchantment of Cotswold.

The next day we wandered over to nearby Oxford since some of my husband's family originated here. We drove around the town, focusing on the tree-lined university-- stately, everything you pictured a British university to be complete with tradition and propriety. When I was college age, women weren't allowed to apply as Rhodes Scholars leading to study at Oxford. Occasionally I think how different my life would have been had these doors been open to me. Happily there are more opportunities for women now.

CROESO I CYMRU—WALES AND FAMILY ROOTS

Our Williams surname is Welsh so we headed west to Wales with a few family names and dates obtained from Stephen's uncle. We passed green rolling hills called the Brecon Beacons National Park, a name that has been rolling off my husband's tongue ever since. The mountain range derives its name after an ancient practice of lighting signal fires on the mountains to warn of attacks by the English. The setting perfectly fit my husband's ideal retirement dream to own acreage and tend sheep. The sunlight in the north was soft, and possessed a warm glow as it danced between the clouds. The fields were a luscious yellow green bordered by darker green trees. It was a breathing John Constable painting with rich golden patina.

By deductive reasoning we discovered that Monmouthshire was the area where Stephen's family originated. On the border between two warring countries, England and Wales, the land was sometimes governed by the British and sometimes by the Welsh. We were looking for the town of Llanelly which appeared on his genealogy sheets, but not on our map.

We discovered that the Welsh double L's were pronounced as an "F." We gave up trying to pronounce locations, and instead pointed to the map. People recognized the name of the township and kept directing us up a hill. After circling five times, my husband was ready to give up. I gently reminded him that we came thousands of miles to find the hamlet, Llanelly, and we would not give up. Finally we turned onto a narrow lane up the mountainside lined by intervening rock walls and hedgerows. We turned into a church with a few houses next to it. We did not realize this was a separate township from the city. This was Llanelly, more correctly the church!

The Llanelly Church was a small structure of gray limestone with irregular colors and shapes. A square steeple touched the road. We got out of the car and walked through the courtyard gate. We picked our way over the stones sloping in a slight incline overgrown with grass. We entered and gazed at the one room chapel cluttered with benches. The rounded nave had no particularly distinctive features, but it was extraordinary to us because it had been the worship house of generations of my husband's family. We had a record that his great, great grandparents were married in this quaint church.

The Llanelly graveyard was jam-packed with headstones. We walked through the yard under the yew trees and noticed names that ran in my husband's family--Lewis, Reese, Williams, and Thomas in different combinations--Lewis Reese Williams, Reese Thomas Williams, William Thomas Reese. But we couldn't match the names with our family dates. We sat on a bench and looked over the fertile green valley below and the surrounding hills. It was a balmy day with clouds pushing across the sky. Nothing was said, yet there was a surge of feelings that this place somehow belonged to my husband. We yearned to know of the men and women who shared my husband's blood.

We watched the sun walk up the hill across the way leaving a shadow in its trail. We reluctantly stood up and meandered over the grassy path past the stone church and back to our car. Although my husband said little on the drive back that evening, he has often spoken of the stone church in Llanelly, and how grateful he was that we persevered to find it.

SWANSEA

Continuing our clockwise travels around Great Britain, we moved on to Swansea, home of some of the best-known Welsh choirs like the Cambrian Male Choir. My husband claims that Welsh choirs are the best in the world. Unfortunately we did not drop in on rehearsals because it was summer break, and they were not practicing.

The camping ground close to Swansea was full so we moved inland and settled for an open grassland field. John was our proprietor, whose only improvement of his campground was a bit of a shack with a toilet, sink, a broken light and cement floors. This was the most primitive of all the places we stayed, but we were content for $15 a night. We were the first campers there but by morning five other families joined us.

Everything was damp with heavy dew when we awoke. We peeked out from our tent. Our camping neighbors had a hard side trailer, and popped their heads out at the same time.

"Good morning!" the man grinned. He had more hair on his chin than on his head. "Where are you folks from?"

"We're Americans living in Germany," my husband replied. "And where are you folks from?"

"Near Pontypool in Wales."

"No, kidding? We just came from there. My great grandparents are from that area," Stephen said, "Llanelly to be exact. It's beautiful there!"

"Aye, really? What a small world that we come from that side of Wales and meet on this side! What is your name again?"

"Williams!" Stephen answered.

"Hmmm, know a few Williams around there. For all we know we might be related."

"We might! So what brings you to this part of Wales?" queried Stephen.

"We're on vacation and we like a bit of change now and then. It's been a while since we've been here!"

"Wonderful, isn't it," remarked Stephen. And I nodded in agreement that it was awesome to be here!

Being somewhat of a romantic, I had brought along a book of poetry by Dylan Thomas, Wales' famous poet. Ironically, Thomas did not speak the native language, but that didn't stop him from creating lyrical lines capturing the spirit of her people. I was in a cloth tent with a flashlight, on dewy grass reading Dylan Thomas to my husband. Could you think of a better way to recite Welsh poetry?

> ...We will ride out alone then,
> Under the stars of Wales....
> Excerpt from
> Author's Prologue

We then headed to Aberaeron, a small coastal harbor. Dramatic brown hills ran into the ocean much like the Mediterranean hills of California. Sheep speckled the landscape. Few cars were on the road. Tourists do not overrun these coastal cities, so as a result there was a calm authenticity about them. As we circulated we heard a lilting language for the first time--Welsh. Despite the British past effort to eradicate the language, it survived.

We kept driving up the coast stopping for a glance at the towns along the way. Aberystwyth was a pleasant coastal city where we found a bookstore and I purchased my Welsh alphabet poster. Stephen noted that the word "Lewis" means "lion" in Welsh, a name that appears in his ancestry.

I trailed after a hunched elderly woman into a deli shop and listened to her order in Welsh. The language was nothing like I had ever heard before. She pointed to a certain meat and cheese and paid for them. When it was my turn I duplicated her order by pointing to the same cheese and meat, which made a tasty lunch that day! Originally I wanted to try the distinctive Welsh food, lava bread, which is made out of seaweed. When I heard that it was an acquired taste, I was glad I had not found the costly item.

We cut northeast back towards England. Due to time constraints we bypassed some of the famous Welsh castles. I wish we had focused our week strictly on Wales. I guess this adds up to cowboy wisdom. How do we get cowboy wisdom? Through experience. How do we get experience? By making mistakes.

THROUGH ENGLAND TO SCOTLAND AND HADRIAN'S WALL

We stopped that night at a commercial campground on the border between Wales and England. I was intrigued by the proprietress, who claimed she had dated Ringo Starr of Beatles fame. She was about the right age, about the right height, and was vivacious enough to overrule our skepticism. Besides we were close enough to Liverpool that it might have been true.

On the road near Carlisle, we experienced one of those marvelous unplanned discoveries. A small board with no pictures marked Hadrian's Wall. Having come from Wales where the language was unintelligible to us, it was nice to understand the signs again. I remembered the name of Hadrian, the great Roman emperor, and asked that we stop.

Stephen protested that we were headed towards Scotland. He sounded just like his father who drove like a maniac straight through a trip with few stops in between. His dad never learned to enjoy the journey, but was only concerned with the destination. My hubby remembers once asking for a bathroom break as a child and being handed an empty can.

I pouted. Stephen relented, turned the car around and bounced down the road toward the Wall. This stop turned out to be one of our most memorable historical learning experiences. The wall was 20 feet thick made of piled stones standing about 12 feet high marking the border between the Roman Empire and the Barbarians. As I looked at the wall with modern eyes I thought, "How could this serve as a barrier?" Then I remembered everything was fought on foot or horse and such a wall would slow down an army in 122 AD. The wall ran across the 73 miles width of England and is considered the most significant Roman structure in Britain. After it fell into disuse, many people removed the stones to use in other buildings. John Clayton is credited with preserving what remains of the Wall today by buying up the land beginning in 1834 until his death. I take pleasure when I hear of Hadrian's Wall knowing we made it there, almost missing this piece of history.

LAND OF BRAVEHEART

We found a campground on the banks of the famous Loch Lomond and I romanticized that bagpipes were playing. Instead we heard the patter of rain on our tent. As the evening wore on the noise reached a crescendo and our tarp was unable to keep the rain out. I awoke floating in a foot of water. Stephen and I dashed to our car and spent the rest of the night drying out. Thankfully, there was a laundromat nearby so we pumped mounds of coins into the dryer and got the water out of most everything. No wonder the Europeans use hard-sided trailers.

Our next day was spent driving as far as we could go. First we drove to Fort Williams bordering the Scottish Highlands, and then on to Inverness. The roads wove their way through barren hills and mountains and we had little competition for the lanes. Few structures predate the 18th century because the Scottish natives had a habit of burning down their towns.

We passed Loch Ness where the monster was said to reside. I squinted, but saw nary a ripple on the water. A strange monster was reported as early as 565 with more sightings in 1871 and studies done as recently as 2001. Scientists speculate there may be animals that are mistaken for the monster, or that wakes from the wind resemble humped animals. In any case Nessie the Monster has brought notoriety to the Lake.

The long drive was broken by rounded barren Scottish hills running for miles with no visible vegetation. We imagined pink and maroon heather blooming on the bald terrain and better understood why their appearance was so conspicuously noted by novelists and poets. Blossoms brought an awakening to the primal moors.

PAPER WEIGHTS

We arrived in Perth and decided to stay the night. We came upon the Caithness Glass Centre known for its glass paperweights. Stephen's late Aunt Donna was an avid collector and we inherited a few collectibles. What a coincidence to find the factory where her pieces had originated. What I took away from my visit, though, was the fact that paperweight associations flourished with intensely passionate members and we knew nothing about them prior to our visit. I suspected specialty interest groups thrived for nearly every conceivable item.

We stayed at a bed and breakfast where the owners, a husband and wife, reminded me of a classic British couple seen on television--he with eyeglasses, slightly balding with a protruding belly grumpily reading a newspaper in front of the television; she, portly with a tinge of jovial flightiness. It was obvious to us that it was her idea to raise a little extra capital by taking in boarders, since he didn't say more than three words to us during our introductions. She, on the other hand, in an effort to offset her husband's moodiness, was overly solicitous of our welcome, prattling without letting us say a word. She led us upstairs to our bedroom, with a double bed wrapped in lacy white eyelet and a four-drawer dresser at the end of the bed. The wallpaper was of pale pink roses on a white background. A crocheted rug was on both sides of our bed. The room was meticulously clean and comfortable, attesting to her virtue as a good housekeeper.

EDINBURGH

The next day we visited the Edinburgh Castle only an hour away, a welcome change from our marathon drive the previous day. This was a genuine castle, not a cinematographic reproduction. Guards in Scottish kilts greeted us. As we crossed the bridge over the moat we saw the statue carved into the wall of the real William Wallace. He was made famous by the movie Braveheart with Mel Gibson. Someone later told me that the guide was wrong and that it was really a statue of Robert the Bruce.

I learned that a tattoo is not always a dye placed under the skin. It can mean a military display at dusk usually of bagpipes and drums. The Edinburgh Tattoo takes place on the Esplanade in the Castle during August. When we lived in Washington, D.C., we watched soldiers in Scottish regalia playing their tattoo and stirring up a patriotic fervor.

We meandered down the main street, called the Royal Mile, which connects Edinburgh Castle with Holyrood Palace at the bottom of the hill. We poked our heads into the shops and priced a kilt for my husband in his Gardner or Gordon clan plaid of deep green. The required yards of fine wool for a kilt was mind-boggling and so was the price! There are many considerations about purchasing a kilt: The weight of the wool; the length of 4 to 10 yards. Some regulation kilts require up to 12,500 stitches and 75 hours to sew with 35-39 pleats. A heavyweight regulation kilt ran around $600. We settled for a business tie in the Gordon clan plaid.

At a corner, a bagpiper was playing away in full force. He wore the bear hat, the braided jacket, the kilt, the socks, the shoes and all the adornments. I thought he was part of Edinburgh's welcome to visitors. When I saw people place money in a small cup, I realized he was earning a little extra money but with such Scottish flair!

At the bottom of the hill sat the Palace of Holyrood, where the royal family resides when in Scotland usually in the summer. The Queen was not visiting, so we were able to tour this small but tastefully decorated castle. I remember the gathered creamy green peacock feathers atop the bed frame, wondering how often they were dusted. Holyrood had a turbulent history with its most famous occupant, Mary, Queen of Scots living here between 1561 and 1567.

At the corner pub, we noticed that our tablemates, two young ladies, were speaking German. So we struck up a conversation with them and learned they were from Switzerland. They were friends from childhood with their families living in the same region for 500 years. It struck me how much of Europe is entrenched in tradition.

ENGLAND

The next day we began our descent down the eastern side of England, stopping briefly at Sheffield noted for their fine knives and where Stephen's brother, Sherm, lived for two years doing volunteer work. This was another ambitious day of driving past lovely English towns. We had lunch in Nottingham, and wondered if we would bump into Robin Hood since my imagination was always active. I was somewhat disappointed that in this center for lace and hosiery there were so many concrete buildings and no dense woods. We went past the city of Coventry where Coventry Carol derived its name. The city's main distinction was that it was the farthest inland city from the sea in addition to having a medieval town center.

We ended our day in the city of Cambridge, famous for its university and cathedral. The famed Cathedral was enormous and awe-inspiring, the seat of the Archbishop of Canterbury, the Primate of All England, head of the Church of England and the worldwide Anglican community. In the courtyard, it seemed there was bright Hollywood lighting and I could picture history relived--bishops marching to and fro in their black cassocks with others plotting diabolical deeds. Thomas Becket was murdered in the cathedral, and King Henry IV and Edward the Black Prince are buried here. Geoffery Chaucer wrote the book, *Canterbury Tales*, about a group traveling from London to Canterbury.

The Cathedral itself has survived numerous fires and is now in Early English Gothic design including flying buttresses, high pointed arches and rib vaulting. It is massive and impressively adorned with soaring stained glass windows. Against the outer walls of the Cathedral were shops from medieval times with their half-timbered fronts. Fortunately these shops plus the Cathedral survived the bombing during World War II avoiding the fate of the rest of the city, which was flattened.

We drove around the grounds of Cambridge University established in 1209 and one of the oldest institutions of its kind in the world. As at Oxford, it is highly competitive to enter this university, so I paid particular attention to the students to see if they appeared any more intelligent than the average. They seemed quite normal to me. I kept trying to drink it all in, but asked myself if I could have handled the weight of 800 years of tradition. I probably would say no since I tend to be more of a free spirit.

LOW ON GASOLINE

It was time to head home. We loaded ourselves onto the Chunnel train and rode under the English Channel back home. Hoping we could find better prices on the Continent we did not fill up our tank of gasoline. It was Sunday but we didn't anticipate that every place would be closed. When we reached Belgium, we were down to the last eighth of our gas tank. We saw a station that took credit cards and quickly pulled up to the pump. We were dismayed to read that only that gas company's credit card was accepted. There was no station attendant. We weren't sure what to do. We had no desire to push the car on the highway when it died. Besides, there was a fine for running out of gas on the highway in Germany.

So we waited. The first person to drive up was a burly man who waved us away. After ten minutes a kindly looking man drove up to the pump. We negotiated to pay him cash in return for charging on his gas credit card. At first he didn't understand what we wanted. We slowed down, talked clearly, and his eyes lit up with understanding. He took our money and inserted his credit card. What a relief!

MAIDEN VOYAGE

It was a marvelous first voyage for us, visiting the land of Stephen's ancestors. We navigated in English, and we gained a better sense of traveling in Europe. In retrospect we have plenty of suggestions for improving this trip, but the important thing was we did it! We ventured off to the unknown and returned more knowledgeable—full of cowboy wisdom!

ITALY

Italian Blitz

September 1998

My mother and son arrived for their first visit to Europe when we had been in Germany only two months. We opted to join for a rushed but affordable commercial tour through Italy. The most difficult part of such a trip was sleeping upright on a bus. My mother came equipped with eye patches, neck pillow and sleeping pills. Stephen, my hubby, faded out quickly and slept the entire trip with no chemical aids. My son didn't fare so well.

Each time I turned around, I saw him staring blankly through the entire night. He later said although it was a fascinating trip, he was miserable from lack of sleep.

FIRENZE

In my mind Firenze in Italian or Florence was located on a hill. I guess I had seen a movie or picture to create that impression, so I was surprised when we pulled up to see the city on an open plain. The Duomo or large dome was the most prominent structure seen in the skyline, built with polychrome marble panels in various shades of green and pink bordered by white. It was designed by Filippo Brunelleschi for a competition. The panel of judges kept turning down the Young Brunelleschi but he persisted and was eventually awarded the contract for his octagonal design.

The Baptistry echoes the dome with an octagonal floor plan. The symbol of eight sides signifies the one day beyond a human's earthly cycle in which Christ rises and lives eternally. It is perhaps best known for its bronze doors designed by Lorenzo Ghiberti, and the masterpiece called Gates of Paradise.

The Old Palace, Palazzo Vecchio, located in the heart of town was the original residence of the powerful Medici Family. Two things surprised me about the Palace: First, its size. This was built hundreds of years earlier when buildings were much smaller than they are today. It must have appeared cavernous to a peasant who lived in a one-room hut. Secondly, the best rooms were located at the third story, at the top of the building at a time when there were no elevators or escalators. Given the cleaner air and the lovely view, I could understand why the best rooms were there. The sun shining that day on the balcony overlooking the city momentarily took me back to how things must have been during those powerful Medici days.

Florence was packed with tourists. It was suffocating, even though it was off season in September. I couldn't imagine what it must be like during the height of the summer! A walk past the Uffizi Gallery was disappointing. The line was so long that I knew I could never sneak a quick visit to see the real Michelangelo's "David." A copy of David in front of the Medici Residence on the Piazza della Signoria helped lessen my disappointment. I vowed that I would return again and spend at least one week in Florence soaking up the important sights.

Our visit to the next church, Santa Croce, Church of the Holy Cross, was like walking through the Who's Who of Italy. It was the burial site of Galileo, Michelangelo, Dante, Leonardo da Vinci, Rossini, and many other notables. It was awe-inspiring. As we left the Church a display of watercolors caught my mother's eye.

"Oh, these watercolors are really well done!" my mother said. She should know since she has her master's degree in watercolors.

"Oh, they are marvelous," I agreed. Stephen and Scott continued to wander down the road, oblivious to the bartering that would soon transpire.

"May I help you ladies?" a blonde, blue-eyed artist asked.

"These are just lovely!" Mom complimented the man, who nodded his head in appreciation.

"Are you from around here?" I asked because I caught a slight Slavic accent.

"Oh, no, I came from Russia. I have been here for eight years," he replied.

"Great that you can make a living selling your paintings," I commented. The artist smiled in agreement.

"I think I'll buy one and you can choose one, too," Mom offered. "I'll pay for it."

She bought the larger watercolor of Ponte Vecchio and I got a smaller one of the Arno River. The painting still hangs in my home today. We finally caught up with the men who were looking at the shops filled with gold-embossed leather bound books and purses--a bit too pricey, but marvelous to admire.

I thought of Cherie, daughter of a friend, who had spent an entire semester in Florence wandering the historic alleys and perfecting her Italian. She had weeks to explore the crooked, narrow streets. I felt a strong sense of envy!

ON TO ROME

The ride through Tuscany to Rome was picturesque. Vineyards created plaited rows against the hillsides. Tall cypress trees hid rust-colored farmhouses. Walled villages with their crenellated castles were silhouetted against the pale blue sky, mimicking live paintings.

We didn't see much of the Eternal City that first night because it was evening before our bus pulled up to the perimeter of Rome. At breakfast our family opted not to go on the scheduled Pompeii Tour. Instead we decided to explore Ostia Antica, another well-preserved Roman ruins 20 miles southwest of Rome.

It was challenging to get to our destination. We had to find the right bus, ride the subway, and transfer to catch the train--all without speaking a word of Italian. Amazingly we did it without much problem.

Riding a bus is an interesting test. Bus tickets are not sold on the bus. You must purchase them at a tobacco shop. Had I not I learned about this procedure from a guidebook, we would have been caught short.

We arrived at Ostia Antica at lunchtime, so we decided on a restaurant located at the entrance to the park. Most of the patrons were locals, which reassured us that our dining would pass high Italian standards. A 25th wedding celebration lent music to the occasion. The waiters wore tunics that added a Roman flavor and showed off their muscular tan legs. The service was good and the pasta was fresh and delicious.

Ostica Antica was the ancient ruin of a large city with apartments, a forum, market, and colosseum. The city fell into disuse when the seaport silted over due to malaria and neglect in the 4th century BC. A local guide would have enhanced our understanding of the place, but it was still interesting to read from the guidebook what Roman life had been like. I remember the rows of walls forming apartments similar to townhouses that appeared very narrow by today's standards. By afternoon we took a break at the colosseum, sitting in the shade imagining the exhibitions that must have been held here. We had covered every inch of the place, and by the end of the day our feet reminded us how many miles we had walked.

Riding back on the train, Stephen and mom decided to return to the hotel while Scott and I decided to see more of Rome. We rode along the Tiber River as the sun set through the smog, the light dabbling through trees onto ornamental bridges. The grand music of *The Pines of Rome* by Resphigi, complete with thundering kettledrums, ran through my head and seemed appropriate to mark our entrance into the Eternal City.

Hadrian's Tomb was an impressive round structure, resembling a cake. Its real name was Castel Sant'Angelo and was originally built by the Roman Emperor Hadrian as his mausoleum. This was the same Hadrian who built the wall in Britain. The Tomb was later turned into a fortress, a castle and is now a museum.

At St. Angel Bridge built to connect the city of Rome to Hadrian's Mausoleum, we saw a Catholic priest taking a photo of a middle-aged German lady.

"Hi, may we shoot a picture of the two of you? It's so much better to have both of you in the same photo," I offered.

"Why yes, that would be lovely. Push this button here," the priest replied. I quickly put the couple in the frame of the camera and shot.

"We are friends from college meeting here in Rome," the priest almost apologized why a celibate priest was with a woman.

"Would you like another one with a different background?" I asked.

"No, one will be fine," answered the woman.

"Where are you from?" asked the priest.

"We are Americans!" Scott and I both responded in unison.

"I'm visiting from Utah," said Scott.

"And I live in Germany," I added.

"Ah, Germany. That must mean your husband is in the military," the priest quickly assessed.

"Very perceptive!" I quipped.

Scott asked, "And where are you visiting from?"

The woman replied first, "I am from Germany."

"And I am a Christian Indian from India," said the man. Scott and I must have both raised our eyebrows, because he quickly added, "My family was converted to Christianity by the Portuguese in the 1600s. My last name is D'Souza. Anyone with that surname is usually Catholic."

"I used to work with a D'Souza in Maryland. He might be your relative," I commented.

"Usually anyone with that last name will eventually link up. Well, it was certainly nice meeting you folks, and thanks for the photo," the priest concluded.

"Nice meeting you folks, too and teaching me about the Christian Indians," I replied.

I turned to Scott. "I am getting really tired, and I think it's time we headed back to our hotel."

Scott and I caught a bus back to our hotel. We were all dripping with sweat from the heat while standing on the bus with no air conditioning. A man with a trench coat over his arm stood next to me. I thought it odd that a person would be wearing a coat in this hot weather. Then I remembered the warning given of pickpockets. Who else would wear a raincoat on a warm day but a would-be pickpocket seeking to hide his loot? I almost wanted him to snatch the used Kleenex in my pocket. I could see his hand very near my pocket, edging closer and closer. I had visions of using my karate chop laying him low to the ground. Fortunately we got off the bus before anything exciting happened.

The next day we toured the Vatican, a small city-state of 110 acres, the smallest independent nation in the world by both population and area. We entered the museum first to try to avoid the crowds. We wandered through the many exhibits and spent a half hour focused on the Sistine Chapel ceiling depicting scenes from the Bible. I was spellbound by Michelangelo's artistic skills, marveling how he painted on high scaffolding while lying on his back. Each of his figures had a power that leaped off the walls and ceilings. The muscular Christ is how Stephen envisions Jesus as an able-bodied carpenter. All the energy and movement stood momentarily suspended as God touched the hand of man to give him life. Genius was the only word that can describe not only Michelangelo's craftsmanship in creating these magnificent human bodies, but his ability to design all these stories into one harmonious whole.

From the Museum we walked to the piazza and into St. Peter's Basilica where St. Peter is purported to be buried. As we entered through the doorway, on the right we saw the Pieta, the stone sculpture carved by Michelangelo of Mary holding the crucified Christ. Unfortunately security was so extreme that we were at least a good 50 feet away from the sculpture. Earlier in the year a man had pounced on the statue and defaced the nose. Still we could appreciate Michelangelo taking a cold slab of marble and creating Mary and Jesus figures so real that at any moment we felt they would inhale a breath of life. The drapery appeared to be silk gathering at the foot of the Virgin Mary and as the light filtered through the thinner stone the marble glowed. My eyes moistened because I felt I was in the presence of true artistry and beauty.

A large window lay behind the altar showing a white dove, which made me realize why I saw so many doves in Catholic churches. A line of people waited to rub the toe of St. Peter's statue, so I dutifully got behind them. I declined to go down to the crypt since I spook easily. I also did not want to climb to the top of the dome with the group, so I wandered the enormous cathedral with its ornate sculptures, and dedications to rich and important people. I think this was a first to see spiraled columns twisted like a loose rope designed by Bernini rather than straight up and down pillars. The soaring dome over the central apse was designed by Michelangelo--I wondered if there were anything the man couldn't design!

We were ravishing. We purchased bread, meat, and cheese from a nearby deli and sat on the outside steps of St. Peter's Square. While munching our sandwiches, we watched the faithful heading into St. Peter's. The nuns were particularly interesting since each order had a distinctive habit, some black, some white, and blue, with varying designs and ornamentations. A navy dress fell just below the knees and the headscarf came just below the shoulders. I recall the long white sari with the light blue trim from Mother Teresa's order. I did not see the full-length black habit often depicted in movies, I suspect because it was still warm weather and less frequently worn.

We joined our official tour group in the afternoon for a trip to the Roman Forum, the Colosseum, Constantine's Arch, Palatine Hill and the Circus Maximus. The Forum was another jumble of ruins. I wasn't too captivated by the local soft-spoken guide, who spoke only loud enough for me to hear every other word. All I could understand was that this was a ruin of stones built by this Emperor or that ruler. Perhaps if I had given it more study I might have better appreciated being on these fabled grounds. It was not until later I found a book with plastic overlays placed over the pictures of the present-day ruins that I began to understand the magnificence of the Roman Forum. In any case, a competent and audible guide is a must.

Within a few hours we saw every highlight in Rome. We saw Raphael the young artist's resting place in the Pantheon, and ate a gelato in the Piazza Navona. Scott and I climbed the Spanish Steps, while the rest waited below. Trevi Fountain was much prettier in real life than the pictures portray. The tradition was if you tossed a coin in, you will return. I threw in a couple extra coins to guarantee my return.

On our last evening in Rome, Stephen led us to an unassuming little family deli on a corner behind St. Peter's. I wasn't expecting much, perhaps a few simple dishes. I was pleasantly surprised. The glass counters were filled with every imaginable pasta, salad, and Italian delicacy. We heaped our plates with homemade lasagna, ravioli, eggplant, and antipasto salads! This was real Italian food at its finest.

The Italians have taken their exquisite cooking skills everywhere they have migrated including Argentina where Stephen lived for a couple of years. He knew that some of the best foods came from the family owned corner deli. Thanks to his knowledge we found a great eatery. We topped our meal off with genuine Italian ice—a perfect finish to a perfect evening.

VENICE

From Rome we again rode the bus overnight to Venice arriving before dawn. Our group clambered onto rowboats for a ride to the Isle of Murano about a mile north of Venice, famous for its glass factories. We were ushered into small wooden buildings. Our host was a dashing young man with a long mane of curly black hair, the type that every American girl swoons over. We watched two older glassblowers make a horse about the size of a fist, using lampworking technique. The blower pinched the glass to create the mane and pulled legs to create a horse. Completed in a few minutes, it all looked so easy, but in reality it takes nearly 20 years to become a master glass blower. Our son was so impressed with the demonstration that he purchased one of the horses.

Years later I had the opportunity to take a glass blowing class. My pieces were crooked, irregular, and obviously made by a beginner, so I can attest firsthand how difficult glass blowing is. However, the experience of twirling molten glass on the end of a rod was also one of the most satisfying things I have ever done-- creating an object of beauty from sand!

The craft has been carried on for a long time. The first glass blowers accidentally set fire to the wooden structures in Venice, so in 1291 the foundries were moved to the Island of Murano. Mother's Day was coming and we purchased a couple of glass bead necklaces. In comparing the Murano made glass with other necklaces, I recognized the extra luster and quality of the beads we had purchased.

Back in the boat we were rowed to the central promenade of Venice where we boarded a gondola. A friend's father who has toured the world, insisted that I take a gondola ride in Venice. I was glad we heeded his advice, because it was a great way to see the floating city. I learned that the left side of the gondola is slightly longer to counterbalance the weight of the gondolier. I was a bit disappointed that our guide did not sing, however.

From the water we could see some homes faced the canals as their entrance, while other houses backed up to them. The rhythmic pushing and pulling of the oar created a natural hypnosis over our group and we lulled ourselves into a peaceful reverie.

Each time we glided under a picturesque bridge, we were traversing between two islands. The founders in 421 built the city on a salt marshland at the mouth of the Adriatic Sea. Because there is no solid foundation, the city is sinking and the water level is rising. Added to that is the fact that there is no sewer system. Waste flows directly into the canal and is washed out to sea with the tides.

When our gondola ride ended, we had a half hour to dash madly through St. Mark's Square or Piazza San Marco, the central gathering place in Venice, peek in St. Mark's Basilica, look at St. Mark's Campanile or tower, and feel frustrated that we couldn't see it all. We did not even venture into one of the glittering shops inside the Piazza. Well, highlight tours are highlights and merely whet our appetite for more.

HOME

We were exhausted but happy to have seen so much. Mom had been hesitant to go, saying she would stay at our home and read a book for four days feeling that the pace was too rigorous, but she was mighty glad she went! In fact, she survived the tough schedule the best of all of us.

On such a quick highlight tour, we had to be able to sleep on a bus or be prepared to tour in a stupor, and there were extra costs for any excursions not included in the original bargain price. My European friends chided us Americans for trying to see too much in too short a time, but the trip delivered on everything it advertised. Yes, we try to cram too much in at one time, but for some, this may be the only opportunity such magnificent sights will ever be seen. Was rushed better than not at all? I think so.

~ THE NETHERLANDS

Holland

October 1998

Holland was one of our four-day weekend trips in our little car. Just inside the Dutch border was a Wendy's food chain. My husband thought he had gone to heaven since this was his favorite fast food restaurant. We ordered our usual bacon cheeseburger, chicken nuggets, side salad, frosty, Caesar salad, and French fries.

A blond employee walked over to our table. "Is everything all right?" she asked us.

Startled I piped up, "Where did you learn to speak such excellent English?"

"We studied it in school, but I am afraid I wasn't a very good student," she replied. Her English was perfect with nary an accent.

AMSTERDAM

Amsterdam enjoyed a thriving Golden Age during the 1700 and 1800s with the Dutch East and West India Companies. The revenue from the ships made the towns so wealthy that folks indulged in many luxuries still seen today, particularly in the fancy architecture.

We arrived early in the morning and headed directly to the tourist bureau. For a small fee we found a bed and breakfast close to downtown. We booked early in the day and got first pick of the price and location we wanted. Our room was located in a guesthouse in a northwest residential section. The house was very narrow, equaling the width of one room. The steps to our bedroom were nearly vertical and the bathroom was down the hall, European style. We were still pleased that our room was clean and adequate, on the second floor overlooking the street.

We took dinner at the bar around the corner from our bed and breakfast. I ordered mussels, which turned out to be the best I have eaten anywhere. I examined the pot to see if I could discover the secret ingredients, but there were only basic spices.

A Scandinavian looking couple sitting next to us smiled and we struck up a conversation. "Where are you folks visiting from?" we asked.

"Iceland," they replied.

"Iceland? Wow! Do you get over here often?" Stephen asked.

"We are Americans who presently live in Germany." I responded.

"Where in Germany?" the wife asked.

"Landstuhl near Kaiserslautern," Stephen answered.

From the puzzled expressions on their faces, I quickly added, "It's about 90 miles southwest of Frankfurt, twenty minutes from the French border."

"We are sorry that our English is so poor," they apologized.

"Well, your English is much better than our Icelandic!" we replied.

Everyone laughed.

The woman continued, "Icelanders work to keep our language pure by not adopting foreign names. As a result many new words are long and cumbersome. For example the word for computer is really long and means something like a machine that can think for itself."

As we traveled we listened for the sounds of each language. The Dutch or Flemish language is related to German but sounds softer. There are a lot of double letters like *oo's* and *aa's* and *van* before names in Dutch.

One of the best ways to be introduced to Amsterdam was from the vantage point of the canal. So we took a water taxi ride, which was very relaxing. We saw ornately decorated homes whose front facades are shaped like steps built during the gilded Dutch Renaissance and Baroque periods. Near the top of many houses was a large hook. Our guide explained that it was a hoist to lift furniture too large to go up the narrow stairs. We understood the challenge perfectly, recalling our bed and breakfast with a stairway barely wide enough for a man to walk comfortably. We saw the canals empty into the sea. We glided through several of the concentric half circles forming the downtown, all built centuries before. The hour ride left us so contented that we had trouble regaining our land legs.

We headed for the Museum Quarter to see the Rijksmuseum— full of the largest and most important works of Dutch painters. The Dutch Masters were the first to use oils in painting, and became world renowned. The museum itself was formerly a red brick castle accented with large gray arches. Our favorite painting was the "Night Watch" by Rembrandt van Rijn, a grand and glorious painting of the town's powerful people. Its colossal size alone commands attention standing at nearly 12 feet by 14 feet. The central figure, Captain Frans Banning Cocq, is dressed in black wearing the stylish lace collar of the day, a large brimmed hat and a red sash draped from his right shoulder. Surrounding him are militiamen, nobles in silks, and townspeople, a total of 34 persons. The color yellow was placed in several strategic places as a symbol of victory. The artist cleverly included himself in the background, slightly above and to the left of the Captain's head, revealing just his eyes, nose and forehead topped with an artist beret.

Rembrandt was an old friend. The National Gallery of Art contains a sizable collection of his works and I would talk weekly to children about aspects of his paintings. Some folks wonder why he painted over 90 self-portraits. Historians are not exactly certain why. One theory might have been to create a visual diary. Another reason for the self-portraitures was that models were expensive to hire. Still another theory is it was propaganda to increase his notoriety. Whatever the basis, the artist left a trail of how he gradually changed his focus from the outward appearance to a penetrating inner self-analysis.

There were boat houses for rent. People actually lived on the canal. Some houses were brightly painted, but most were a basic black or brown. I wondered what they charged for rent, and how the utilities were handled. I thought of my friend, Julia, who loves to live on the water. She regularly sought houseboats as her living quarters. She claims that living near the water calmed her ruffled nerves. I wondered how she would fare in Amsterdam.

Amsterdam is a city best seen on foot after being on the water. We walked until our feet were thoroughly worn out. There was much to poke our heads into—shops, museums, galleries, eateries. I most enjoyed our evening walks over canals that had twinkling lights gaily reflected in the water. Workers coming home for the day often carried a bundle under their arms, a stick of bread perhaps. With the sun fading, people turned the lights on inside their homes, and we were able to peek at what appeared to be miniature house settings.

HAARLEM, TULIPS, AND THE HAAG

It was my turn to drive. At one point I got confused and turned onto a wide lane made of bricks. I was noting how lovely the road was when Stephen began yelling as several cyclists rode straight toward us. I had driven onto a bicycle path! Fortunately I was able to resume our position on a proper road without mishap, accident, or injury.

Everyone rode bicycles in Holland—children, adults, and grandparents--cycling paths were often broad. The terrain was flat so pedaling was easy, and it didn't pollute the environment. With gasoline so expensive, it was more economical as well.

Haarlem was about 20 minutes west of Amsterdam. The Dutch also gave this same name to the colony they established in America. The town was surprisingly quaint. Built in the 10th century, the city earned its income by levying tolls on the highways, and then developed into a cloth making center. The story was told of Frederick of Toledo who besieged the city for eight months. He promised amnesty if the city surrendered. Believing the empty promises, the city capitulated. Frederick reneged on his words and slaughtered over two thousand of the Calvinist citizens. So much for the integrity of someone's word.

The purpose of our visit to Haarlem was to see the home of Frans Hals, the painter, whose realistic characters usually wore a wide lace collar. We found the museum on a side street but it was closed on Monday. We paused a moment to look up and down the old street. Many houses had half doors that often appeared in Dutch paintings, with the lower half closed and the upper half filled with ruddy-cheeked peasants.

We continued driving on to Leiden and Lisse, home of the famous Keukenhof Gardens and springtime tulips. Each year of our assignment in Europe, I made reservations to visit the Gardens, only to cancel them at the last minute. To my disappointment I have yet to see these massive floral displays.

An acquaintance once told me she didn't like tulips, but after seeing seven million of them in profusion she confessed to gaining an appreciation. If you purchase a bouquet, it may likely be from Holland since they are the largest flower wholesaler in the world.

After Lisse, we headed southwest to the Hague, a very subdued gray city and home of the international world court. After driving around and around unsuccessfully trying to find The World Court, we gave up and moved southeast to Delft.

DELFT AND KINDERDIJK

Delft porcelain is noted for its cobalt blue designs on a white background with a high glossy glaze. Picture a windmill in deep blue on white tile and it is probably Delftware. The ceramics were modeled after the imported Chinese porcelain of the 17th century. I asked my husband to stop at the factory. The tour was short so I spent most of my time in the gift shop hunting for something fitting to my budget--a Dutch shoe magnet.

As I studied the map of Holland, I saw towns that lent their names to cheeses like Gouda, Edam and Limburg. I wondered aloud if it would be worth it to purchase cheeses in those cities as a souvenir gift, but decided it would be too smelly in the car.

We swung southeast traveling home when we spied a small sign with the word "Windmills." Stephen and I quickly glanced at each other, nodded in agreement and began following the sign. The road twisted and turned through cities and fields for 20 minutes occasionally reassuring us with another small sign. I clapped my hands with joy when I saw the blades of our first windmill. Then we saw another and another till there were 19 gray windmills lining the main channel beside the Molenkade River. This was Kinderdijk.

Because Holland is at the mouth of the Rhine River, much of the land is below sea level and these grand windmills kept the ocean off the land literally creating Holland. We walked inside one large mill built around 1740. I was surprised that people lived inside. The quarters went up and up with little space since the large water wheel and gears took up most of the room.

Kinderdijk had the highest concentration of windmills in the country, and was a fitting finale to a quick but engaging tour of Holland. We finally felt we were in classic Holland. Ironically, no English guidebook described the park.

BY CANAL NEXT TIME

Holland dominated the seas for hundreds of years and I felt a sense of history everywhere I turned. This tiny country was delightful and easy to navigate since the people were friendly and spoke excellent English.

The Dutch claim Holland has been resurrected from the mouth of the Rhine River. One of their favorite sayings is "God created the world. But the Dutch created Holland."

The country deserved more than a long weekend look. I may do it next time as a friend did, and take a slow barge down the inland waterways in the Dutch tradition!

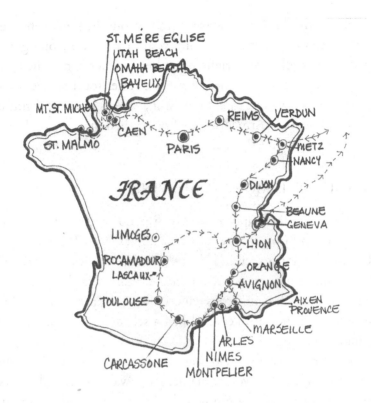

Viva La France
In A Car!

February 1999

THE AMERICAN WAY

My husband's idea of a vacation was how many miles could he put on our 1998 Sentra. We quickly learned that driving in Europe is not the same as driving in the western United States. One hundred miles in the southwest takes roughly 90 minutes. In Europe because of narrow, winding roads, small towns, and three hours of traffic on the road, it always took longer.

Being the novices that we were, we outlined an ambitious tour of central, south and southwestern France in one grand sweep. After all, it was right next door to Germany where we lived. Being off-season, there were also fewer tourists. We loved being able to wander the cobblestone streets without fighting masses of people. Armed with a French dictionary, a good road atlas, and lots of nerve we drove off for a week of adventure.

BURGUNDY IS MORE THAN WINE

The drive took approximately five hours from Landstuhl, Germany, to Lyon, France, our first night's stop. The Burgundy Region of France reminded me of the classical France we Americans reminisce--a bucolic life set against castles and fields of grapevines. The numerous wineries were tempting to visit, but since we were not drinkers and had a schedule to keep, we kept going.

Further down the road was the town of Dijon where the famous mustard derives its name. This was the capital of the region and the gray government buildings conveyed an important air. We pulled into the village and drove around the center. I expected to see more signs advertising the mustard, but there were few. Stephen also boycotted my purchasing a bottle of the yellow sauce, saying we could buy it at home, and we didn't need the added weight.

A hop, skip and a jump brought us to the town of Beaune known for the famous Hotel Dieu, founded in 1443 as a hospital with the most remarkable roof tiles. The multicolored Burgundian tiles scattered across the roof formed a panoply of geometric colors. The hospital is a medieval jewel surrounding a central courtyard with a pharmacy, a Roger van de Weyden painting, a chapel and hall for the poor. It surprised me how tall the ceilings were, considering it was a hospital and difficult to heat during the winter. Today it is a museum. Walking through the handsome rooms of hand carved paneling reminded me more of a church than an infirmary, although both are used to heal, one the body, the other the spirit.

Our French lunch was superb and at a reasonable price. I tried out my limited French on the young waitress.

"*Je voudrais le menu!*" I floundered slowly.

The waitress did not answer, but merely smiled.

I tried again, "*Je voudrais le menu, s'il vous plait!*"

This time she handled me two menus, but more as an automatic reaction than as a response to my French request. Oh, well, I tried.

Someone told me that the "plate of the day" was the best deal when eating, which included a soup or salad, an entrée, and dessert. We had a creamy mushroom soup, a cut of chicken and potatoes with a creamy white sauce doused with wine, and a sorbet for dessert. The price is a bit more than we pay for in America, but the quality is always excellent upholding the French reputation for superb dining.

THE RHONE RIVER VALLEY

We hit the road again heading for Lyon nestled on the banks of the Saone and Rhone Rivers. It is a pleasant city of manageable proportions. We immediately headed to the highest hill in town, the home of the Notre Dame de Fourviere--symbol of Lyon with its gaudy turrets and crenellations of marble and mosaic. The vantage point offered a view of the city and the valley. The streets below had a characteristically European air without the rush of a larger city. I kept reminding myself that the word Hotel de Ville was city hall, not a place of accommodation.

My mind considered the Romans to be found only in Italy. Yet, Romans remains were scattered throughout France and nearly all of Western Europe. In Lyon there is a large Roman amphithe-

ater built in 15 B.C. that seats 10,000 persons. An engineering
marvel, it is still used for performances today.

Textiles are an important product of the region, since the
trade center of Lyon was on the silk route. But today we visited
the Musee des Beaux Arts located in a former abbey and considered second only to the Louvre in importance in France. We
wandered its hallowed corridors, through the 14th century paintings, the Etruscan, Egyptian, Phoenician, Sumerian and Persian
art, as well as some of the richest 19th century collections of works
by Veronese, Tintoretto and Rubens to Braque, Bonnard, and
Picasso. I acknowledge I do not remember much because my feet
were so tired. Amazing connection between head and feet, isn't
there?

I convinced my husband to patronize a famous restaurant
listed in our guidebook. The building resembled a large open
box with high, high ceilings. Waiters in black with white shirts
bustled about. We were seated at a booth with wooden partitions
and began studying the menu. A waiter passed by balancing a
large platter of sausages, and cut meats over a plate of sauerkraut.
For a moment, I thought I was back in Germany, since this was
identical to dishes there. Again, I was learning that political borders do not mark food borders. We ordered escargot swimming
in garlic butter for our appetizer. We sopped up the remaining
butter with chewy French bread, indulged in meat dishes of suc-
culent lamb and savory salmon, topped by a creamy flan dessert.
Delicious!

South of Lyon is the town of Vienne which has one of the
highest concentrations of Roman architecture extant anywhere
with the Temple d'Auguste et Livie, the Theatre de Cybele, the
Theatre Romain, and the Pyramided du Cirque, once the center-
piece of the chariot racetrack. Pontius Pilate is buried here--the
Roman governor of Judea who presided over the trial of Jesus
Christ and ordered his crucifixion.

All of this reminded me how extensive Roman holdings were around the Mediterranean Sea and beyond. Textbooks rarely convey the immensity and power of the Roman Empire. Traveling in person taught me that during an age without planes, telephones, or telegraph the Romans were able to hold their empire together for hundreds of years.

We continued south on highway A-7 an excellent divided highway. Our next major stop--Orange.

THE PROVINCE OF PROVENCE

Orange was a neatly dressed city. As we walked through the town we felt it exuded order and calm. Its largest attraction is the Roman Theater with a Statue of Augustus Caesar, considered one of the finest in the whole Roman Empire. Built against a hill, it is a 1st century structure with perfect acoustics and is still used for programs and concerts. We sat a long time admiring the complete sculpture of Augustus Caesar with arms and legs intact in a niche above the theater. Most copies are minus the arms or even the head. The white marble of the statue contrasted with the reddish colored stones. Peering over the walls of the theater, we saw roofs, chimneys and television antennae poking up against the skyline.

We drove several times around the Triumphal Arch, a much smaller version of its sister arch in Paris. Perhaps it was the combination of balmy sunshine and pleasant pastimes, which add to our memories of Orange.

PAPAL POWER

A hop down the road brought us to Avignon. Not being a scholar of papal history, I learned an entirely new chapter about the Catholic Church.

I am not sure if I ever had a world history class, but I am certain I had no idea of the significance of Avignon when we arrived. As far as I was concerned the center of the Roman Catholic Church had always been in Rome. But from 1309 to 1377, seven French popes moved their operations to France at Avignon because of a great internal strife called the "Western schism" or the "great controversy of the antipopes." Pope Clement V was elected but there were violent protests in Rome about the voting, so he moved to Avignon.

In front of the Palais des Papes is a stone plaza with little greenery to welcome visitors. Looking at the church, one could tell that it had been added upon at different times with no coherent planning eventually evolving into a fortress. I felt no warmth emanating from the building. In fact it seemed infused with a cold, stark, almost foreboding aura.

After paying our admission fee, we assembled in the waiting room full of flags and antique furniture. Our tour conductor was knowledgeable, spoke excellent English and I could hear him well--three desirable traits in a guide. He guided us up and down stairs and through a maze of halls and rooms. Everything was on a grand scale. My favorite was the medieval cloisters near the library, repeating arches facing the courtyard of Palais Vieux. As the stories unfolded, I realized that popes commanded armies and possessed as much ambition as any king. They were more than spiritual leaders.

We ended our tour at the Great Chapel, which was sparsely furnished. We were told that the room was once lavishly decorated before 1789 since one of the reigning pope's philosophy was to serve God through luxury. What an interesting concept! During the French Revolution the room was destroyed and never refurbished.

Nearby was the Rhone River and we climbed the Saint Benezet Bridge. Construction began in 1177 but through the years, floods and lack of upkeep swept several of the supporting pillars away leaving only four so its span reached halfway across the river. Built underneath was a little chapel, large enough for one standing person. I am always amazed what people can conceive and do.

NIMES—THE AQUADUCT

Nimes is considered part of Languedoc-Roussilon Region, but is only about an hour west of Avignon. I vividly remember the Maison Carre--a little square building and one of the best preserved temples in classic Roman tradition located downtown. Inside was a barren square room. Still I am pleased with the memory perhaps because the proportions were so perfect and also because I felt I could tuck it in my back pocket and take it home with me. We drove around gazing at some of the Roman sites. We got out to see the amphitheater, and, lo, and behold, there was a large plastic bubble tent in the center. We asked the guard what was happening and he replied that a major tennis match was being held there. We later saw it on television and marveled at the French use of their antiquities.

Our main destination here was on the outskirts of Nimes called Pont du Gard, a large Roman viaduct still standing after 2,000 years. The viaduct stood 160 feet high and was made of enormous blocks of stone, some weighing 6 tons. We wondered how the stones were hoisted without the aid of modern day machinery. Three levels of arches, one on top of the other used natural gravity to convey water for the 31 miles to Nimes. Pont du Gard stands as a testament to the greatness of Roman engineering.

LOOKING FOR VINCENT

We went to Arles to see the residence of painter Vincent Van Gogh. I think I found the house where the painter lived but there was no marker to confirm our find. I later learned that the original corner building had been destroyed and what now stood there was a large four story business building. While Van Gogh lived in Arles he produced 750 paintings and 1600 drawings, a prodigious outpouring of creativity. I was a bit disappointed that there was so little in the city to remember one of its famous residents, at least I could not find much information telling me about him.

We toured the great well-preserved amphitheater with an empty niche. Eventually we began to see so many amphitheaters that they started looking alike to us. I understand that there are over 230 Roman amphitheaters scattered over the Empire. The open structures were not for chariot and horse racing, which were called circuses but were used for public spectacles including sports, games, and displays.

At the Museon Arlaten our lovely young guide wore a black dress adorned with the local lace collar covering the shoulder and dropping in the front to form a deep V. This fashion was also common in other parts of France and Belgium. The collar reminded me of Van Gogh's painting of Madame Ginoux pinpointing the canvas to this region. It's too bad that Van Gogh did not share in some of the financial gains his paintings have produced for its owners. A canvas of Van Gogh recently sold for $40 million.

Not speaking French was a decided disadvantage. It kept us from meaningful interaction with the local people, almost as though we were in a plastic capsule, merely making observations like space aliens. I did make use of my little French, making reservations at our hotel. I literally counted on my fingers to retrieve a number, *un, deux, trois*.... I could not simply pluck it out of the sky, but had to begin counting again with number one for each number needed; *un, deux, trois, quartre, cinq, six, huit;* and again *un, deux, trois*, for 383.

MARSEILLE

On my first trip to Europe my train passed through Marseille but at the crack of dawn, so I didn't see much. I could technically say, however, that this was my second trip to Marseille but Stephen's first. We drove onto the lovely harbor of Marseille. The water in this harbor was crystalline blue and private yachts lined up in neat rows. Shops and hotels fronted the edge of the water. The industrial shipping port was further down the shore and is the largest in France.

We stayed at a hotel a street off of the harbor. The advantage of our location was that we could walk to the harbor and we had parking for our car. We wandered down to the wharf area and randomly selected a restaurant. The food was deliciously fresh! I had yummy scallops sautéed in butter and Stephen had fried halibut.

The most conspicuous landmark in Marseille is the Notre-Dame-de-la-Garde on the hill overlooking town. It is not a light airy design like Renaissance architecture, but one with substantial weight of the Neo-Byzantine period. From the church's balconies, we saw the island of If, or *L'Ile d'If* where the story of the Three Musketeers took place.

Marseille is an interesting crossroad. Many of its immigrants are from Algeria. It is not French in feeling, but rather a city of commerce. We got to Avenue Prado and saw a bit of non-touristy Marseille filled with Arabic speaking folks.

Stephen's nephew was living in Marseille for a year doing volunteer work for his church. We surprised him with a short visit. We were glad to see him looking well. He beamed with pride and reported how happy he was with his service. I wanted to take him to lunch but his schedule was booked. We were envious of his excellent French.

ONTO CARCASSONE

We backtracked up through Arles and Nimes then down the French coast near Montpelier, capital of the Languedoc-Roussillon Province. Stephen often repeats a story about this area regarding Simon de Montfort and his Catholic crusade against the Cathar heresy (1209–1229). Simon conquered towns to clean them of heretics. When he arrived in Montpelier his men asked him how to distinguish between the infidels and the faithful. His order was: To kill them all, because God will know the difference!

We got a flat tire, luckily only a block away from a car repair shop. We walked over to the two-car garage owner and tried saying "new" like it said in the dictionary. The repairman got a puzzled look on his face. Finally we quit trying to pronounce the word, and pointed in our French dictionary to the word "tire," and then to the collapsed tire on our car. A look of understanding spread across the man's face.

He immediately took our tire and in a few minutes it was repaired. We were a bit nervous that we would be charged tourist prices, which was at least double or triple the going rate, but the man was honest and we paid the regular price.

It took about another hour and a half to reach the citadel of Carcassone. The fortified French town was better than a Disney set because it was authentic! It has served as a watch base since the time of the Roman Empire because of its strategic location between the Atlantic and the Mediterranean, and on the road between Spain and the rest of Europe. An outer wall encircled the perfectly restored medieval town its ramparts forming the actual walls of the city. Entering through a low archway, we were immediately seized by a time warp and thrown into medieval France. Every vendor was dressed in period clothing and ancient music filled the air. A jester in purple and yellow bowed to us. Even though the shops were all touristy, it was well worth a day and the price of admission to walk back in time.

The next day, we turned our car north and began our journey home. We drove through lovely boulevards in Toulouse where Francois, our French friend, was born. North of Toulouse the divided highway ended, turning into a two-lane country road. All the tourist traffic, farm equipment, utility trucks, and semis shared the road with us. It was a slow drive, taking us much longer than anticipated to reach our last two planned stops.

On long trips we will often alternate drivers. My husband has a habit of telling me how to drive--"You are too close to the middle line," or "You are following the truck too closely," and "Don't grind the gears!" Finally I pulled the car over and got out.

"What are you doing?" Stephen asked.

"Since you think I can't drive well, it's your turn again," I quipped. When it was my turn again, Stephen didn't say a word about my driving.

LASCAUX AND ROCAMADOUR

The scenery was pastoral so the added time in the car was not a hardship. The region seemed untouched by the hustle and bustle of modern life. Small farmhouses dotted the roadside. Hand-painted signs at nearly every farmhouse advertised duck pate or *foie gras*, a regional specialty made from the liver of a duck that is force-fed corn. Animal rights' activists' say that force feeding is cruel and some countries have banned the product. We didn't speak the language so we could not make adequate inquiry or a good bargain, so we passed on this regional dish.

We headed towards the great cave of Lascaux, since this was the beginning of man's first known art work on cave walls dating to the Paleolithic Age some 16,000 years ago. Four teenage boys chasing their dog discovered the rooms in 1940. The actual caves were closed to the public due to deterioration from the carbon dioxide of visitors, but another site was created replicating the original called Lascaux II.

We navigated our way to the tourist entrance and walked into a darkened cavern. The guide switched on the electric lights revealing a cave with a low ceiling. As we walked into the various sections we marveled at the long horned cattle, deer, and even a rhinoceros found on the walls. The early artists painted by fire light using charcoal and ground colored stones, capturing the essence of an animal in a few strokes. In many ways their stylized animals had a sophistication borne of keen observations. Some scholars assume these caves were sanctuaries where early man left imprints of his beliefs and knowledge. As I gazed at the walls I asked myself why is there always an urge to create, a need for expression? Why would someone stand in a darkened room working under torchlight drawing animals and figures of men?

I have taken several art history classes and they all began with drawings from this cave. It felt like I had completed a full circle to have sat in a class and learned about such places and then to stand near the actual site. I had a quiet satisfaction almost a sense of accomplishment arriving at such a place. Education can be dangerous by fomenting unrest, teaching us about other people and places making us move beyond our own complacency. For others like me we develop a desire to see it all!

Back on the road we made a beeline for Rocamadour. We would not have given a second thought about the place except that Francois told us we had to see it. We took our friend's advice and found the town a few miles off the main highway near Cahors. This is a famous French pilgrimage center honoring an ancient grave and sepulcher for St. Amadour, a Christian hermit. Built into the side of a steep hill are a series of chapels wrapped by a winding path with the final church located on a rocky peak high above the scenic Alzou Valley. Inside is a wooden Black Madonna reputed to have been carved by St. Amator. I panted climbing the stairs so I couldn't imagine the pilgrims traditionally climbing the stairs on their knees in humble homage.

As we reflected upon our many travels, Rocamadour often pops up in our memory. It was an unexpected surprise echoing a familiarity to St. Michele on the west coast of France except built into a hillside and not an island. It reinforced the fact that recommendations by local folks carry real weight and if possible should be followed.

The drive through France was an incredible trip, admittedly much too rushed. The people were as warm and inviting as any in Europe. Any one of the French regions we visited would have made a marvelous vacation in and of itself. If I go again, I'll do it the French way--enjoying more by seeing less! And my husband no longer makes marathon driving journeys.

The Republic Of Georgia,

May 1999

A GEOGRAPHY LESSON

Where is the Republic of Georgia? Formerly a Soviet satellite country east of the Black Sea, it is bordered by Turkey, Armenia, Azerbaijan and Russia. It is the ancient land of Colchis where the mighty Caucasus Mountains soar, and where Jason the Argonaut found the Golden Fleece.

We went to visit our dear friend, Goga, and his parents. We first met the family when the older brother, David, attended school in the States and introduced his younger brother to us. We had known the family for about eight years, making any visit memorable!

REFINED PALATE

Georgia is noted for its food and hospitality. This is a result of their philosophy that a guest is a gift from God. My 80 year old aunt toured the Soviet Union and declared that only in Georgia did the food taste any good! As one of the few wine making regions in the Soviet Union, Georgia was also the only national champagne producer.

If you don't get an invitation to dinner in a private home, you will miss the essence of Georgia. Dining is an experience, not simply an act for nourishment. It is a ritual requiring several hours. At one meal I counted 14 different dishes, and probably missed a few more. When we ran out of table space, cups were inverted and dishes piled in layers on the table. Up! Up! Up!

Walnuts were used extensively as well as cilantro, tomatoes, onions, all varieties of meat, vegetables, pomegranates, beans, hot peppers, mint, and basil. Nothing was overly spicy but each dish had a distinctive flavor. A favorite snack of mine was *churchkhela*, walnuts strung on thread and dipped in a thickened grape juice. Although the snack does not look appetizing, it keeps for a long time without refrigeration and was used by soldiers during war campaigns. My Georgian friends know that more than silver and gold, the gift I most appreciate when they visit is my *churchkhela*.

An entire art of dining has developed into a science. Presiding over the dinner was the *tamada* or toastmaster. He was responsible for the toasts made to various people in a specific order. No one offers a salute without his permission. With each pledge, the glass must be completely drunk, bottoms up. A *khantsi,* or a ram's horn, was used to honor a special guest. In return the guest is required to empty the horn to the last drop, a hefty feat in anyone's country. Needless to say, Georgians know how to hold their liquor. They are also masters at how to create a conviviality, almost a bonding!

"GAMARJOBUTS!" HELLO!

Our flight on Austrian Airlines took us briefly through the Vienna airport and then three more hours to Tbilisi, capital of the Republic of Georgia. When we landed on the tarmac, a VIP truck was waiting for us, compliments of Goga, our host. As we climbed the stairs to the immigration office, there was Goga in a suit and tie waiting to greet us.

"Eliska, welcome to Georgia!" and he embraced me in a big bear hug. "Welcome, Stephen!" and shook hands. The last time we saw him, Goga was a student running around in jeans, now he was a married businessman. He had filled out around the waist, as good husbands do, but he still had that wavy auburn hair, clear blue eyes, and infectiously funny smile.

Nicky was also there. He was another student that we had befriended in the States. He was now a champagne maker. He also represented the darker Georgian blood with black hair, eyebrows meeting at the noseline, and a ruddy complexion in a 5'11" frame.

Goga and Nicky represented the genetic strains that flow through this region. The Caucasus women like Goga's mother, were noted for their blond hair and blue eyes. Nicky's family represented the influx of the Persians and other peoples from the Gulf area. Both men married accomplished women from good families. Interestingly both wives were their husband's opposites in complexion: the swarthy dark haired man, Nicky, married a blond haired woman, while Goga with his auburn waves was wed to a dark haired beauty.

"Goga, that was quite a welcome, shuttling us across the air field in a VIP van!" I exclaimed.

"Yes, I wanted to make your arrival special so I pulled a few strings. You know how it is done here in Georgia. It is who you know!" Goga beamed.

"I am finally here in Georgia after hearing about it for years!" Stephen smiled.

Goga whisked us off to the city. As we left the airport I thought of our military friend's experience. Landing in Tbilisi when the Soviet Union was breaking up they had to buzz the runway to chase the cows off before they could land. Things had improved.

"How are your parents?" I inquired.

"They are doing well. Dad is back directing work in the factory that makes metal parts, and Mom just retired," Goga answered.

"What did she do?" Stephen asked.

"She was a physician, but they made no money since it was socialized. The last few years she earned enough in a month to buy a loaf of bread. Pitiful! Private doctors are doing better, though." Goga commented.

We drove on a four lane highway and soon were on Rustaveli Street, the main downtown thoroughfare. The avenue broadened and the shops took on a more sophisticated look. The major government buildings were located here as well as the opera house. There seemed to be more activity than when I first visited in 1994, an indicator that the economy was improving. We drove past the university, and past more modern shops selling jeans and western apparel, and finally into the parking lot of their apartment building. The high rise looked much the same as it did on my first visit except with more cars in the parking stalls.

Goga had tried to spearhead the neighbors to clean up the apartment building and install a new elevator, but only a few responded. He ended up shelving the idea. During Soviet times, hallways of the high rises were never cleaned or beautified. It was always a pleasant surprise to find the inside of a private apartment spotless and well decorated.

The following few years after the collapse of the communist government were financially difficult for people in the former Soviet States. Many were unemployed and people survived by selling personal possessions or receiving help from their children living abroad. Things were so tough that Goga's father once wished that Stalin were back in power, because at least there was food on the table. In baby steps, Georgia seemed to be moving forward. New businesses had sprouted on Rustaveli Street, and more cars being driven.

"*Gamarjobouts!*" as I hugged Ia, Goga's mother. "*Rogo ga hart?* Hello! How are you?" I blurted as I hugged the father. Goga then made introduction of my husband to the family. And we got to meet Goga's lovely wife and newborn son.

Goga's wife was petite and slender with shiny black hair cut in a bob. She had large dark eyes fringed with long eyelashes, a real beauty. She did not speak English, only Italian and Georgian. Her father was a wealthy manufacturer so she had many opportunities to travel abroad.

The newest member of Goga's family, Little David, charmed us all! He was only four months old and already half of his mother's height with a bundle of dark hair and dark eyes. He made little noises with the cutest smile and his eyes would light up at the sound of a human voice. His mother was only five feet four, but they say that his maternal grandfather was tall.

"A new couch?" I asked Goga.

Goga proudly beamed, "Yes, I bought this and a new dining table for my parents."

"Ah, life at your company must be good," I said.

"It's not bad," Goga confidently admitted.

On my first visit to Georgia I had been impressed with the devotion and fierce loyalty that the children exhibited towards their parents. It was not just Goga's family or Nicky's but everyone I talked with had strong bonds of affection. So it was natural that a second son, Goga, would willingly purchase furniture for his parents.

Goga was as flamboyant and generous as ever. Instead of putting us up in his parents' apartment, he rented his neighbor's unit for the week. He paid the widow to stay with her daughter for the duration of our stay. What can I say? For convenience? Excess? Originality? We thought it was pretty fun having our own penthouse with two bedrooms, a living room, dining room, and kitchen--right across the hall from Goga's parents!

Dinner that evening was at a traditional Georgian restaurant located near the Metekhi Church and Mtkvari (Kura) River. The restaurant consisted of a series of small cabins where guests could have all the privacy they needed.

The meal included traditional dishes like *badrijani,* baby eggplants stuffed with ground hazelnuts, *chakapuli,* a lamb stew, *khackapuri,* a cheese pie made of dough, *mtsvadi,* a lamb shishkebab, and *pkhali,* minced spinach mixed with ground walnuts and topped with pomegranate seeds. As usual we had to loosen our belts to devour all the food!

We were joined by Nicky and other friends we had met in America. I first met Dr. Gogi when he was a Fulbright scholar in Washington DC. He was a mature man with a wife and two children, not a young student like my other friends. And he knew everyone in government.

To illustrate his broad network, several years back on a Washington DC subway I bumped into some tourists. I helped them decipher the metro map and asked where they were from.

"The Republic of Georgia!" they replied.

"*Gamarjobuts! Rogo ga hart?*" I said greeting them in Georgian.

Their mouths dropped open and disbelief filled their eyes when they heard their native language coming from the lips of a Japanese-faced American.

"Don't you know that all Americans know Georgian?" I kidded them. Later in our conversation, we realized that we all knew Dr. Gogi, that is how well connected he was.

TBILISI

Georgian legend tells how Tbilisi was established when King Vakhtang Gorgasali shot a pheasant that fell into a hot spring. When the bird bounded out, apparently healed, the king believed the waters magical, and established his capital near the Mtkvari River. We heard that the sulphuric waters were soothing and healing even though we were unable to take advantage of them.

Our first full day was filled visiting tourist sites in the capital with our friends. We visited the large ethnology park, whose emphasis is on culture rather than chronology. Houses have been reconstructed from all parts of Georgia. According to Goga it was the first park of its kind in the world, although the Norwegians claim to have been the first. Georgia has the most varied building materials of any of the ethnography parks we have seen—wood, stone, and plaster shaped in squares, cones, and rectangles. We were impressed with the wide variety of building styles in this old Silk Road country.

Georgia was for centuries the crossroads for many conquering nations including Persia and those from Europe. The city has been destroyed nearly 30 times over the last 1500 years. The Hittites, Assyrians, Scythians, Cimmerians, Persians, Arabs, Turks and Mongols have all left their mark. Through it all, the Georgians have tenaciously clung to their culture, religion, language and traditions.

A tour of the newly restored Narikala Castle yielded a new cathedral that was built over the old foundations. During my first visit there was only rubble. Through the diligence of university students and archaeologists, the church was rebuilt with a high retaining wall. Dr. Gogi, our professor friend, noted all the donors on the plaque posted inside the church. He sarcastically commented that they were all well-known politicians, who had donated nothing to the building but merely wanted their names immortalized.

Goga, Nicky and Nicky's older sister Nino, and Dr. Gogi met us that evening. Nino was named after Saint Nino of Cappadoccia who brought Christianity to Georgia in 330 AD. Our Nino looked unbelievably good, her thick dark hair in a modern bob and her large dark eyes surrounded by long eyelashes. She had spent a year doing a fellowship in Budapest, and San Francisco, earning her doctorate in chemistry.

We met at the Hore-Hore, "Singing" Restaurant. It appeared to be a nondescript square building with simple tables and chairs. An occasional piece of artwork or craft enlivened the yellow walls. In the center was a large open space reserved for dancing. The ambiance came from the customers who sang, and danced along with the marvelous group of musicians. Georgians are known for their fine voices and nearly everyone in the restaurant joined in. The famous ballet choreographer George Balanchine was a Georgian. Unfortunately, my friends represented the non-singing, non-dancing Georgians. As expected, the restaurant heaped more food before us than we could handle, and we rolled out of the restaurant bursting!

MTSKHETA

On a weekend outing, Goga, Nicky and Nino, and Dr. Gogi and his wife, Nia, accompanied us to two of the oldest churches in Georgia, located an hour west of Tbilisi in Mtskheta. It was good to see Nia, Dr. Gogi's wife, who was now working at the US Embassy. She was dark haired, tall and slender with a gracious elegance about her. I have always admired her unruffled demeanor.

The churches were hundreds of years old, built before the 1400s out of local stones. At times such churches disappeared into the terrain since they were the same earth color as their surroundings. At the Djvari Church, Church of the Cross, the small but sacred stone structure was perched high on a hill. The entrance was through a rock patio matching the color of the medieval church. Inside was simply designed with a small screen separating worshippers from the priest's corner. The room was cozy and could probably hold only fifty standing worshippers but today we were the only visitors. Several icons of stylized madonnas and saints with halos were painted on the walls. Candles were lit on a narrow table. There were no benches, following the Eastern Orthodox tradition of standing during a church service.

We walked behind the church onto a balcony that overlooked the valley below where we fought a stiff wind. We were surprised we had driven so high on the mountain at least 2,000 feet above the valley floor. The original worshippers 600 years ago had to walk by foot or ride a beast of burden to reach this remote church. We did not stay long since the wind kept whipping our hair stinging our faces.

In the valley below was the Svetitskhoveli Church where the coronation and burial of the kings take place. Nicky and his wife were married here. The current cathedral was built in the 11th century although the site dates to the 4th century. Since it is believed to be the burial site of Christ's mantle, it is considered one of the most venerated places of worship in the country.

This church was six times larger than the Djvari Church on the hill. Its large barren grassy courtyard was surrounded by a ten-foot fence. As we approached we could smell burning incense and we saw a few people milling about. We followed a priest who wore a long black tunic to his ankles over dark pants and a standing cap on his head. His mustache and beard were scraggly and I wanted to fill in the white spaces of his beard with eyebrow pencil.

It took our eyes a moment to adjust to the darkness of the interior. There were no electric lights. Shafts of sunlight, like beams through dark clouds after a storm, fell on four priests practicing their melodic hymns. Their voices blended, rising and falling with such power that when they stopped there was an empty silence. Georgian harmony is known over the world, and perhaps on other planets. According to Goga a recording of Georgian singing was sent on a rocket into outer space.

Some differences exist between the Roman Catholic Church and the Orthodox although their origins are the same. Orthodox priests can marry and raise a family. The sign of the cross is made with two fingers from right to left, unlike the Western Church where one finger moves from left to right. And incense is burned during Orthodox services.

We wandered over to the river where many families were milling about. To my surprise we ate again, more than your imagination can fathom. At a small takeout stand Nicky ordered *khinkali,* Goga's favorite dish, dumplings filled with ground beef, pork, lamb and spices, which looked like large ravioli. These dumplings were boiled and eaten with a dish of fresh greens, watercress, basil or local produce. *Shish kabobs,* or meat on skewers, was another main dish—a decidedly Persian influence. We sat at a table on an open veranda and stuffed ourselves until my stomach ached from overeating. We were so full that we almost couldn't walk.

We kidded Nicky that he ought to go into politics. We could not walk 20 feet without someone saying hello to him. He engaged in long conversations with numerous people at the river.

On the way home we stopped at the champagne company where Nicky was an officer. He showed us his big office complete with private bath and bottles of the most delectable champagne.

Since Russia was a closed country during the Cold War, most of Russia's stock of champagne came from Georgia. Nicky's father was a winemaker and the gene ran in his family.

To top off the evening Dr. Gogi, invited us to his house for dessert. Dessert was not just one but four choices, typical of abundant Georgian hospitality. I was beginning to understand that unless the guest aches with the pain from overeating, Georgians will consider themselves poor hosts.

AN AUSTRIAN PARTNERSHIP

The one place Stephen wanted to visit was the Caucasus Mountains. They rise from the base of the valley to over 16,000 feet above sea level breaking into breathtaking snowcapped peaks. He wanted to find the highest peak in Georgia. Goga, the consummate host arranged a day off from work to take us.

I expected to see sparse settlements on our drive northward but instead we saw dense concentration of homes and people in the valleys. Spacious square farm houses were made of stones and plastered over. As we began climbing in elevation the houses finally disappeared.

We drove to a ski resort in the Caucasus Mountains where Goga had honeymooned called Gudauri, a joint venture between the Soviets and Austrians. The resort was closed in May although scattered snow still remained on the mountain. The hotel was European in ambiance with indoor pools, a sauna, a whirlpool, two indoor tennis courts and bowling lanes. We wandered around hoping for lunch but no services were available.

We headed further north. We drove over an incredibly narrow gravel mountain pass that Coke trucks careened down with abandon. I'd call it an unpaved country road in the States with sharp switchbacks. As we questioned the number of accidents on such a road, we came upon a truck tipping over at a 45 degree angle. Men were clustered around propping it up trying to save the cargo. We did not linger to find out if they were successful. I hope they were.

The first time Goga drove this road he was returning from Moscow late at night. He was glad that the darkness hid the deep chasms and challenging road conditions. Otherwise he would have lost his courage.

We reached the northern part of Georgia, near the Chechnya border. Fortunately the civil war had not escalated yet. Unfortunately, the highest peak, Mt. Shkhara at 17,059 feet, was shrouded in clouds and could not be fully seen. We lingered for a while and then turned the car around. We noted numerous glass greenhouses where tomatoes appeared to be growing.

A large monument in the usual oversized Russian mode was off the road as we came down the mountain pass. The parking lot was spacious but empty. We stopped and walked through the crunchy snow to examine the artwork more closely. The round memorial was several hundred feet in diameter with fabulous mosaics celebrating the friendship between Russia and Georgia. It seemed odd that such an expensive structure appeared to be abandoned, not located near any population center, or seemed to serve any real purpose. Its message was ironic now that Georgia was struggling to get out from under the shadow of Moscow.

SARKATVELO--GEORGIAN FOR GEORGIA

Goga tried to teach me some Georgian. Only five million speakers of Georgian exist worldwide. The language is distantly related to Basque in Spain. Some of the sounds were literally swallowed or were mere clicking noises. Part of my problem learning the language was that I couldn't justify this guttural tone as a letter.

When Goga's older brother, David, was graduating from Georgetown University, he invited their father, Jamal, for graduation. For my preparation I hired a private Georgian tutor, who taught at the State Department. When Jamail arrived in Washington, D.C., I was able to carry on a basic conversation-- aided by lots of hand gestures. Unfortunately language is a perishable skill. I could not repeat my performance today.

KAHETI

Dr. Gogi, my husband, Stephen, Goga and I drove to Kaheti a city east of Tbilisi to gain a glimpse of Narikala Fortress, a stone edifice that protected the Georgians from the Persians during their numerous wars. Persia seemed so far away, yet they were Georgia's breathing enemy for centuries. We also visited the spacious house and estate of one of the famous national poets and philosophers, Chachavadze. Names ending with *dze* or *vili* were usually of Georgian origin. In Georgia the people greatly respect and honor their writers and poets, enabling Chachavadze to enjoy this comfortable standard of living.

We ate a dish of *kachipuri*, a lamb stew with greens. We also ate sour green plums and the long curved traditional Georgian bread, *shotis puri*. Made of flour, water, salt, and yeast, the bread's curled ends result from baking in ovens narrower than the rolled dough.

The drive home was on a mountain road that the natives said cars could pass, but there were many potholes in the road. While Goga artfully dodged the road's deep caverns, the rest of us enjoyed some dramatic views of green mountains with pastoral settings. Trees hung their white blossoms over our path and sheep wandered here and there. The sun shone softly through billowy white clouds. Occasionally a shepherd wearing a woolen cap would pop his head up and wave. It was a picture waiting to be painted.

Goga is a real jokester and storyteller. He recited joke after joke all the way home to Tbilisi. He entertained us for over two hours and we laughed and laughed until our cheeks were tired from grinning so hard. It's challenging enough to be funny in your own language, alone in another, but Goga succeeded. I'd share the jokes with you except as soon as I hear a funny story, it evaporates from my brain. In other words I don't remember.

Again more eating. Dinner was at The Cellar Restaurant. As Nia slid into the booth, she noticed that her boss sat at the next table. How funny! We ate the traditional Georgian fare of dumplings, shishkabobs, eggplant, pomegranate garnishes, and walnut filled vegetables, and then rolled out of the place from too much food.

TOURIST DAY

Goga took us to the most dominant sight in Tbilisi—the big radio tower on the hill overlooking the city. When he was a child his parents would take the tram car up the slope and the family would play in the children's amusement park, and eat at the restaurant. The park was abandoned during the 1992-1994 Civil War over ethnic tensions when two provinces, Abkhazia and South Ossetia, broke away from Georgia. Bullet holes were still imbedded in the walls, paint was peeling, and neglect was apparent. No one has refurbished the park. According to Dr. Gogi the city was holding out for the biggest bribe.

Georgia enjoys a Mediterranean type climate so it was usually pleasant. However, it rained on Wednesday making it a perfect day for indoor shopping. Goga and Stephen indulged my whim and we went downtown to tourist shops on the main boulevard. I picked up the usual souvenirs, and little stuffed dolls in Georgian costumes. The dolls were adorned like ladies-in-waiting with long gowns topped by a headdress from which flowed a long veil. The male doll had dark full pants and dark shirt with billowy sleeves and wore a small pillbox hat.

Tbilisi has come of age--we ate lunch at the new McDonald's. When the chain first opened in 1999 you had to wait hours in line. Now the place was fairly empty since the average Georgian can't afford to eat there. Dr. Gogi shared his perspective again that a Georgian will spend nearly an entire month's wages to see and be seen at the latest venue and then eat beans the rest of the month.

The three-story, domed, and glass lined building was quite a swanky McDonald's, located next to one of the city treasures, the statue of founder, King Vakhtang Gorgasali. Many citizens protested a commercial building next to one of the city's most historic statues, but capitalism prevailed. I guess someone knew the right officials to bribe.

NICKY

Nicky's family invited us for dinner. The family lived in an apartment building across a gully from Goga's place. The outside resembled the remnants of a war zone, cement rubble and gray everywhere, but once inside the apartment, it was richly decorated with rugs and carved wooden furniture.

It was great to see his family again. Everyone looked exactly the same as five years ago except now Nino and Nicky both spoke English.

Their mom was a physicist by training but she chose to become a mother of two children. Her handsome dark eyes and hair indicated the Persian influence. She was on the quiet side, and since she spoke no English, our communication was always limited to smiles, pats, and nods of appreciation.

Their father, on the other hand was an extrovert. A small businessman he had large grey eyes, a shiny bald head perched on his slender body and a nose that curved down. He was formerly a wine maker and kept a private stock of the finest wines, but now ran a small business that managed to stay afloat as Georgia left the Soviet Union and struggled towards a capitalistic society. I never pinpointed the nature of the business, partly because we couldn't converse without an interpreter, and partly because he may have wanted to be vague. Many businesses had ties to the Mafia.

The grandmother was visiting from the far eastern side of Georgia. She had pale raisin-like skin and wore a kerchief on her head. She came up to my armpits since she was hunched over, but her eyes were bright and her handshake was as firm as ever. I was pleased that she remembered me from my previous visit. On that visit to her farm I remember there was no indoor plumbing, but everything was very neat and well tended. We had a marvelous dinner that evening with several other invited guests whose relationship I never established. At breakfast the next morning, those guests chased away their hangovers with shots of vodka.

I kept apologizing for how much work we created by visiting (a very Asian trait). There is so much work involved in preparing the food that we rarely saw Nicky's mother sit down at the table. In fact, she had invited her sister to help her in the kitchen. Nicky reassured me that it was a nice change to have visitors.

On our next-to-the- last day in Georgia we stopped at a newly opened restaurant for a snack of *kachipuri,* consisting of a round flat bread with an egg in the center, a regional dish from Batumi on the Black Sea. There were no special spices, but it tasted fresh. In typical Georgian fashion, the restaurant was swarming with people since it was a new locale to see and be seen. Goga even let us pay for some of the food, since we were so insistent. Georgians usually won't let you pay for anything. We had to be careful not to say we wanted anything, because before we knew it, it would be ours.

We repeated that we wanted to treat everyone to dinner. After our persistence, our friends relented and took us to a pizza joint that many foreigners patronized. We had a pleasant meal with good food. The bill was very modest and we felt it was a poor pay-back from us for all the incredible hospitality we had enjoyed.

FAREWELL PARTY

The end of the week came so quickly! Truly the days dash by when you are enjoying yourself. Goga and his parents insisted on hosting a farewell party, attended by people we knew and loved. There was Goga with his wife and baby, Nicky with his wife, Dr. Gogi and Nia, his wife, Goga's parents, Ia and Jamail. Later Dr. Alex, a professor I had met on my first visit, stopped by. I swear when I return to Georgia I will wear only elastic waistbands. Once again we ate until we couldn't eat any more.

Through the week we noted that Georgia has made some economic recovery since its independence from Russia. There were glimmers of prosperity here and there, but the overall progress was much slower than I had hoped. Fortunately our individual friends were all doing well and each one seemed healthy and prosperous.

We gained a new appreciation and understanding of the word *generosity*, and loved learning so many new things about history, geography, and culture. Later we would return home and post the map of Georgia and her alphabet as reminders of great friends in an exotic part of the world.

After the many dishes of food were consumed, and our belts were loosened, the toasting began in earnest. Goga gave the honor of the *tamada*, the toastmaster, to Dr. Gogi, and afterwards complimented him on his sensitive handling of the evening. In the States, toasting, if done at all, is more a ritual ceremony often coming across as rote and flat. By giving a toast to someone, the words form a bond and a feeling of affection. We toasted their generous hospitality, their kindness, their attention to detail, and most of all their friendship. We felt a closeness that will forever tie these wonderful, warm-hearted people to us. We counted our blessings, not our calories after having been to Georgia!

Russia

June 1999

A PARTYING CLERK

The Austrian Airlines clerk must have been partying the night before. Even though the ticket clearly stated "Moscow through Vienna," he labeled Stephen's luggage for VIE or Vienna. Given the grief I experienced the last time I was in Moscow when I had to wait three days for my lost luggage, I hand carried my bag. We arrived in Moscow but Stephen's luggage was still riding on the carousel in Vienna. So Stephen had to wait a day and a half for his luggage. Fortunately an extra set of underwear and clean clothes for him had been packed in my hand carry—a lesson learned from experience.

Part of the problem getting our luggage through Russian customs was that we carried a half dozen bottles of water with us. In Germany, it was difficult to find non-carbonated bottled water, so we brought our own to Russia. Perhaps the customs inspectors had read too many James Bond novels and thought we were transporting heavy water used in making plutonium for nuclear weapons. Being an "exotic" Asian woman with a tall handsome military officer, we might even have passed as spies!

We also got a good dose of Russian customer service. We contacted the tour company about the delayed luggage, and they said it was the airline's problem. We kept calling the airlines and each time someone would answer, "Please call back in an hour or two." Stephen heard this at least four or five times. The tour company tried calling for us, and finally said that it might be best for us to go to the airport in person. Mind you, the airport was 40 minutes away by taxi and we didn't speak Russian. Thoughts of spending three or four hours at the airport was frustrating, but we needed his luggage. Since creative solutions were rather sparse we went. With relatively little hassle we got Stephen's bags. Twice I have been in Moscow and twice lost luggage.

MOSCOW

Everything in Moscow was on a monumental scale. Downtown streets were ten lanes wide and the buildings seemed never-ending. Red Square was a dramatic center to Moscow with its open parade grounds ending at St. Basil Church. The Church was built in 1555 and was noted for its colorful onion domes painted green and yellow, lapis lazuli and white, and red and black. The tallest tower was painted in a multitude of reds topped by a golden onion dome. Red Square is often considered the central square in all of Russia deriving its name from an old Russian word that meant *red* or *beautiful*. The adjective beautiful was applied to St. Basil, and somehow transferred to the plaza surrounding it. The square separates the Kremlin from the shopping district of Kitay-gorod. We were thankfully there in summer. I shiver at the thought of a bleak cold winter with Siberian winds howling.

We stayed at the massive Hotel Russia, which could accommodate 6,000 guests, and wasn't as bad as the tourist books described it. One called it an eyesore and another recommended a compass to find one's way around. We were pleased to have a private bath with running hot water, since we don't take anything for granted when traveling. There was no air conditioning but the windows opened to allow the summer breeze to waft through. The hotel's main virtue was its central location next to Red Square. Stephen and I managed several trips back and forth between sightseeing to grab a snack, phone about the lost luggage, and take a shower or nap.

KREMLIN

Even though we were fatigued from jet lag on our first evening, we walked entirely around the Kremlin, a triangular shaped complex of government buildings including the official residence of Russia's President. Within the Kremlin Walls are four palaces, four cathedrals and the Kremlin towers. The city was shinier and brighter than I remembered from my previous visit four years earlier. Much of the communist grime was gone and there was new construction. It was a lively Sunday summer evening so throngs of people milled about the plaza, talking, flirting, and enjoying the fountains.

We ran into a Lenin impersonator who earned a little change posing with visitors for a photo. He had Lenin's high balding forehead, the soft cap with a brim, and costume to match. He was so charming that we succumbed and had our photo taken with him.

The next morning we enjoyed an excellent orientation tour of the city with our tour group. I had never reached the outskirts of Moscow on my first trip so this was a treat for me.

We drove around the outside of the Kremlin, past the Pushkin Museum, Tolstoy's House to Novodichy Convent, by the stadium, by the University of Moscow now called Losomonov, past Arbat Street, Treykov Street, and the White House. The White House was their Parliament building, a large square office building that still bore the black smoke from the shootings that had occurred. Parliamentary opponents to President Boris Yeltsin led an armed uprising in October 1993 that lasted ten grisly hours with tanks punching holes in the front of the White House.

In the afternoon we left the tour and headed out on our own, our focus the Kremlin. Once inside the Kremlin Walls we visited the Armoury, which started as storage for the royal arsenal, and now was a museum displaying the most exquisite silverwork, plus the gowns of Catherine the Great. Like so many of the royal families who didn't always speak the language of the people they ruled, Catherine was German by birth.

A RECORD BREAKING SPRINT

The next morning we returned to the Kremlin and walked around several 13th and 14th century churches inside the compound. Although we entered the Kremlin Walls we were turned away at the entrance of the churches. We didn't speak the language so we couldn't ask why. Finally we slipped in with another German tour group and gazed at all the ornate paintings. Filled with icons and candles the churches were intimate spaces, not the soaring cathedrals of Europe.

Stephen still kids me that he never saw me run faster than at the Kremlin. We bought our tickets at a kiosk about 300 yards away from the entrance of the Armoury. When the entrance guard saw my large duffel bag, he said I had to check the bag back at the ticket building. The Armoury was closing in five minutes, so

I sprinted to the kiosk and back to the gate in record time. This was one exhibit I was not going to miss!

We were here to see the Russian State Diamond Fund, home to Russia's most important and impressive treasures--diamonds in the crown jewels collection. As we walked the corridor guards lined the airtight rooms every ten feet. Glass showcases displayed the finest treasures. One royal crown was entirely of diamonds. The largest diamond in the world was atop the Russian scepter—the Orlov Diamond! The helmet of Yaroslav II, the sabers of Kuzma Minin and Dmitri Pozharski, all famous rulers, and the fabled Faberge eggs were on display. After being in these rooms I could understand why there were mystery movies involving Russian diamonds. Surrounded by such amazing wealth my imagination couldn't help but shift into high gear.

I ask a lot of questions. Today's was: why do kings always hold a scepter in their right hand and an orb in their left with a crown on their head? The scepter, originally a long staff or rod, has come down through antiquity as a symbol of power used by the King of Persia, the Greeks, Etruscans and Romans. The orb or round ball was another representation of potency and also the visual token of holding the world. The cross on the orb was a Christian emblem of God's dominion over the world. A king or queen received their crown at a coronation ceremony legitimizing their authority. The crown, scepter, and orb were established symbols of royalty and power.

Our eyes were bedazzled by the wealth we had seen, and once outside we had to squint for a moment. We meandered around the Kremlin Wall to Red Square., and decided to peek inside Lenin's Tomb. No cameras were allowed and there was no check-in kiosk. So while I dashed in, Stephen held our cameras. Then I held the equipment while he peeked inside.

When I walked downstairs into the mausoleum I was the only person in the dark sunken room. I paused through the hazy light to gaze at Lenin. The soldier on guard snapped his fingers and motioned for me to keep moving. I think it's because the body was really a wax figure and they didn't want people to observe it too closely, at least that was a joke a friend told me. Lenin has been on display since 1924 and there is speculation that parts of the body might be fake. The next day we had extra time and there was no line, so we went through the Tomb again. We also wanted to be sure we saw it all because the guards made us hustle so fast. Afterwards we strolled along the headstones near the Kremlin Wall and read the names of the leaders of Russia including the infamous Stalin.

In preparation for this trip I read an epic novel on Peter the Great (1672–1725), which helped me understand the long history of what I saw. One man, Peter, albeit king, had moved a massive feudal country, uneducated, untrained, uncivilized, and superstitious, into contemporary European culture, westernizing and expanding her into a major power. It was a tremendous feat! Such a simple thing as shaving men's beards and wearing Western clothing met fierce resistance from his people. Standing nearly seven feet tall, Peter the Great was a visionary. He recognized Russia's need for a warm water seaport and fought for one near Azov in the Black Sea. He patterned his city, St. Petersburg, after Amsterdam where he spent time as a young man. He was ruthless when people crossed him, but he achieved phenomenal success in making Russia a European power.

On our own we bravely rode the Moscow subway. I remember thinking how fast the escalators ran over long steep inclines. They clacked since they were made of wooden slats running parallel with the railings. We arrived safely at the Pushkin Art Gallery where paintings by Matisse and other famous Impressionist painters hung. The building lacked air-conditioning which made it tiring to tour for any length of time.

Americans may not be aware that our American National Gallery of Art evolved from purchases made from Russian collections. During the Russian Revolution of 1917 Bolsheviks sold the paintings to collectors to raise hard cash for the revolt. Andrew Mellon, American banker and avid art collector, acquired many of these paintings among them Raphael's *St. George and the Dragon*, Botticelli's *Adoration of the Magi* and Titian's *Venus with a Mirror* and several Frans Hals and Rembrandts--making it one of the greatest art transactions in history. Mellon later donated his entire collection to the new National Gallery of Art in Washington, D.C.

We found Leo Tolstoy's simple Moscow house on our own. Tolstoy's principal dwelling was in the country south of Moscow but to placate his wife who tired of rural life he maintained a house in the city. I had just finished his book on tape of *Anna Karenina* so I paid special attention. The two-story house was sparsely furnished but contained portraits of his family and his writings. It was not the objects we saw but what had transpired here that intrigued us. Tolstoy regularly entertained composers like Rachmaninov and Rimsky-Korsakov and writers like Chekhov and Gorky. Artists cannot generate ideas in a vacuum so they always seemed to congregate and feed on one another's creativity.

We walked to Arbat Street a picturesque pedestrian mall noted for its excellent craft stores and entertainment. We dined at a Mexican restaurant owned by a Cuban. Naturally when Stephen finds someone who speaks Spanish, he engages them in conversation. It took me a while to absorb the fact that a Cuban from a warm tropical island would move to freezing Russia but then I remembered that Cuba was also a communist country. I assumed that the blanks in our host's life story were highly classified. For a brief moment the idea of him being a KGB spy fluttered through my brain. Anything is possible.

On my first visit to Moscow, David, my Georgian friend, had accompanied me to Arbat Street. A bundled peasant woman with lines of hard living on her face, approached us selling a *matruska*, nesting dolls, made of black lacquer. Each of the twelve dolls portrayed a Russian tale. David whispered that in order to survive many people were selling family treasures on the street. He knew the value of the *matruska* doll and encouraged me to purchase it, which I did. It was not inexpensive, but it was a rare treasured piece.

DAS-BE-DAN-YAH (Good-bye)

St. Basil has been closed all week. On our last day it opened to the public. The church was the striking landmark at the end of Red Square with fabulous colored onion domes. Napoleon wanted to dismantle the church and move it to France. He lacked the technology so he ordered it bombed. A sudden rainstorm drenched the gunpowder saving the church. Napoleon then changed his mind about razing the icon so it comes to us intact.

A funny story was told by our guide of a native Russian who while traveling abroad came upon a photograph of a gaily-painted church.

"What's this photo?" he asked his friend.

"Don't recognize your own church? It's St. Basil in Moscow," the friend retorted.

The traveler was embarrassed that he didn't recognize his own sanctuary, because he had known it only as a gray color. Right there he resolved to restore St. Basil to its original bright grandeur and fulfilled his promise years later.

The Church is so prominent on Red Square that once inside I was surprised at its cloistered feel. I had expected an expansive interior to match its reputation. There was one large central dome with eight smaller galleries surrounding it. All the rooms were painted an eggshell yellow and had simple repeating motifs. Inside the top of the largest cupola, the rounded ceiling, was an icon of Christ with a stylized halo circling his head, his nearly touching eyebrows hanging over beady eyes, the left hand holding a Bible and the right raised in blessing. Considering the church was nearly 450 years old, I should be amazed that the church was still standing!

The tour group graciously consented to give us a ride to the Treykov Gallery even though we had not signed up for this specific tour. This gallery featured all Russian artists. It was an impressive display including artwork that could be termed true masterpieces. But they were unfamiliar to us since there was not much communication between East and West. It amazed me how isolated we can become as a people, not knowing what is happening on the other side of the world as if there were a tangible wall of silence.

We had dinner at Pushkin Square at the largest McDonald's in the world. We found the meals comparable to the West. For whatever it was worth, 24 rubles equaled $1 and my hamburger cost about 56 rubles.

On my first visit to Moscow, I ended up having to find dinner on my own with everyone else in meetings. A women's group needed one more person to get a group discount on flights and asked if I would go. I agreed since I was already planning to fly to the Republic of Georgia and was curious to learn about Russian women's issues. I had no host during my stay so I had to fend for myself. I went to the nearest McDonald's. I figured I could point to pictures since I didn't speak or read Russian. I remember the server's confused looks when I resorted to hand gestures but at least I didn't starve!

OVERNIGHT TRAIN

We took a train to our next destination--St. Petersburg. The engine, a rounded military shaped bullet painted a dull green, reminded me of the engine from old Russian movies. It was so incredibly hot at the station, hotter than a sauna, that rivulets of sweat ran down people's faces. After the train got moving, it cooled down to the point that we became cold matching Russia's extreme temperatures.

In the narrow train passage we met some Australians. Their group had been traveling for nearly three weeks. They began in Hong Kong and traveled by train to Guangxi, Xian home of the terra cotta soldiers, to Beijing, to the capital of Mongolia to Lake Bakaal, largest fresh water lake in the world, and then through Siberia. They had toured Moscow and were now on their way to St. Petersburg. What a long, ambitious trip! One woman on the tour got so accustomed to the train lulling her to sleep that she had difficulty sleeping in a regular hotel bed.

We shared our train compartment with another couple, Renata and Arno our 20-something companions. He was a tall skinny student in Berlin and she was equally thin. Both were raised in East Germany and were fluent in German and Russian. They agreed that speaking Russian gave them a decided advantage while traveling. The train beds were quite comfortable. Exhaustion also makes sleep more appealing. Although I slept happily through the night, Stephen complained that he woke up at every train stop.

A PLANNED CITY

Our hotel in St. Petersburg was the Pulskaya, a joint venture of Finland and Russia. The rooms were larger than in Moscow. However, the hotel was not as convenient with a 40 minute subway ride to the center of town instead of a five-minute walk across Red Square.

In front of the hotel was a dramatic memorial honoring the 900,000 people who died in the 900-day siege of St. Petersburg during WWII from September 8, 1941, until January 27, 1944. Nazi Germany encircled the three million inhabitants of the city who refused to surrender despite an unusually cold winter and little food. It is estimated that over 641,000 to 800,000 civilians perished, but the city is proud of its fortitude.

St. Petersburg was called Leningrad for a time then changed back to its original name. It was a city planned by Peter the Great. He wanted the city to be styled after Amsterdam, so there were many canals. Most of the major edifices were low square buildings in baroque-federal style. The city had a uniform look since it was built in one period rather than over centuries. Many in our group felt Moscow had more vibrancy, but St. Petersburg's major sights were truly outstanding.

On our first afternoon, Stephen and I braved the subway on our own using a guidebook and my limited knowledge of the Russian alphabet. The only signs written in English were name brands. We walked the canals and found our way to Pushkin's house, home of one of Russia's greatest poets. He enjoyed near-idol status and his home was an opulent 12-room mansion on the Moika Canal. Also quite an artist Pushkin illustrated his writings. Tragically he died at age 37 in a duel fought to defend his wife's reputation.

We wanted to visit Church of Our Savior similar to St. Basil in Moscow. We stood at the entrance booth and started to pay our 30 rubles. The woman refused to sell us tickets. Instead we were directed inside to purchase our admission at 250 rubles for foreigners, more than eight times the local rate. I sort of understand why they charged foreigners more, and didn't mind at the Kremlin, but to see one more church? I contented myself by looking at a mosaic icon through the iron fence and leaving.

This may have been the church my girl friend, Jo, visited in the 1980s while Russia was still governed by the suppressive communist regime. Jo recounted how people seemed almost afraid to talk to her because secret police were watching their every move. She felt such a heavy numbness in her heart. People's eyes were dull and listless as if hiding their true feelings. In this church she had a brief encounter with a white haired dowager. A slightly bent woman dressed from head to toe in black approached my friend and squeezed her hand totally unafraid. She babbled in Russian pointing to the front and then upwards toward the heavens. Jo looked into the woman's face and saw a glimmer of light in her countenance. She felt the spirit of hope for the first and only time in Russia in that woman's eyes. According to my friend it was no coincidence that a church was the only place in godless Russia where a spark of freedom could survive. When her group left Russia and flew into Finnish air space the entire planeload of passengers erupted into a spontaneous cheer. Everyone was relieved to be away from the heavy-handed oppression they had all felt.

WORLD'S LARGEST REPOSITORY

Thursday found us at the Hermitage, the world's largest art museum. A brass band in front of the gallery entertained waiting patrons, playing every foreign tune they could think to cater to paying foreign visitors. They got the biggest tip from the Koreans for playing *Arirang,* a famous folk song.

We climbed the wide marble stairs up to the ornate palace. The summer heat was oppressive. Only one restored section had air conditioning, nonetheless we pressed onward. We managed to beat the crowds to the Matisses, the core of the Impressionists section. Many of these paintings have toured in the United States so it was like a reunion for me! I was a little shocked that the paintings were often hung right next to a window with no ultraviolet protection. Renoir's famous *Boy with a Whip* was in dire need of restoration with large cracks in the oil. Other paintings were behind glass and the strong glare made it difficult to see. It was still a great treat for me!

A one-time stroll through this museum could not replace the opportunity to feast for days on these great works. As a volunteer docent in Washington, D.C. at the National Gallery of Art, I was regularly exposed to world-class art. Each time I noticed a little more in every painting. Great art continues to touch our souls giving us something new to savor each time we view it. I am grateful for the opportunity to visit the Hermitage but I left aesthetically hungrier than when I had arrived.

IT'S ABOUT PETER

The Venice of the North, St. Petersburg, was literally created from a swampy bog. Poor living conditions and widespread disease took a toll on many of the peasants trying to build this city of canals. Peter the Great pressed forward with his dream. It was amazing to consider what one person with absolute power can accomplish in a short time, compared to a compromising republican government. Peter could be criticized for his callous punishment of those who disobeyed or betrayed him. Yet examining the other side of the argument, what if Peter had never lived and accomplished all that he did, where would Russia be today?

Saturday was the culmination of our visit to the magnificent mansions of the Peterhof and Catherine's Palace located west of St. Petersburg. The Peterhof is often coined, the Russian Versailles, famous for the spectacular fountains surrounded by gilded figures on the shores of the Gulf of Finland. The dramatic Grand Cascade is a series of steps with water spraying upward flanked on each side with life-size statues in gold leaf. I was surprised to learn that the fountains operate without the use of pumps relying instead on elevation and natural spring waters.

The Grand Palace looks imposing from the gardens yet is relatively small and narrow. The Chesma Hall is decorated with12 large paintings of the Battle of Chesma a naval victory for the Russians over Turkey in 1768-1774. The Picture Hall was another noteworthy room with over 368 paintings mostly of women. What was remarkable was that only one model was used for most of the paintings. The amber room was robbed by the Nazi during World War II and is now being restored with genuine amber pieces covering its walls. Impressive!

I am especially fond of the wooden parquet floors made of ornate and intricate designs throughout royal residences. Not only did the craftsmen know their various colored woods, but showed incredible skill in fitting the pieces together. I kept reminding Stephen that the carpenters didn't have electric band saws in those days, and that everything was done by hand.

Catherine's Palace next to the grand Peterhof was being restored so many parts were closed to us. Photographs showed how thoroughly the Nazis destroyed the residences, and how much time and money it has taken to restore the sumptuous palaces.

WHITE NIGHTS

We were in St. Petersburg during the White Nights when the sun dipped on the horizon for a mere 30 minutes and then reappeared essentially creating nearly 24 hours of sunshine. It was fun having light that late. However, after a full day touring, we were wiped out and confess that we never saw a sunset. It's hard work being a tourist!

Next to our hotel was a typical Russian style grocery store. One of the most interesting experiences on a trip is to peek into the activities of ordinary folks. We were impressed with the cheap prices of food, but then again we made more than $100 a month, which we heard was the average salary.

Our only free morning was Sunday, so we dashed to the cemetery where several famous musicians were buried: Tchaikovsky, Rimsky-Korsokov, Murgorsky, and the writer Dostoevsky. My mother and I went annually to the famous ballet, *The Nutcracker,* with the music composed by Peter Tchaikovsky. I also studied the piano and grew to love the little excerpts from his concertos. There was much contrast in his music from the light to the ponderous. Tchaikovsky was such a part of my childhood that I had to have a photo next to his tomb.

I wondered why artists of all persuasions when using paints, music, or drama have such a burning need to create, almost a compelling drive to share this melody, this painting, or play. It becomes a powerful compulsion in their lives, not totally propelled by monetary reward. Creating art is a difficult lifestyle, but I am grateful I am the beneficiary of their passion.

We slipped into a church while religious services were being held. Everyone stood. The room was dark except for the hundreds of dancing flames on lit candles and the smell of wax scenting the air. The women all wore head scarves. A choir provided the melody, voices blending so harmoniously that we didn't miss the organ. Every face reflected a devout piety. A feeling of peace attended the service.

RUSSIA IN TRANSITION

As a child I had considered Russia as one unified country. When the Berlin Wall fell in 1989 and the Iron Curtain was lifted, I was surprised to discover the many republics and ethnicities that had been under Russian domination, were each now asserting its independence. It was a keen reminder of how quickly we forget history if we are not paying attention.

We saw great monuments to the past rulers, yet we only skimmed the surface of the heart and mind of the Russian people. They now struggled to make it economically as Russia is lurching forward to an open market economy. I was not certain if the reserve of her people stemmed from a natural inclination or from having lived with repression for so long. It is as if their harsh climate was reflected in their outlook and philosophy. I have heard it said though I did not witness it, that among friends the chill disappears and Russians become a jovial and lively people.

Much of Russia's story has been one of suffering, so its writers, musicians and artists have drawn their creative works from heart-wrenching events. To me it seemed there was no lightness, only a fathomless depth.

If I were to describe Russia in one word, it would be IMMENSE. Everything in Russia is expansive, from the geographic size of one of the world's largest countries, its gargantuan monuments, its massive roads, and its long and turbulent history. Most important is the widespread tenacity of her people against natural and man-made obstacles, retaining their identity and forging ahead.

The Baltic States—
Lithuania, Latvia, Estonia, And
Helsinki, Finland

July 1999

BALTIC STATES

Vilnius? Riga? Tallinn? Most Americans looked puzzled when we mentioned these names, wondering where on earth we visited.

These Baltic States were not to be confused with the Balkan States where the Kosovo fighting occurred. The Baltics—Estonia, Latvia, and Lithuania--are by the Baltic Sea and Finland. We had friends doing volunteer work in Lithuania so we decided to visit these former Soviet states.

VILNIUS, LITHUANIA

From the air, we spotted cultivated fields with clumps of trees dotted by lakes and rivers--an idyllic landscape. Stephen's brother had once visited here during the winter. He reported only four hours of daylight, and a blustery cold wind. I was glad to see green everywhere and plenty of summer sunlight.

Our American friends, Dee and Beverly, met us at the airport. We knew the couple from our first tour of Maryland. Dee was a retired scientist and amateur basketball player. Beverly was a daily swimmer and never without a smile. Although they were a decade older than we were, we bonded with them. They had volunteered to serve a mission for their church and were stationed in Vilnus. I laughed to think that they had requested an English speaking area to serve. Yes, they spoke English, but everyone else around them spoke Russian or Lithuanian. An interpreter usually accompanied them on official business. Otherwise Dee spoke clear English and hoped that people understood him.

Hailing a taxi was a challenge, because many cabs lack meters and drivers can charge what they like. Dee found an honest driver after negotiating in the street, and we headed for their apartment. The flat was a leftover from communist era days, but was clean and spacious. The ceiling was 12 feet high, and the interior doors had glass in them. The furnishings were sparse since our friends volunteered for only 18 months. We tossed our suitcases into our bedroom and handed them two boxes containing Mexican food, enchilada sauce, tacos and other American items. Until recently, such delicacies were unavailable in Lithuania. Beverly immediately said, "Oh, I can invite some fellow Americans for dinner. They will love it!" She always thought of others.

Dee drilled us on our pronunciation of "Vil-NEE-us," the capital of Lithuania.

"No, the locals say Vil-NOOSE," he corrected us.

"Vil-NOOSE," we parrotted back.

I wanted to see something unique to the region so off we went to a small amber museum. The museum/shop explained the history of *Gintaro*, also known as Lithuanian amber, sometimes called Baltic gold or fossil resin. Most genuine amber on the market is from this part of the world. The color ranges from black to a clear yellow. When real amber was burned, it smelled like pine pitch.

I noticed long legged, dark-eyed beauties on the street chatting on cell phones.

Everywhere in Lithuania people talked on the wireless phones. Later I read that this country has one of the highest cell phone usages in the world.

We met an older American and his grandson at lunch one day. The man was born in Lithuania but emigrated as a child. This trip was a coming home present he gave himself. This tall lanky grandfather got a twinkle in his eye when he told us, "Had I known the women were this attractive with such short skirts, I would have returned to Lithuania much sooner. There's so much scenery!"

We were happy to accompany Dee and Beverly to their church meetings. We joined in the congregational singing in English. He told us there was always one hymn sung in Russian and the other in Lithuanian to appease both groups. Because Lithuania had so recently been communist, we expected only a stark room for the church services, but were pleasantly surprised to find a new chapel building. We supposed there would be few members, and were amazed by the good-sized congregation of 60 persons. Dee conducted the meeting with the help of an interpreter.

Since our American friends did not have a car, we boarded the intercity bus the next day and took a 40 minute ride to Trakai. They invited an engaging young college student, Anna, to join us as an interpreter.

At one time Lithuania covered Poland to the Black Sea and was the largest kingdom in Europe. Trakai was the capital of the great realm with an old medieval castle still standing. The red painted edifice had been lovingly restored and now stood on an island surrounded by a clear lake, perhaps a moat.

Along the shore were restaurants, and we indulged ourselves for lunch. I chose a mushroom salad with eggs and a bit of onion. We also had beet soup with sour cream and fried potatoes. I love eating at these places! Not only is the food fresh, delicious and filling but cost only $35 for five people!

We did not want to overstay our visit with Dee and Beverly, so we planned to head out that afternoon--our next destination Panavezys. We needed to get to the Vilnius station to catch our bus. We couldn't find a taxi, honest or otherwise. On a whim I raised my hand as a young man drove by in a beat up car. He stopped and when we explained our plight, he agreed to transport us. We crammed into the car sitting one on top of another. By some miracle, we arrived on time. We wanted to pay our impromptu taxi driver. His eyes opened up like saucers and he refused any money, but we insisted. After all, he helped a stranger in need. Can you imagine stopping someone like that in the States?

Beverly and Dee gave us a departing hug. We felt we had accomplished our "mission" by delivering two boxes of American and Mexican food to them.

PANAVEZYS, LITHUANIA

We took the chicken bus to Panavezys, two hours north of Vilnius, where our other American friend, Renee, was based. I say chicken bus because there were live animals on board including squawking fowl--the freshest way to transport meat without refrigeration! The bus stopped at every turn collecting colorful creatures, human and otherwise. There was no air conditioning and it was quite warm. My battery operated fan came in very handy.

The ride felt nostalgic. Every inch of soil was farmed with scattered horse-drawn wagons or plows. Some bus stops were only a simple bench sitting in a field with a few houses nearby. We wondered where these people came from and where they were going. My memory conjures a farmer sitting on his three-legged stool in the middle of a field milking his cow.

Renee met us at the bus stop, bubbling with smiles! She was a Peace Corps volunteer helping to teach business and English classes. We had met her through Stephen's older brother.

We walked the city square of the fourth largest city in Lithuania. We ate Panavezys pancakes for dinner, sometimes with potatoes added to the mix and topped with fresh fruits or with salty toppings like salmon. The food was good, although I would prefer it a tad spicier. Renee confessed that she missed her bottle of hot sauce. How fortunate that our gift box for her contained the spicy condiment!

Renee took us to her apartment in a high rise complex, a studio with a curtain sectioning off the bed area. The walls, furniture, curtains and bedspread were all olive green. She confessed her dislike of the Soviet era color making her seasick at times. However, it was spacious, clean, and had running hot water.

A host family helps a Peace Corps volunteer to transition into the society faster. Renee said her Lithuanian family had really helped her get over the homesickness everyone experiences abroad. The gracious family invited us to share some "tree" cake, *pyragas*, a national delicacy, and diet Coke at their apartment. The "tree" was a tort in ever-larger circles piled on top of each other to form a pyramid standing nearly a foot high. It was yummy if on the sweet side.

The hosts were a classic Soviet couple. The wife was short, stout, with bleached blond hair, and clear blue eyes. He was slightly taller, balding, sported a paunch, and was expansive in his smile. Their two children, a boy about ten and a girl eight, looked well and healthy. To counter the sweet torte, the mother fed us some homemade pickles that had no vinegar and were absolutely delicious. Trying to figure out what gave the pickles their tang we used broken Lithuanian and English and a dictionary. We deduced one ingredient was horseradish leaf. I still think of those as the best pickles ever.

The next day Renee asked a former English student of hers, Vladis, to drive us an hour away to the Hill of Crosses in Saulis the top tourist site in Lithuania. Much of Lithuania was on a flat plain so any change in elevation was quickly noticed. As we neared our destination we saw a dark mound rising on the horizon. Thousands of crosses of every size, hue, and material were crammed together in remembrance of the many who suffered years of persecution under the Soviet regime. Large wooden crucifixes were strung with smaller rosaries. It appeared to be a manmade forest. The Soviet leaders tore down the crosses several times, but each time they stubbornly re-appeared. The officials finally gave up and let them stand. As we gazed at the pastoral landscape surrounding the forest, it was difficult to imagine what horrors were memorialized.

Vladis, the English student, was a muscular five foot eight and in his mid-thirties. Renee whispered that she thought he was a lawyer but wasn't exactly sure what he did for a living. He had served in the Soviet army, yet was a patriotic Lithuanian. The country's hatred of communism was well documented and we saw very little evidence of Russian occupation remaining. The people were freer thinkers in this country, so they suffered more oppression under the brutal hand of the Soviets. Ironically Lithuania is one of the few countries to grant all of its Russian residents full citizenship. Other Baltic States have denied full status to their Russians creating ethnic tensions.

Part of the beauty of traveling on our own was the spontaneous, unplanned event. Vladis knew everyone, as though he were a politician. He suggested that we roast shishkabobs at his friend's cabin located in the middle of a small lake, even though his friend was back in the city. We all agreed. We dashed into a grocery store and purchased the necessary supplies.

Once at the lake he suggested we all go swimming. None of us was prepared with swimsuits. I looked at Stephen then at Renee. We all shrugged our shoulders and dove in the water with our clothes on. It was summer so the temperatures were pleasant. The laughter was infectious! We giggled like a group of school kids. As the sun set low in the horizon, we emerged from the lake and shook ourselves off like little puppies. We got the barbecue going and ate the most delicious beef, onions, tomatoes, and zucchini! We watched the sun set reflect in the water over snippets of broken English phrases. After the sun was securely settled in the west, we shuffled home to Renee's filled with laughable memories of our Panavezys visit!

RIGA LATVIA

For our farewell breakfast we ate Panavezys pancakes stuffed with a cottage cheese filling. We bid Renee good-bye and boarded the bus north for Riga, Latvia. The fare was $8 per person for a two-hour bus ride.

On our journey we visited with the young man across the bus aisle. He was Lithuanian studying polymer physics in Stockholm. To reach Sweden he would ride over 20 hours on the bus.

When I travel my passport is always by my side so at the Lativan border it unnerved me to surrender it to the customs official. The guard disappeared into a big official building while we waited inside the bus. Thinking of black markets and forged documents, I wondered if I would see my valuable document again. Finally after 20 minutes the guard re-boarded and handed out all the passports. I let out an audible sigh. I am certain that not many Americans travel by bus through this border, preferring to fly, so we probably raised a few eyebrows in the immigration office.

RIGA, LATVIA

Riga was a bustling seaport for the Russians. Peter the Great used it as the linchpin in his plan to open his country to the West. Fortunately for us the bus terminal was centrally located. We were able to store our bags and walk to most of the sights. We wandered through the city and by chance ended up at the Relocation Museum, the most visited tourist site. Had we tried to find it, I am certain we would have gotten lost. The display chronicled the history of the Russian and German occupations and the ensuing mass deportations and deaths. The museum was a sobering reminder of man's inhumanity to man.

On display were relics of items made by the Latvian prisoners. Even in oppression and miserable circumstances, these prisoners created beauty. One admirer built a silent keyboard for a famous pianist and composer who had been forced to work in the mines.

We met an American couple who were probably Silicon Valley yuppies from the look of their expensive perfectly matched biking outfits. They were cycling across the Baltics on vacation. They remarked how flat Lithuania was compared to Poland intimating how boring the country appeared to them. Too bad they did not know our friends there who would have made their trip definitely more interesting.

While we waited for our midnight bus ride to Estonia, we ate an incredibly filling Latvian dessert, a cream with raisin sauce, bread and berries, almost a meal in itself.

TALLINN, ESTONIA

The bus tickets north to Tallinn cost us $10 each. We managed the overnight ride on uncomfortable seats with wires poking through. Perhaps we were mastering the art of sleeping upright! Or was it merely exhaustion? At any rate, we slept through the night.

Renee had given us names of budget accommodations in the heart of the old city of Tallinn. The Peace Corps workers had a network and passed along good deals to each other. One travel guidebook rated our hotel as rock bottom cheap. The only drawback was that the entrance was shared with a topless bar located a floor above us. I felt a bit uncomfortable entering, but the rooms were clean and the price was right.

Our exploration of Tallin began with a climb to the upper hill where many Germans lived long ago. Beginning in 1346 for 500 years the Germans dominated commerce, the government and the Church making the Estonians little more than serfs. The German heritage is still strong enough that we occasionally spoke German words to obtain directions.

The older section of town containing cobblestone streets was totally surrounded by an old stone wall. It was easy to transport our minds to the days when kings and queens reigned. When the Iron Curtain fell we were pleasantly surprised to discover a rich culture and fascinating history of this area. I always associated the communist regime with cold steel rather than with flesh and blood tapestries.

The people, especially the women, seemed taller than elsewhere in Europe, evidence of Nordic influence. Many of the people looked American to us, not having a distinctive European appearance like the Germans or Russians. And yes, they used cell phones here but not as often as the Lithuanians.

We rode the public bus to Kadaka Torg, the marketplace, a large covered pavilion. The bus driver, an older man, spoke a little English. He told us that nearly all the shoppers on the bus were from Finland. The Finnish cross the Gulf of Finland for bargain shopping since it was so expensive in Scandinavia. Inside the market were incredible shops of food, clothing, and crafts. We looked long and hard at the hand-knitted sweaters but finally decided we didn't need any.

I remembered a travel show which followed a line of longitude down through Tallinn. We watched the program with fascination. My husband and I never dreamed we would someday be here!

HELSINKI, FINLAND

We stayed four days in Estonia since we felt prices would be more reasonable than in Finland. Our assumption was correct. But we still wanted to visit Finland, part of Scandinavia. So we caught an early express boat to Helsinki across the Gulf of Finland and in 1 ½ hours reached the city.

We wandered Helsinki's port and its open air market where we met a man selling thistle flowers. He proudly told us that the State of Hawaii requested his thistle seeds for their botanical garden. We ate smoked salmon, potatoes and salad for $5 from a street vendor. We boarded the T3 Trolley, a tram on a circular track running through the entire downtown. This was an easy way of seeing all the major sites. The city's architecture looked more restrained and had a reserved northern feel.

We had read that the tall handsome Finns were highly infatuated with the tango, an Argentinean dance. We felt it a rather sensual dance for conservative people, but that was its appeal—it allowed reserved people to express their emotions. Unfortunately our time was too short to see the dancers in action.

Someone once told Stephen that Helsinki was the book capital of the world. As we entered a large bookstore, a young clerk asked if he could help us. Stephen proceeded to ask for an obscure medical volume printed a few months ago. I nudged him. Why would he request such a specialized book? Stephen replied, "Someone told me that I could purchase any book in Helsinki and I want to see if it's really true!" Ten minutes later the clerk appeared carrying the six-inch wide tome. We were both impressed! Yes, if one bookstore carried such a highly specialized book, then Helsinki can keep its claim as the world's book capital!

MISTAKEN FOR A NATIVE

Since Stephen was a classical music buff, we went to Jean Sibelius' home, *Ainola*, outside of Helsinki. This famous composer's song, *Finlandia*, became a rallying tune for the Finnish people during occupation times. The hour long bus ride gave us a glimpse of suburban Helsinki reminding me of America during the 1950s with modest size homes and neatly tended yards.

After we paid the admission fee, a young lady handed my husband a brochure in Finnish.

"Ah, thank you but I need a brochure in English," Steve said.

"I am so sorry. I thought you were Finnish," the receptionist stammered.

Stephen beamed. He felt complimented he was mistaken for a native.

The house is named *Ainola* after Sibelius' wife. It was lovely and homey--truly a refuge for a creative composer. It was built of rugged Finnish native timber and stones with balconies, gables and verandahs. The two stories were simple, but the library was enormous contained over 3000 volumes. Sibelius required tranquility and the house was peaceful, but the city is now encroaching up to the property lines.

For our return trip to Tallinn, we took the ferry back. We recognized others passengers from the morning's express, following the same schedule as us.

A FIRST FOR US

Kadriog Park was in a ritzy section of Tallinn. Enjoying the quiet morning we strolled around and poked our heads into whatever caught our fancy. Peter the Great, built a palace here but spent very little time in it. Now it served as an art museum. We circled the president's palace, up the path to a monument dedicated to those who perished in a ferry accident, and then continued along the shoreline to the bus stop.

What happened next was not typical but does happen in former Soviet bloc countries. Since the front of the bus was so crowded we boarded from the rear. Stephen made his way to the front to purchase our bus tickets. It seemed he was taking a long time, but I thought he was just talking. Then he waved me over and told me that a group of uniformed men was preventing him from leaving the front of the bus until he had paid each of them $50. They demanded payment in dollars, not their currency. It was our last day in Estonia, and he showed them his empty wallet with a lone $20. They didn't bother to ask me for money even though I was carrying the lion's share of our cash. They grudgingly took the twenty. I was angry, but my husband said it was better to surrender the money than escalate the conflict. He was right.

We reported the incident to the tourist bureau, although we knew nothing would be done to pursue the issue. It was illegal to extort money like this but it happens. So a word to the wise--if you see several uniformed men in a front of the bus, immediately get off and wait for the next one. We were thankful no one was hurt.

Food is a remarkable comfort. We ate our last final meal at Vaenama's, Grandma's, which helped to calm our ruffled nerves. The tourist bureau recommended it for indisputable Estonian food. The meal of meat, potatoes, onions, carrots and bread were similar to American fare, but fresher with no preservatives. The meal was delicious, filling, and reasonably priced.

We caught a taxi and in a few minutes were at the airport close to downtown. A new terminal was being built next to the old one. Things were looking up for Estonia!

INDEPENDENT THINKERS

The Baltics were emerging from their post-communist economic doldrums faster than other former Soviet bloc countries. This was in part due to its industrial base developed during Russian occupation plus there is a higher ratio of progressive thinkers. They were moving rapidly but there will still be a generation's time needed for the transition.

The people were all friendly and accommodating. Many, however, were insulted if we greeted them in Russian. Only in the northernmost part of Estonia did we see any Russian newspapers. Most have turned their backs on the former Soviet Union and now face westward to Germany and the United States.

The Baltics were a bargain! While getting there was somewhat expensive, rooms and food were affordable, although I suspect that prices will eventually catch up with Western Europe.

We had not known what to expect, since information is limited. Our trip turned out to be fun and satisfying! Having American friends located in these remote places gave us a personal glimpse of daily life. Their friendships blessed us with a remarkable journey.

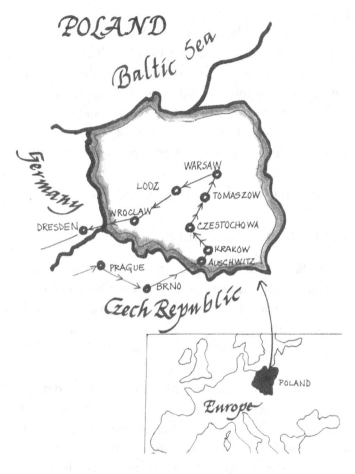

Ode To Poland

August 1999

YOUNG AT HEART

When Ingeborg boarded our bus at the Heidelberg Train Station, we knew we were in for a very special weekend trip. At the youthful age of 84 she was still directing tour groups! When

102

we later chatted on the subject of age, she said keeping active was the key. She certainly practiced what she preached.

We still had never entirely mastered the overnight bus ride. This time, we had our eye patches, earplugs and pillow, but forgot the sleeping pills. Somehow we got in enough winks that we were fairly coherent for morning breakfast at the Hotel Florin in Olomouc, Czech Republic. This city, however, still suffers from economic repression illustrated by its drab sooty buildings. The blooming flowers in the nearby park provided a pleasant contrast to the dreariness.

European breakfasts were filling with breads, meats, cheeses, hard boiled eggs, vegetables, yogurt and drinks. Filling up our bellies helped us survive the long days since lunch stops were unpredictable.

As we rode along, I found it interesting how different countries stack their hay. Each region has its own peculiar method-- rolling, mounding, cubing, or whatever. Here the hay was thrown over a stake with three crossbeams resulting in a six-foot high mound. In Yugoslavia, before it broke into various states, the hay was hung on a clothesline-like apparatus. This little detail has always intrigued me.

We were on our way to Poland, a country that had retained its distinctive identity even though it did not politically exist for 100 years. Its conquering neighbors Russia, Prussia and Austria divided the country among themselves. It was not until after World War I that Poland became a nation again.

MEMORIAL TO HORROR

Our first stop in Poland was the city of Oswiecim where the infamous Auschwitz concentration camp was located. As we rounded the street corner to the Camp we saw castle turrets welcoming us. It appeared to be like any other tourist site, until we saw the barbed wire quickly dispelling any notions of the place being a typical haunt. We crossed under the sign "*Arbeit Macht Frei*" or "work makes you free." The dormitories housed various exhibits of shoes, luggage, and clothing collected from the victims. Our young tall Polish guide mechanically walked us through the exhibits of gas chambers and photographs of the deceased. The room of human hair piled in mounds behind glass affected me the most. Before these victims were gassed their hair was shorn and sold for making carpets. I wondered how I would feel discovering that the rug I bought was made of human hair from a murdered prisoner. I still shudder writing about it. We began to see the one million massacred not as numbers but as individuals with hopes and dreams and fears.

We then rode two kilometers to Birkenau, a much larger camp. A lone train track ran to the brick gate, and we were reminded that victims from all across Europe had been dropped off here like cattle. The passengers would walk to the chambers from the trains innocently thinking they were taking a shower. Instead they were gassed to death. Those that lived for whatever reason were shot on the spot.

I thought about the soldiers being ordered to exterminate people and quietly obeying those commands. A part of your brain has to shut off in order for you to carry out such a diabolical deed. We say we would never do such a thing, but it isn't until we are in the midst of the situation that we really know how we will react. We hope that we will make the right choice, but we never really know until the moment arrives.

People were sometimes so moved by the visit to the camps that they didn't speak to anyone for hours Ingeborg told us. I had visited the Washington D.C. Holocaust Museum and vaguely knew beforehand what I would see. For some in our tour, it was the first time they witnessed the horrors of madmen. We were all subdued after the visit.

Two large busloads arrived filled with young teenagers from Israel to honor the dead. Dressed in white sweatshirts they laid flower wreaths of pine needles and chrysanthemums against the fence. They will hopefully keep the memory alive of those who perished, so we don't repeat this atrocity again.

I was struck with the irony of what I saw. On one side of a dirt road was Birkenau a place of senseless death. On the other side were bushels of new potatoes being harvested by a Polish family, a continuation of life.

POLISH JEWEL

Our ride to Krakow took us through a countryside full of homes in various stages of construction. Ingeborg said it has been several years since she was in Poland, and found the economic recovery encouraging evidenced by the building taking place. In earlier years the Poles could not obtain building materials even if they could afford them.

We arrived in Krakow and could see the church steeple at Wawel Castle, but the driver never got close to it. He was lost. Our faithful Ingeborg had difficulty remembering how to reach our hotel. On top of that the brakes began to wheeze and sigh each time the driver applied pressure. At times it felt like a comedy of errors. We lurched around the city with noisy brakes that drew attention to our bus. We saw the steeple from north, south, east and west before we found our hotel. We ended up only a kilometer from the heart of the city, after having had an unplanned view from the four cardinal points!

Ah, Krakow was a jewel of a surprise--a monument to the heart of the Polish empire. Fortunately it was not bombed during the two world wars and comes to us historically intact. The south view from the lake was the most striking of Wawel Castle and the Cathedral where nearly every Polish king is buried. Warsaw was the large and powerful political capital but Krakow was the classical capital and cultural center.

Stephen and I threw our bags into our room and ran for the trolley while there was sunlight. We did not want to waste a minute of light. A trolley slipped off its track creating a trolley-jam, so we ended up riding a bus. A kind Polish gentleman told us where to get off, and we were lucky to end up in front of the Florian Gate in the heart of the city. A flourishing welcome for us after a long day! Wandering down the street we came upon the large market square, the Rynek, with its wondrous Cloth Market, the Sukiennice, in the center. The facade of this long building laid out in 1257 definitely caught our attention sitting in the middle of a large empty plaza. The rounded tops, which were echoed in the arches at the pedestrian level housed dozens of tourist shops where I purchased a hand carved wooden statue of a baker. I wanted to bundle up this building along with my baker, and bring it home.

We wandered around seeking more than a beer garden for our dinner. We chanced upon a most peculiar little dive located behind a hamburger stand. There were nine tables crowded into a tiny room, which appeared to be a cafeteria. I giggled when I saw a bearded Japanese man checking his dictionary and glancing up at the billboard menu in Polish. Forget trying to read the menu. We simply wandered among tables and pointed to the food we wanted. We ended up with a delicious chicken rice soup and *pirogi*, Polish dumplings made of boiled pastries filled with potatoes and onions. It cost all of 6.4 Zloty or $1.50 to feed both of us.

Somehow in our miscommunication we ended up with two huge plates of *pirogis* instead of one. We offered the extra plate to our tablemate, a hunched older woman with a headscarf. She hesitated, her head lowered. She sighed. Then with great gusto she wolfed the entire plate down finishing before us. She was clearly hungry. Not speaking any Polish, we could not ask her about this establishment. We did not know if it were for indigent people because many local customers wore patched clothing. All we really cared about was that the food was tasty, and it didn't make us sick.

Our formal tour began the next day in the Jewish Ghetto, where Stephen Spielberg filmed the movie, *Schindler's List.* The Gothic buildings crowded around a large open courtyard. At one time nearly one-third of the population in the city was Jewish.

Then we wandered through the ornate cathedral on the hill, I recalled learning about Queen Jadwiga through James Michener's book, *Poland.* She was the beloved queen of Poland who lived 1374-1399. Her husband, Jagiello, was from Lithuania. I took satisfaction knowing we had visited his castle home in Trakai, Lithuania.

Even though it has been hundreds of years since Jadwiga's death, she was still revered by the Poles. One example of why was when she sold the court jewels and used the money to establish the University of Krakow. Such thoughtful acts reveal what caliber of woman she was. The original school building still stands and I felt it had a hallowed aura. Nicholas Copernicus, the famous astronomer, attended the University she established from 1491 to 1495. He wrote his then unorthodox theories of the universe but wisely requested they never be published until after his death. In this manner, he enjoyed a rather peaceful life, and was not persecuted as a heretic.

CZECTOCHOWSKA

I hadn't the faintest idea what to expect in Czestochowska, which was halfway between Krakow and Warsaw. When we arrived we learned there was a famous cathedral housing a Black Madonna. When a young lady inquired why the Poles made such a fuss about the Black Madonna, I smiled, because I had silently asked the same question. The mysticism that surrounds such icons often seemed more amazing than the icon itself.

The day of our visit coincided with a major holiday for worshippers. Thousands of Polish farmers swarmed around the basilica giving thanks for their harvest. Poland is 95 percent Catholic, and these were some of the most devout. We recalled Pope John Paul was from Poland and had trained in Krakow. We could tell that the men were not entirely comfortable in their ill-fitting suits. The sun-creased lines on their faces and their toothless smiles attested to their hard lives.

I don't recall ever feeling so embarrassed as when a guide took our group to the front of the cathedral to see the Black Madonna. Thousands of Polish farmers crowded in line for hours to get a glimpse, and we tacky tourists jumped the line to the front. One young lady said she felt so self-conscious barging in front of the worshippers that she forgot to look at the fabled icon. Had she looked she would have seen that the Madonna was not a sculpture but a flat painting darkened with time. Originally from Constantinople, it had been transported here in 1382 and become the most revered ecclesiastical icon in Poland.

The devotion of the people was what made the visit memorable. Their clear eyes devoutly stared at their Madonna. Their weary patience was born of life on the farm. And their humility dressed their demeanor. Had the worshippers not been present, our visit to the shrine would have felt ordinary.

WARSAWA

During World War II over 85 percent of Warsaw was leveled. I was certain of no rubble, but not sure if the Poles had rebuilt a concrete jungle and called it a city. I was relieved to find a modern and attractive capital.

Ludwig, our local Warsaw guide, joined our group and made the tour fun. Wearing a straw hat from Mallorca and sporting a white goatee, he launched his spiel. He was a law graduate of Krakow University but during the Russian occupation was demoted to a baker. He says his cakes were reserved for the enemy--heavy like lead, and tasted awful. After spending three months in the United States he was firmly convinced he loved America. Ludwig was as spry as Ingeborg, whom he would whisk by the arm, and off we would dance to the next site.

All the monuments were about the anguish of war--to fallen heroes, Jewish ghettos, Unknown Soldiers graves, and the site of the Warsaw Uprising. The two exceptions were the monument built for Chopin, the composer and the birthplace of Marie Curie's, the physicist. Curie was the only woman ever to receive two Nobel prizes, one in physics and the other in chemistry. Old and new towns formed a wondrous maze of medieval streets.

We boarded our bus-with-the-sighing-brakes for Wroclaw. Although the bus ride was five hours long now most of the passengers had gotten better acquainted with each other. The sound of conversations was scattered throughout the bus.

WROCLAW

The most popular dishware among the American wives was Polish Pottery. On our several shopping trips to Boleslaweice, Poland, we turned before the city sign of Wroclaw and never made it into the downtown. I expected Wroclaw to be a grimy industrial town. Again, I had another pleasant surprise awaiting me.

Our hotel in Wroclaw was a remnant from bygone Soviet days, large and old. Wide hallways were made of worn wooden planks that squeaked when we walked. Our room was bare except for the bed. The location was excellent, however. A short ten-minute walk landed us in the center of the Market Square, the largest city center on our trip. Each of the three-and four-story buildings was original medieval architecture.

My imagination was tickled. It reminded me of a Disney set with colorful buildings, narrow and tall with flourishes and curved roofs. However, these were genuine. Bands playing lively tunes lent a festive air as well as the throngs of people drinking and laughing on a Sunday evening!

After dinner Stephen and I wandered towards the Odra River. We passed the University of Wroclaw and then crossed the bridge to the Church of St. Mary on the Sand and the Holy Cross Church. It was almost a fairytale walk with reflections on the river, twinkling lights and cobblestone streets. At any moment I felt a hooded medieval monk would rush by and a knight errant on horseback would clop, clop, clop down the lane.

The bridge was filled with huge spiders and their webs. Artificial light shone directly on the concentric circles making them glow. My husband is a real arachnid lover. He launched into his little lecture on spiders--how the spun silk is stronger than an equivalent steel cable and that the funnel web spider of Australia is the most poisonous in the world. One Christmas I bought a video on spiders for our nephews and nieces. Stephen was such an enthusiast that he plucked the arachnid video out of the gift basket and kept it for himself.

BOLESLAWIEC

Two years earlier I had joined a group of women on a Polish Pottery shopping tour to Boleslaviece. We rode all night, shopped all day, and returned home that evening. We stopped to buy more Polish pottery. The shopping fever is infectious and Stephen got in on the buying melee. He selected a series of cereal bowls and in less than two hours we filled three boxes full of pottery and crystal. While my husband paid in one store, I dashed to another to begin filling more bags. It was excellent teamwork.

The earthenware holds up well and is popular in the States where it costs many times over what we paid in Poland. Most importantly Stephen didn't complain about the money spent, but gloated what great bargains we managed to find.

EPILOGUE

Our long weekend was an ambitious trip, covering much of Poland in a short time. It gave us a snapshot view and an insight into the rich heritage and history of Poland. Gone were the stereotypes of impoverished Polish farmhouses, grandmothers bundled in scarves, and cabbage soup. Now my images are of castles, kings and universities!

Austria, Hungary, Slovakia, And The Czech Republic

August/September 1999

PLAN B

A planned commercial tour didn't materialize. So we tossed our baggage into the car and put Plan B into operation--the triangle of Vienna, Budapest, and Prague creating our own itinerary day by day.

AUTOBAHN 6

On our first day we drove Autobahn 6 across the middle of Germany to the Czech border. For lunch in Regensburg, we enjoyed some stomach-challenging sausage, delicious but heart-burning, in the oldest restaurant in the city, the Wurstkuche. We set out to find for ourselves if Stephen's co-worker had truthfully extolled Regensburg as a picturesque town. The Dom or Cathedral is pure German Gothic begun in 1275 and completed in 1634. The Rathaus, the city hall, was spectacular with its ornately painted tower. It was located right next to the Steinerne Brucke a stone bridge built in 1135-1146 with arches spanning the river and decorated with statues, the prototype for the famous Charles Bridge in Prague. At one time wealthy families competed to see who could build the highest tower in the city. The honor went to the Goldener Turm, or golden tower built in 1260. In many ways, there was a Czech feel to the city—a hidden Bavarian gem visited mostly by German tourists. After the end of the walk, we agreed that the city had great allure with its old medieval buildings and steep hills falling into the Regen and Danube Rivers.

We drove further down the road and spent the night in Passau at the confluence of three rivers, the Danube, Inn and Ilzd. We took a 40 minute ferry ride to see where the rivers joined. The Inn River originated in the Alps glaciers and appeared silvery in color. It contrasted with the muddy Ilzd originating in the Bavarian Forest in Germany. We saw an unusual number of bicyclists riding alongside the Danube River between Passau and Linz, Austria. Some hailed from as far away as Vienna. All ages were pedaling the bike paths, not just young fitness fanatics.

We stayed in a cyclist hostel on the river--The Rotel Hotel. The width of the room was exactly as wide as the bed, allowing no space between the wall and the mattress. We had to clamber over the bedding to reach our pillows. The bathroom and showers were communal but the price was right for DM 25-30 a night, twelve to fifteen dollars.

We learned that Rotel sponsors tours throughout the world with clients sleeping in red buses with bunks especially designed for the trip. I love to thumb through their travel catalogue listing the wide and unusual offerings like one journey from Tripoli in Algeria, traveling south through Chad and the Sahara, ending in Ghana. Another tour went through Uzbekistan to Kyrgyzstan, and into Muslim China going through fabled Tashkent.

FOLLOWING THE MUSIC TRAIL

On the road to Vienna we passed a billboard advertising the home of Anton Bruckner, an Austrian composer known for his symphonies, masses and motets. Being footloose and fancy free we made an impromptu decision to stop at his birthplace. We followed the street sign near Linz and discovered the modest schoolhouse in Ansfelden where Bruckner was born. A trail then took us over the hills through the forest to St. Florian's Monastery. Bruckner played the organ here and is appropriately buried beneath the organ inside the church.

After a traffic jam, which they say happens often in Vienna, we arrived at our campsite. Europeans camp to save money. Many pulled hard-side trailers complete with satellite dishes towed behind their Mercedes. The cost to park a trailer is $20-30 versus the hotel charge of $150 per night. We weren't so lucky to have a trailer but we had a fold up. We pitched it right next to another making for wall-to-wall tents in the campground. Clean showers and restrooms were provided, so it was not really roughing it.

At night the campground was a society unto itself with children playing and grown-ups chatting at portable picnic tables. Laundry hung from a circular clothesline. One couple sipped wine by candlelight. We laughed to see the top-of-the-line Lexus and a Mercedes in the parking lot. Several American backpackers found their way to our site. An entire spectrum of travelers enjoyed the same communal grounds.

Traveling on the Vienna subway was the most economical way to get around we had read, so the next day we took the advice and rode the underground around Vienna. Our first destination was the Schonbrunn Palace, where the Hapsburg Dynasty came to hunt and later to live. Their family ruled for almost 700 years. If you get the principals confused, you are not alone. One of the best known royals is Elizabeth of Wittlesbach nicknamed Sissy, Empress of Austria. She was the daughter of a German duke who married into the powerful ruling family of Austria. As empress she was known for her unconventional behavior and also for her attractiveness, intelligence, simplicity and kindness. Her husband, austere Franz Joseph, remained devoutly faithful to her. She hated the intense scrutiny of the court saying it felt like a gilded cage. She ate very little to maintain her stylish figure and she had one daughter that died in infancy and one son who later committed suicide. Still Sissy traveled extensively. Sadly she was stabbed by an insane man. The life of the popular Sissy ran parallel in many ways to the life of England's Diana, the Princess of Wales--both women of extraordinary beauty, natural grace and popularity who defied convention. Unfortunately both tragically died young.

The Schonbrunn Palace also bears the mark of Maria Theresa, a powerful empress who bore 16 children. She converted the hunting place into the Schonbrunn Imperial Summer Residence. She transformed the palace and garden into the Rococo style eventually having this period named after her--Theresianian epoch. These palaces, Versailles, Peterhof, Munich's Summer Palace as well as the Schonnbrunn followed the floor plan of their day, a long corridor running through each adjoining room, making for easy tourist flow.

On our next day we did the full whistle-stop tour of Vienna. We should have first taken a trolley to gain an orientation of the city layout. We did that at the end of the day. Our first call was at the Silberkammer, the Imperial Silver Collection, and the Kaiserappartements, the royal apartments. The Silberkammer contained enough gold, silver, and crystal service to satiate the appetite of the most ardent collector. A short illustration of its excess--the elegant table service for 140. Imagine having a sit down dinner for that many people!

Stephen climbed the church steeple of St. Stephen while I poked my head into nearby shops. We saw the famous Ankar Clock of 12 carved bas relief figures hung over a small bridge-way between two buildings. While admiring the timepiece, a couple in front of us struck up a conversation. We learned they were from Haifa, Israel. They directed us to the Vienna Clock Museum a few streets over and luckily we followed their advice. We found the museum located in an old narrow building with three small floors of clocks on display. It was interesting to see the many shapes, and sizes of clocks that actually functioned. Early chronometers, and sundials began the exhibition moving to the 16th century when public buildings began displaying clocks. Of course a Black Forest cuckoo clock was among the collectibles. I especially liked the tiny pendant watch in the casing of a violin. The best lesson we learned-- a clock design is limited only by the imagination of its creator.

We grabbed some yummy pastries, since we did not want to waste more time than necessary waiting for lunch. Each flaky morsel literally melted in our mouths, and I still salivate at the thought. Delicious! Then we walked to the Vienna Opera House--one of the busiest in the world. It produces 50-60 operas per year, approximately 200 performances. During our tour I was most impressed with the back of the theater. It was actually larger than the stage to accommodate the myriad of scenery and backdrops. I was also amazed that the floor dropped to the basement creating more storage.

Two famous events in Vienna were closed in August—the Lippanzer Stallions and the Vienna Boys' Choir. One tour agent gave us a tip. If we flew on Austrian Airlines we could stop in Vienna for no added cost on future trips. So maybe next time we'll do that.

A SPICIER VENUE

We hopped in our little car and headed further east to Budapest, Hungary. I was not quite prepared for the invasion of European chain stores throughout suburban Budapest. We spotted CORA, OBI, IKEA, and AUCHAN, and others. Without question, this former Soviet country has rapidly turning into a capitalistic society.

Somehow I had a romantic classical picture of Buda and Pest, two cities divided by a river and finally joined by a bridge. The city has retained its glorious old-world flavor only in the city center. Many compare Budapest with Prague in the Czech Republic. One friend loves Budapest but hates the tourists in Prague. Another friend who lives in Prague, naturally loves that city. Others prefer Budapest's quieter pace. All agreed that the architecture in both cities was enthralling.

Even though we knew all the museums were closed on Monday we climbed Castle Hill. Our ears sharpened at the cacophony of languages. When the sound was unfamiliar I asked what language was being spoken. Two stand out in my mind, Macedonian and Slovenian. Many different tourists from the former Eastern Block nations were here. Why not? It was a natural extension of neighbors visiting neighbors.

We walked the perimeter of Budapest's walls near St. Stephen's statue, the patron Saint of Hungary who at the end of the 10th century was crowned as its first king. We ambled through the colorful medieval houses in old town. After we had exhausted ourselves, we descended to the river level at Margaret's Island where there was a lovely city park. Golf carts and tandem bikes were available to rent but we didn't indulge. Our energy level dictated that we sit on park benches and watch others.

We were hungry in Hungary, no pun intended. I read somewhere that the Germans called these people hungry and the name stuck. It was time to find a place to eat. We caught a trolley car shaped like a rounded bullet, and headed for the top half of the trolley circle. Stephen thought this was heavenly civilization because we found a Pizza Hut, McD's and Wendy's along the same boulevard. I insisted that we have a Hungarian meal. Operating off of hungry stomachs we tromped down to The Little Piper Restaurant listed in my guidebook. We managed to find the place. When we arrived there the establishment was dark. The sign on the door simply stated that the owners were on vacation. So I gave in. We backtracked and ate at Wendy's.

We had a bit of a problem finding our bus stop back to our hotel in the dark. As Stephen and I studied our city map, I was surprised that two smiling Hungarian ladies volunteered to help us find our way. Usually older ladies in their 70s and 80s don't help strangers, especially foreigners. I guess they reflected the friendlier attitudes the Hungarians possessed. The women pointed us in the right direction, we caught our bus and made it back to our hotel.

The Hungarians are a conglomeration of many cultures that have conquered and remained in former Roman Pannonia. It seemed to me that they were shorter and stockier than we've seen elsewhere. There were blondes and brunettes with blue eyes and then there were darker complexioned Hungarians as well. The people call themselves the Magyrs. Their Ugric language was related to Finnish, because they were thought to come from the same area near the Aural Mountains. They were a little pocket of Uralics surrounded by a sea of Slav speakers.

For lunch the next day we again walked down to the river near Margaret's Island where we found a Hungarian restaurant. My husband murmured we paid a lot for sausage and beans, goulash soup, chopped-up peppers and fried pancakes. Perhaps it was pricey, but it was the real McCoy.

James Michener's book, *The Bridge at Andau,* described the Hungarian 1956 uprising against the Russians, and the brutal retaliation that occurred. Over 30,000 lost their lives fighting. Another 10,000 were killed when tanks destroyed building foundations and the houses collapsed on the occupants. Stephen consented to take me to the intersection where all of this happened. No sign, statue or plaque commemorated the courageous stand made by the Hungarians with homemade bombs against Russian tanks. I tried to envision these implements of war rumbling down a commercial street and creating havoc. One day life was normal and within 20 hours the Hungarians were under the repressive domination of the communists. In Europe, war is an ever-present specter.

I'm an idealist. It's difficult for me to understand the greed, the envy, the power struggles, and the hunger for dominance that underline every past conflict. War is grown children squabbling without adult supervision. Rulers lob armaments against each other and it's the common people that get caught in between. All the energy, time and resources gone into war could have been directed to peaceful pursuits like developing medicines for illnesses, finding alternative energy sources, and increasing food production. The more extensively I travel the more I realize how fleeting empires and kingdoms are, none lasting forever. The battle may be won but ultimately it's all for naught--the temples still crumble and the sovereigns die mortal deaths.

BORDER CROSSING

The European Union has spoiled us by eliminating long arduous border crossings. By contrast, we were abruptly reminded of former times as we entered and left Slovakia. We waited for an hour both entering and leaving. As we got to the immigration booth we were summarily dismissed after becoming ten dollars lighter and the guard a little richer.

We ate lunch in Bratislava, capital of Slovakia. The town seemed quiet with few people milling around. We ate at a hamburger joint, pretty much the standard fare. We strolled the main street and spotted familiar international product names like Coca Cola, HP, and Fiji film. The town was pleasant but nothing immediately caught our eyes. According to our Czech friend, Eliska, when the Czech Republic and Slovakia separated, the Czech Republic kept most of the resources and the tourist sites with the agrarian plots going to Slovakia.

DEKUJI--THANKS

We continued to the Czech Republic through Brno up through Hradec Kralov on a two-lane road littered with cars, farm trucks and traffic. It was slow going. We saw several new industrial plants, indicating positive economic growth for the Czech Republic. We arrived in Nova Paka in Bohemia to stay with our friends, Karel and Eliska, both in their early thirties. We met Eliska when she was a graduate student at the University of Texas. A mutual friend told me about her and we met over hamburgers. We solidified the friendship when she expressed a wish to build a small library of English books for her church in Prague. I sent out fliers asking for donated books, and then persuaded a local choir to hand carry three or four books on a concert tour to the Czech Republic. Over 500 books were delivered to Prague.

Eliska and Karel were really good sports to let us stay with them in their spartan Soviet-style high-rise apartment--a living room, one bathroom, one bedroom and a narrow kitchen. Everything functioned well and we were comfortable. Their fold-down couch was boxy looking but surprisingly comfortable and we slept well on it. Eliska confided we were the first guests they had ever entertained. I wanted to tell her how much work hosting was but decided to let her find out on her own.

After a light dinner, we all drove to a nearby park with red sandstone cliffs. It was refreshing to walk among the evergreens and not see another soul. At the end of a 15 minute walk, we had a view of the emerald valley below as darkness slipped over us. The leaves crunched under our feet. There was just enough light for us to follow the path back to our car and to bed.

Eliska prepared a typically high-caloried, fattening breakfast full of yummy meats, breads, cheese and spreads. I hoped we didn't cause them to exceed their budget too much. They were a young couple just starting out and prices were high. We bought extra sacks of groceries as gifts for them to use so I hope that helped.

Fortunately both of them spoke excellent English which allowed us to converse, since Stephen and I speak not a word of Czech. It is always interesting that Europeans learn to speak good conversational English, while we Americans can barely function in our mother tongue. I regret that we don't emphasize foreign languages more in American schools. We could learn from the Germans who teach English at age nine. By age 13 students are encouraged to master French or Spanish, a third language. Multilingual speakers have a decided advantage in our international world.

The couple asked us to step outside to see their "new" used car. Such transportation was a status symbol. They had saved their money for a long time and found a good deal. I remember their car being very faded, shaped like an old Studebaker, but of

Russian make. It had definitely seen many miles and I silently prayed it would not break down soon.

Eliska knew of my desire for Bohemian crystal since I had mentioned it in an email. While Karel was at work, she suggested we drive an hour away to Turnov, a resort town. There were only two crystal stores, but the prices were good. Stephen soon participated in the buying by picking up a lovely aquamarine glass dolphin. I purchased some water glasses heavily engraved at the base in traditional ornate Czech designs. We also checked out a glassmaking school and were impressed with the graceful contemporary designs. The artistry was top quality.

On our ride back, we stopped at the striking Hrad Trosky, an old castle ruin. I had seen pictures of the two stone buttes, but didn't realize that a palace had lain between them. Two natural basalt pillars anchored a rectangular, two story palace, a formidable defense begun in 1396. The lower rock, the Baba, stands around 160 feet high with the Virgin pillar, a little taller. We climbed several wooden stairs to a platform that gave us a panorama view. Rolling Czech hills dotted with dark verdant forests sprinkled with patchwork farms and villages. Standing so high we felt every blast of wind, so we could not admire the view for long.

I wished I could adequately describe my feelings about being in Bohemia—paradise? These were the same mountains, hills, and trees found throughout the Czech Republic, but the spirit of the area was so inviting. Friends giving us a personal introduction helped, but I sensed it was more than that. It was as though my inner soul spoke to the trees, the rivers, the hills, and the serenity. The land reciprocated with an internal feeling of calmness. I wished I could pinpoint it—a rural rusticity? A special bewitchment? A magic spell? In any case, I fell under its enchantment.

We felt a tug to stay longer, but as the saying goes, "after three days fish and guests stink." So we moved on to our next destination--Prague where my American friend, Karen, lived. We said *Dekuji*, good-bye in Czech, gave everyone a hug, and headed down the road.

PRAGUE

Through gently sloping hills and a golden sunset we left Nova Paka and drove directly south because road construction blocked our usual route. As we neared Prague the land flattened. After missing several turns and driving on one-way streets, we found Karen's apartment. We lugged our bags upstairs to the third landing and found a spacious apartment with two guest bedrooms. The bathroom door blended so perfectly into the woodwork that you couldn't find it if you didn't know it was there.

Karen worked for an American company and had lived in Prague a year. I first met her when she was preparing to do international work in the Republic of Georgia. Some disliked their assignment in Georgia, feeling as though they were camping out. Not her. She learned the difficult language and felt the warmth of the people. How wise to approach living in a foreign land with the attitude that you will love it despite inevitable setbacks.

We slept in the next day and were totally lazy. Karen had already left for work but thoughtfully left us change for the trolley and a street map. We found our way downtown and wandered up and down the old town and into the famous shopping district, St. Wencelas Square. Hordes of tourists surrounded us, but the winding, twisted streets were still a delight. On a previous visit we had seen the castle and the famous Astronomical Clock on the central plaza, so we skipped them this time.

We met Karen at her office, climbed the hill behind her building, and took in a bird's eye view of the castle across the river with its mob of tourists, the Charles River Bridge with its many statues, and old medieval shops. Prague has been a cultural center for centuries with hundreds of concert halls, galleries, music clubs and festivals as well as an educational center with 11 colleges and universities. A marvelous ambiance resides here. We walked to a nearby shopping plaza and grabbed a pizza that was delicious and lived up to its title of El Diablo—super spicy!

Karen took the afternoon off and suggested we tour the Old Jewish district. In the olden days, all Jews were required to remain within the confines of the Jewish Ghetto comprising only a few square blocks. This restriction survived for hundreds of years. They were only allowed to work in limited professions, and commerce was one of them. Ironically that was where all the money was and Jews became very adroit at handling capital.

Our tour began with a visit to the old cemetery with headstones tilting to the right or left and crammed like sardines in the small plot. We peeked into all the synagogues with the most memorable being the Spanish with its Moorish and Islamic designs. All seven synagogues are in use but attendance is sparse. During the 18th century more Jews lived in Prague than anywhere else in the world. Today only about 1700 people are associated with the faith.

As an Asian, I can better understand when I am discriminated against, because I am physically different from the Caucasian majority with my almond eyes, my sallow skin color, and my straight dark hair. I can understand when Africans are set apart because we can readily see their physical characteristics. But many Jews appeared Caucasian in their appearance. Why then were they segregated as a people? I am not condoning these practices, but merely citing what I perceive as a strange origin for prejudice. Even if there was a long history of persecution, my question was how do you distinguish Jews from the regular populace when they are all mixed in together? The answer is that you can't tell the difference if they change their name.

WIDE PATHS

Despite the spur-of-the-moment beginning we were tickled with our impromptu trip. Over a long weekend by car we covered four countries each distinctively different from its neighbor. It amazes me that people living so closely side by side can develop such vastly different cultures, customs, languages, food, and traditions. We recognized that our wanderings were making us grow. Traveling is like taking a wedge, opening up your brain and pouring in more awareness, consciousness, knowledge, understanding and sensitivity. Of course, with some folks the medicine doesn't take effect and they remain the same. I like to think that Stephen and I were good "patients," absorbing all that was out there!

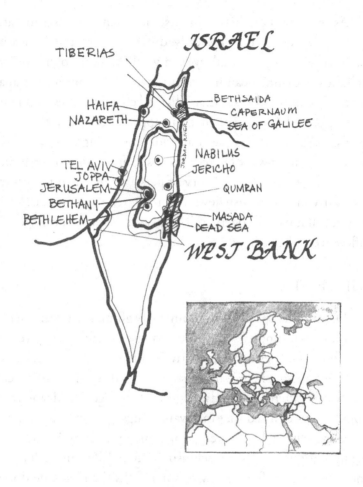

Our Pilgrimmage To Israel

November 1999

Israel has a long history literally built layer upon layer. As one civilization was destroyed, the conquerors built their new kingdom upon the rubble of the vanquished. After many millenniums, Jerusalem lies atop archaeological treasures from periods including the Canaanite, Hebrew, Assyrian, Persian, Babylonian, Greek, Egyptian, Syrian Seleucid, Hasmonean, Roman,

Byzantine, Arab, Crusader, Maluk, Ottoman Turk, British and now the nation of Israel.

Many approaches exist for a visit to Israel. As an archaeologist, one could find several lifetimes of digs. As a religious scholar, one could spend eternity ferreting out the Jewish, Christian and Muslim religions--especially as they interrelated with one another. The naturalist could soak up plenty of sunshine in pursuit of animals and fauna. But for us, we went as simple religious pilgrims with a group organized through the chapels at our base.

Places that we read about in the newspaper--The West Bank, Golan Heights, Gaza Strip, and Palestine--suddenly had a geographic fixity. Names from the Bible such as Jerusalem, Bethlehem, and Nazareth became real. The land was arid, so dry that one 16-old marveled, "How could such a barren place be the stage for so many conflicts?" I am still trying to answer that one.

Our guide was Father Paul from Athens, Greece. In his tiny five-foot frame was packed more energy per molecule than any other individual I have met. He kept those of us 30-40 years younger, breathless from the grueling pace he set. He really knew his way around, too, taking at least four groups a year to Jerusalem. Father Theodore also accompanied us.

All guides must be certified in Israel. There was no guarantee you would be matched with a guide of your faith. On previous visits, several in the group noted that a non-Christian would guide Christians. This could be distracting at times, because the guide would lend an air of cynicism during his lecture. Many said it was better to know your guide ahead of time.

JERUSALEM

We landed in Haifa and rode an hour on the bus approaching Jerusalem after dark. We caught glimpses of orthodox Jewish men darting through the streets in their black garb, top hats, and long side curls. Next to them were Arabs in loose flowing robes. The streets were narrow, and the buildings all of pale limestone. We arrived at Notre Dame Guest House across the street from the walled Old City. It felt like a momentary blip in time being in a city that I had read and heard so much about. I pinched myself not certain if this was reality or a dream.

We learned that some of the churches were closed in protest because the Islamic faith wanted to build an enormous mosque in Nazareth in front of the Church of the Annunciation. It was not important to the protesters that this was a busy tourist week before Christmas. Fortunately for us, the closed churches were the only demonstration we witnessed. We were grateful that there were no bombs blowing up or tourists being shot while we were there.

Old Jerusalem is entirely hemmed in by a formidable stone wall with a total of eleven gates. Our foray into the Old City began at the New Gate. We found ourselves on narrow streets punctuated with steps, tromping through the Arab Souk or market. Although many of the merchants wore western dress, older men wandered the stalls in traditional Arab headgear a large square piece of cloth anchored on the head with cords. The smell of exotic fragrant spices like cardamom and curry permeated the air while merchants' voice called out in English, German, or Spanish, trying to lure tourist into their stores. I kept reminding myself that we were on the eve of the 21st century, and not the middle ages.

Occasionally a small truck hauling merchandise would bounce precariously down the market steps honking its way past the milling crowds. The market was built when donkeys brought in the merchandise long before there were any trucks. This was creative adaptation.

THE WAILING WALL

Our next stop was the Wailing Wall, perhaps the most sacred of Jewish places. Here Jews come to shed tears for the lost Temple and perhaps for some of their history. In order to enter all visitors passed through modern metal detectors. Armed guards stood along the northern wall. It felt painfully incongruous going to a religious site surrounded by implements of war.

Formed by large blocks of limestone, the Wall was actually the west side of the large Temple complex. I had seen many pictures of the Wailing Wall, but didn't realize it stood 65 feet high. A large sandstone plaza sloped down to the Wailing Wall ending at a small stone partition, a *mechitz*, setting off the prayer area. Men worshipped on the left and women on the right.

It was a Monday when Bar Mitzvahs were taking place at the Wailing Wall--the Jewish rite when a 13-year-old boy becomes a man. Large, ornate Torah scrolls were brought out on tables nearly as tall as the youngster carrying the sacred scriptures. Male family members robed in skullcaps and ceremonial clothing gathered around to hear the young son read revered passages. The females leaned on the partitions. Beneath their feet were coolers loaded with celebration food.

I walked to a little room off to the side where paper was available for writing a small prayer. I quickly wrote a few lines, I covered my head with a scarf, and knelt at the Wall. Hundreds of handwritten petitions were tucked into every crack. I placed mine in a vertical slot, whispered a few words, bowed and stood up. I stepped gently around those swaying in invocation and joined our group back on the plaza.

HEZECHIA'S TUNNEL

We slipped out the south gate, called Dung Gate, named because of the garbage that was dumped over its edge. From this vantage point we were able to get a clear view of the hill on which Jerusalem is built on. We scrambled through some of the "City of David" excavations that were being conducted. King David, of Biblical times, built his city on the side of the hill because there was a water source vital in this parched land.

Further down the hill we came to the entrance of Hezechia's underground tunnel. During a wartime siege residents could quench their thirst by diverting the available water outside the walls to the city through the tunnel. We remembered our flashlights but I forgot my waterproof shoes. Fortunately, I was able to borrow a pair of old shoes three sizes too large for wading in the water. Feeling like a duck, I began to waddle through a manmade tunnel hewn in the side of a hill.

The water came up to our knees and at times to our thighs. The tunnel zigged and zagged but considering that the work was done by hand with crude instruments through solid rock, it was a remarkable feat. The two ends met in the middle of the hill without much deviation. I read James Michener's *The Source* in preparation for our visit to Israel. Several chapters described this tunnel and the men that carved it. I almost felt the presence of the fictional characters chatting, shouting, hammering and struggling to create this underground water source. I pictured them stripped to the waist with their long hair plastered to their heads from sweat, working in flickering torchlight.

We walked for 40 minutes, sometimes needing to duck because of the low ceiling. At one point our guide had everyone turn off their lights and hold hands walking through the water. This was not fun, but it did prove how black total darkness is. The kids in the groups said wading through the tunnel was the best part of the day.

The tunnel ended at the Pools of Shiloam where Jesus told a blind man to wash the mud from his eyes and regain his sight. Today the stone corridor and porch steps were empty. Next to the pools was a little Muslim primary school with the children being dismissed for the day, a juxtaposition of religions sharing the same ground.

ON OUR OWN

We had a few hours on our own in the evening. We found the Pools of Bethesda, now located inside a convent but it was closed because of the protest. So we passed through Stephen's Gate (my husband liked something with his name) and caught a taxi. Our driver, in true Arab business style, offered us an extra tour and a stop at a tourist shop. We politely declined wondering how much of a cut these folks receive if they deliver a vacationer. He took us to the Mount of Olives across the Kidron Valley where we stopped to take panoramic photographs of Jerusalem. At the end of our ride my husband confused the exchange rates and mistakenly ended up tipping our driver almost as much as the fare. No wonder they liked Americans in Jerusalem!

After the sun dipped below the horizon, I convinced my husband to return to the Wailing Wall. We entered through Damascus Gate and made a beeline for the site. The floodlights were on and a few guards wandered above. Save for three men in long beards rocking in fervent prayer, we had the place to ourselves on a clear Israeli night without the distraction of crowds and noise. Stephen and I simply sat there without saying a word. The solitude felt like true worship.

Reluctantly we rose and left. We climbed stairs to the walkway of the old city wall. We caught glimpses of the twinkling city below and beyond, giving us a different perspective. Many times Jerusalem felt surreal with brightly lit plazas and exotic figures in robes walking down darkened paths. Three young boys noisily tossed a soccer ball. I discovered a little bookshop and bounced down the stairs. To my delight, I found a Hebrew poster for my alphabet collection. Later we were told us that the stairs to the old city wall are difficult to find. I am certain had we been looking for the entrance, we probably would have missed it. It was pure luck we discovered the stairway!

DOME OF THE ROCK

The most distinctive sight in Jerusalem is the gilded Dome of the Rock located in the southeastern Arab sector on the Temple Mount also known as *Al-Haram es Sharif.* This octagonal structure was used for private prayers. We were required to remove our shoes to enter, while our guide guarded our cameras and bags. The stained glass windows inside were elegant, and the entire edifice was exquisite. Hundreds of elegant Oriental carpets lay around a large flat stone about 20-30 feet in diameter. According to legend, this was the rock that Abraham climbed to reach Mount Moriah to offer up his son, Isaac, in the Christian world, and in the Muslim, his son, Ishmael. An angel of the Lord intervened staying his hand and telling Abraham he had passed his test. Some maps indicate this as the center of the earth and also where Mohammed ascended to heaven.

We heard the call to Mecca. In Israel they face south to pray. Just then a group of young schoolgirls in uniforms came fluttering in to the Dome bringing smiles to our group as each comely, dark-eyed child skipped by.

Across from the Dome was another edifice for public prayer, a square building with rows of carpets called the al-Aksa Mosque. Today it was empty. We wandered to the front noting all the smaller personal carpets laid out in long rows, and observed an artist on scaffolding painting symbolic art on the upper walls.

Some tourists wore odd-looking green skirts, tubes of green material with elastic on both ends. It took me a while to realize that if the guards felt you were dressed immodestly while visiting the mosque, they asked you to cover the offending part of your body. If you wore shorts, you had to cover your legs. Some of the women in our group wore sheer blouses and were asked to don these modesty covers. The dress code is very strict in Muslim areas.

MARY AND MARTHA

On the other side of the Mount of Olives was the small town of Bethany a suburb of Jerusalem with narrow, winding, and dusty streets, the Biblical home of Mary and Martha. Lazarus was raised from the dead here. A small sign suspended from a bare bent rusty pole directed us to the Tomb of Lazarus. Descent began directly off the street without a sidewalk to buffer us from moving cars should one appear. We carefully stepped down steep-hewn stairs of red sandstone descending two stories and were told this was where Lazarus awoke from the dead. I felt a bit skeptical, because the real site could have been any number of places. Some say that sites may be of dubious origin, either based upon hearsay or arbitrarily designated by Helen, the mother of

Constantine. At least there was no charge to enter the cave, and we got a feel for underground burials.

We plodded back up the steps and trudged a few hundred feet down the hill to a little tidy Catholic Church. Light filtered softly through yellow and black stained glass windows. We had no sooner settled in our seats for daily mass when the loudspeaker next door blasted the muzzein's call to prayer. I plugged my ears to muffle the megawatt sounds. No one slept through *that* mass.

GARDEN TOMB

On a free afternoon my husband and I debated where to visit. Father Paul suggested the Garden Tomb. We were not certain of its significance, but went based on his recommendation. We walked to the Garden maintained by a London Society located north of the Damascus Gate. A worship service in the garden was concluding so not to disturb them we skirted along a footpath to the far edge of the property. The area resembled an undeveloped gravel pit until we noticed that the rocky escarpment was shaped like a skull. The overhanging cliff was marked with hollow indentations that resembled eye sockets, nostrils, and a mouth. It slowly dawned on us that we had reached Golgotha the "place of the skull" where Christ may have been crucified. It was an unexpected find, and left us with an eerie feeling.

With the formal services concluded, Stephen and I had the Garden all to ourselves for half an hour. We followed the little path back into the center and found the sepulcher where it is believed Jesus was buried. Hewn into the stone were two small adjoining rooms, one spacious enough for several people to stand and the other side containing a rock table where a body could be laid. Outside were guiding edges for a large rolling stone to cover the opening. Being there made it easy to imagine that first Easter morning with the resurrected Christ talking to Mary.

There is controversy where the actual crucifixion took place. It is a fact that the executioners would always crucify outside the city walls. Some say that this disqualifies the Church of the Sepulcher as the crucifixion site since the Church stands within the city walls. Defenders say the city walls have since been moved, ransacked and destroyed.   Still others claim that Golgotha near the Garden Tomb was the true site. This is a good illustration of how history can easily be altered and forgotten.

ISRAEL MUSEUM

On another free afternoon we wandered on our own to see the Dead Sea Scrolls, manuscripts from the Qumran community nearly two thousand years old. Discovered in 1947 the nearly 1000 documents have unearthed religious and historical events and doctrine. They are considered one of the few remaining manuscripts of holy scripture written before 200 AD.

We planned to catch a bus to the museum, but couldn't find the stop. We kept asking people for directions and they kept telling us to go a few more blocks down the street. Then another pointed in the same direction. By the time we got to the Knesset, the Israeli Parliament, we saw the museum. Although we ended up walking the whole way, which was not our intention, the bonus was that we saw the city and residential areas up close.

The Dead Sea Scrolls were located in a building modeled to look like the clay jars in which they were found. After nearly two thousand years, another voice spoke to us from the dust paralleling scriptures found in the Bible including the coming of the Messiah. Before their discovery the earliest known Bible dated from the 9th century. Fragments of the scrolls were displayed like a huge jigsaw puzzle, millions of pieces painstakingly reassembled. The clay jars were real but only copies of the manuscripts were displayed to preserve the originals.

Even when we travel with a formal tour, we carry a travel guidebook. In our spare time, the book gives us ideas of what to see allowing us to enjoy sites we might otherwise have missed. It was fun to compare our tour's itinerary with our guidebook and feel satisfied that we saw the highlights.

DEAD SEA AND MASADA

The story of the Good Samaritan is one of the best known parables in the Bible. Two people, a priest, and a Levite, men sworn to help others, bypassed the beaten man who had been robbed. The Samaritan, a despised enemy, took compassion and nursed the man back to health. The parable illustrated the principle that an outcast person or group can show behavior superior to those who merely claim to possess virtue.

We stood at a lone outpost in the middle of a waterless wasteland before the descent into the Dead Sea, and were told that this was the spot where the parable took place. Though the location may have been questionable, the powerful meaning of the parable was not.

From Jerusalem to the valley floor of the Dead Sea was a difference of nearly 4000 feet. In a yellow school bus with stiff hard seats we dropped and dropped and dropped in elevation from the Judean Desert at 2500 feet above sea level to the Dead Sea at 1240 feet below sea level, the lowest spot in the world. We passed barren hills, occasionally occupied by Bedouin shepherds. Finally we reached the Jordan River Valley at the bottom. The day was smoggy and unfortunately limited our view so we simply had to take our guide's word that the famed city of Jericho lay to our left. We turned right going south on the western shores and passed the Qumran Hills where the Dead Sea Scrolls were discovered. The haze obscured any clear glimpses of the Sea but blended into the horizon line until we couldn't tell when the sky ended and the water began. Salt crusts glazed the rocks. A dust seemed to cover everything.

We reached a prominent outcropping. A mythical aura surrounded this mesa. This was Masada the holdout where a thousand Jews barricaded themselves in 73 A.D. against the Romans. Roman engineers spent three years building an enormous dirt bridge to the top of the mesa that still remains. When the soldiers finally broke through the gates, they found every one of the Jewish citizens had committed suicide rather than be subjected to slavery. The rallying cry through many wars afterwards was "Remember Masada!"

The first to build on Masada was the paranoid King Herod. To shield himself from his many enemies he had two elegant palaces built in the remote region. The northern palace was used in summer, and was in three tiers built into the face of the mesa. The western palace was a winter retreat. Herod spared no expense using the finest and costliest materials, which was partly why the people hated him. Almost nothing remained on the mesa today of his lavish excesses. Only one ruin remained intact enough to visit--the bathhouse.

Pilgrims usually walk the 30 minute hike up the mesa. Fortunately, I was able to take a cable car and avoided the hot sun. Once on top it took imagination to picture the sumptuous buildings that once graced the top, since there was only rubble.

Our bus lumbered over to a little oasis on the Dead Sea, the world's saltiest body of water with 30% salinity. There were lovely change houses and showers and soon everyone was in a bathing suit. Our group wanted to swim in the Dead Sea but we all quickly found out you cannot swim. You can only float on the Dead Sea. If the water gets in your eyes, it stings because it's so salty. The water was liquid but loaded with so much mineral that it felt almost like a soft jelly. I tried to float but felt I would capsize so I treaded instead. One gentleman read his newspaper while lying on his back. I lasted about 20 minutes before I began to itch. I rose out of the Dead Sea and walked the hundred yards to the showers scratching all the way.

GARDEN OF GETHSEMANE

The next day we arrived at the top of the Mount of Olives across the Kidron Valley from Jerusalem. Our plan was to walk down the hill touring the sights along the way. We stopped at a stark little building made of cement walls with no roof, no altar, and no foliage. This was supposedly the place where Christ arose into heaven earning it the name the Mount of Ascension.

Down the hill we reached the Garden of Gethsemane. The old knarled olive trees in the garden not only gave us shade but helped me visualize where Christ suffered before being crucified. We knew that the trees, which can live 300-600 years, were not witnesses the night Christ was betrayed but I imagined they were. The medium-sized chapel, the Church of All Nations, was lovely with curling arches and stained glass windows, but was too crowded with tourists to offer any meaningful reflection. Back outside we found the Lord's Prayer inscribed in multiple languages along the garden wall. We challenged ourselves to guess the language, and were surprised we could identify most of them.

As I gazed across the valley to Jerusalem the golden Dome of the Rock sparkled in the sunlight. We noted the numerous gates. The one facing the Mount of Olives was sealed called The Mercy Gate. According to local legend this is where the Lord will enter when He comes again. As I gazed upon this town it was difficult to understand why hundreds of battles have been fought here and why there has been so much blood spilled. It was not a place of sweeping vistas or great beauty. It had no strategic location. Yet its historical importance is undeniable.

BETHLEHEM

Bethlehem was in Palestine, so barbed wires and armed guards marked the entrance to the city, a stark contrast to the sleepy hamlet depicted in Christmas carols. Like neighboring Jerusalem this city was compact and was also located on the side of a hill.

Our first stop was Rachel's Tomb. Rachel was the second and beloved wife of Jacob or Israel of the Old Testament. Jacob worked seven years to earn her hand, only to have his father-in-law trick him by placing the older sister under the marriage veil. Jacob then worked another seven years to marry Rachel. I thought some of the old Biblical characters rather deceptive and wondered about in-law relationships.

Once inside the Tomb we were not certain what we were seeing with several coffins in the long room. We finally deduced that the one coffin elegantly draped in velvet with a woman wailing over it marked Rachel's grave. We paid homage and left.

One astute young person remarked, "They ought to leave a lot of the spiritual sites untouched." Instead huge monumental churches are erected nearly obliterating the spot. The birthplace of Jesus was a case in point. On one side was a Greek Orthodox Church claiming to house the manger, and connected to that was a Roman Catholic nave which also claimed to be Christ's birthplace.

Our group huddled for daily mass in a tiny basement corner of the Catholic Church where Christ was supposed to have been born. I watched tourists descend the stairs to pay homage. Christ was born at the gold star one group was told, so each pilgrim tenderly touched it. The next group lacked a guide so they wandered around trying to locate the sacred site. I couldn't blame the unsuspecting tourists since the spot believed was the birthplace was obscured with velvet, candles, and flowers.

Finally back outside it was a relief to be away from the noise echoing off the marble walls. As we walked through the alley behind the cathedral the merchants cried out, "Father Paul!

Father Paul!" They knew our guide and that he brought paying tourists. We poked our heads into one shop with every conceivable figure carved out of olive wood—the Pieta, Mary Magdalene, Mickey Mouse and Garfield the Cat from the sublime to the comical. We told ourselves we were "just looking." But when we saw a lovely olive wood nativity set we couldn't pass it up. It has become our treasured Christmas keepsake from Bethlehem and the Holy Lands.

BACK TO JERUSALEM

An incredible number of Biblical sites exist in Jerusalem. We saw a room that might have been where the Last Supper was held. Devoid of any furnishings that would have helped me envision Christ breaking and blessing the bread and wine, it seemed only the cold empty room that it was. We also saw Mary's Tomb. If the sculpture were any indication of actual height, Mary was a tall woman. We visited the church courtyard where Peter was said to have denied Christ three times before the rooster crowed. There was also the prison where Christ was held before he saw Caiaphas the high priest. These were all pretty much just rooms without furnishings or adornment. It is the events that transpired which gave us meaning.

We meandered among the white coffins we had seen from the Garden of Gethsemane. These cemeteries were far different from ours. White coffins were not buried, but placed above the ground. There were no plants or trees, just stones. We saw the grave of Oskar Schindler, the hero of the movie, *Schindler's List* who helped save many Jews by hiring them at his factory and then shipping them out of the country during WWII. We followed tradition and placed a small pebble on his tomb as a tribute to his courage and humanity.

We finally made it into the Church of the Holy Sepulchre which was closed all week due to the protests. This was the traditional site where Christ was said to have been crucified and buried. The Church was a maze of many religions competing for a corner. We waited a while to duck into a small sepulcher where Christ was supposed to be buried, large enough for only one person at a time. Then we climbed stairs to a small platform competing to be Golgotha, the crucifixion place. Apparently some Roman general had leveled the hill trying to ward away believers of Christ. It was difficult to get a sense of awe associated with the sacred site where Christ died. Too many contending religions were crammed into a small space. Instead of a sacred shrine it felt more like a bazaar with people vying for a piece of real estate. And it was not proven to be the actual crucifixion site. Candidly I liked the Garden Tomb better.

NORTHWARD

After several days in and around Jerusalem, we headed northward towards the Sea of Galilee. No one needed to tell us when we were in an Arab or in an Israeli sector. Our bus driver who was a Palestinian Arab, apologized, "I am Palestinian, but I am embarrassed our sections are cluttered with garbage. It looks terrible!"

Indeed the roadsides looked like a landfill full of cans and bottles, while on the Israeli side were profuse flowering plants and tended gardens. As we drove further north the barren grey hills became lush with greenery, farms and banana plantations.

The fabled River Jordan was a clear green not much wider than 90 to 100 feet. A relatively shallow river of about three to ten feet in depth it flows for some 70 miles between Israel and Jordan. We stopped for those who wished to be baptized in the River. I noticed a large group of Americans from the South in line before us. I asked one older woman, "What have you seen in Israel while you've been here?" She replied in a deep southern drawl, "Honey, I don't know. My friends will tell me when I get home!"

We stopped by Jacob's Well. It was still giving pure water after 3,000 years. This was where the Samaritan woman gave Jesus a cup of water, and he then told her of her life. She quickly spread the word that she had met a prophet. Today a church covered the well.

Father Theodore, the other young and quiet Greek priest on our trip, said, "This was an authentic site!" as a few of us gathered around.

"Why do you say that?" I asked.

"Because they cannot move a well."

We all nodded our heads in agreement.

The Sea of Galilee was a peaceful place. We could see the other side of the lake, which now touches the country of Jordan. It was calm today, but the serenity was deceptive because sudden storms can stir up the water and make it hazardous. Another interesting fact was that the bottom layer of the Sea of Galilee was salt water fed by underground springs, while the top layer was fresh water. By keeping enough fresh water on the surface, the two layers did not mix. The region seemed sparkling and alive. I could understand why Jesus loved Galilee.

One of my favorite places in the region was a little church on the north side of the Sea of Galilee, were Jesus was supposed to have told Peter "upon this rock I will build my church." The well-appointed décor was a perfect size for two dozen parishioners. I believe, though, it was being surrounded by the people we had grown to enjoy during the week that made it memorable.

We drove further on to Tabgha where the Sermon on the Mount took place. A miracle took place here when five barley loaves and two fish fed 4,000 followers. As the sun sank lower in the horizon the water glimmered with dancing colors. We wandered down to the water's edge and heard the lapping of the water on the rocks. Reed-like plants created a curtain of living lace over the water. I pictured fishermen pushing their boats from the shore ankle then knee deep in water. I could envision Christ walking these shores better than at any other place on our trip.

We backtracked to the western hills where we spent the night in Nazareth at the Casa Nova Guest House, across from the largest cathedral in Israel. We later learned that the mosque site being protested throughout Israel was located down the hill from our quarters. The apparent issue was that the finished mosque would block the view of the cathedral. There is so much irony in religion which preaches tolerance and love, yet finds it so difficult to implement.

As we neared the city center in the open square, 20 Muslim men were reciting their evening prayers. Cars zipped by and the city noise was a dull roar. Across the street from the bowing worshippers was a pastry shop that sold the most delectable morsels. The name of the store was unknown, but my fingers knew how to point to this yummy delicacy that appeared to be strings of phyllo dough dribbled with honey.

We did a short tour of Nazareth. After a visit to where Mary and Joseph were believed to have lived, we went to the city well that had existed for centuries. Most likely Mary came here for water. I thought of Father Theodore's words "you can't move a well." It seemed that Jesus lived the majority of his life on the side of a hill in Bethlehem, Nazareth and Jerusalem.

FAREWELL TO ISRAEL

After a packed week of activities, it was time to return to Germany. Little did I guess our adventures were not quite over. David Ben Gurion Airport proved to be our final hurdle. We gasped when we were told to be there three hours early, but we really needed the time. First of all, we stood in lines forever. When we finally reached the end of the line, custom officials made us open our bags and grilled us with an incredible number of questions. We were required to unload the entire contents of our suitcase, the one we had just packed at the hotel. Then we waited in another line for the airline to give us our boarding passes. All this took more than two hours.

We finally reached the counter only to be informed that the airline had oversold the flight and run out of seats. Another lady, Lauren, and I did not mind staying overnight. My husband who had patients scheduled needed to get home the next day.

With incredible ineptitude the airline could not find anyone willing to give up their seat for a later flight. They never announced the offer over the loudspeaker. After 20 minutes of frustration, the ground staff found Steve a flight to Paris on Air France and ended up flying my husband home first class. He later told me at Orly Airport two drivers were waiting with a taxi to drive him from Paris to Landstuhl, Germany. The drivers took full advantage of no speed limits and made a normally five hour trip in three. Stephen got home about three in the morning. What a taxi ride to remember!

My friend from the ticket debacle, Lauren, and I checked into a five-star hotel on the beach of Tel Aviv. Rarely do I get to spend time in a luxury hotel, so I cursed in frustration because it was dark when we arrived and dark when we left at 3 am.

We did have time to do a little touring. Lauren and I sauntered over to the restored Jaffa port, poked our heads into a few shops and then had dinner. It was a long haul home to Germany from Israel arriving by train at 3 pm that afternoon. It left me exhausted, but I cheerfully remind myself that I got to see a little more of Israel.

It was incredible to think that we could crowd so much into seven days. We also learned that Father Paul would return again the next week with another tour group. We marveled at his zest! We felt a deep sense of gratitude having walked the Holy Lands, to be in places that we have heard about all our lives. We saw firsthand the cultures, religions and history playing a daily part of Israeli life. Most importantly, we felt a vibrant energy emanating from the people. How appropriate that we were there just before Christmas, giving the season extra meaning for us that year.

Egypt

February 2000

LAND OF THE PHARAOHS

We arrived in Cairo at night. The boulevard from the airport showed Egypt at her best with glitzy stores and fine government buildings. The majestic draping palm trees contrasted against the smaller trees trimmed like pillbox hats. Minarets broke the skyline every thousand feet. Traffic jammed the streets at ten o'clock at night. I kept thinking, "Omar Sharif, Omar Sharif."

My husband, son and I crossed the bridge over the Nile. Somehow, I expected this river to be grander and wider for all the legends that have emanated from it. The Nile, the giver of life, looked like any normal sized river. The fanfare of trumpets was missing.

As we rounded the corner to our hotel, I gasped! The Pyramids of Giza were flooded in lights. Before us lay 4,000 years of history! I stared for a moment in disbelief that these were the real pyramids of the pharaohs. Was I really awake?

We had made our travel arrangements through a German tour company, who contracted with an Egyptian company. Our group was composed of 30 Germans and only five Americans. Even though we flew together and stayed in the same hotels, the company provided different guides, one in German and one in English. Since there were only five Americans, we essentially enjoyed a private tour of Egypt.

The others in our party were Richard and his wife, Wii. Richard was of African American descent but had a fair complexion. His mustache had more hair under his nose than he had on his shaved head. He was retired from the military, but was stationed in Germany because of his wife's job. We quickly learned, nothing seemed to harry Richard being so kindhearted and he clipped along at his pleasant, unhurried pace the entire tour.

Wii, Richard's wife, was a native of Thailand, a wiry Asian woman who managed recreation programs in Germany. She was on the Olympic volleyball team for her country, and somewhere along the way, she and Richard met and married.

CAIRO

We spent our first night in Cairo in a Western style hotel. We ate a Western style breakfast and spoke English. The hotel was a hushed, sterile world. It was not until we loaded ourselves into our little white tour van, that the full force of Egypt hit us.

We were stuck in traffic! Dented cars of various vintage were crammed on narrow lanes! Arabic words were flung into the air! The noise was a constant rattle of horns blaring, drivers shaking their fists, and then totally disregarding traffic signals--if they could move at all. One daring driver raced along the median. I was surprised there were not more accidents.

Men and women in long dark robes wove in and out of crowds, some deftly balancing baskets on their heads. Western dress was equally apparent. To my eyes, the buildings and streets had a brown or gray cast making the scenery almost monotone in color. Egypt was like a midpoint of Eastern and Western society, modern yet traditional; impoverished, yet wealthy, and above all, fascinating!

Our first stop was the musty Egyptian Museum, a good beginning. Its very size was mind boggling. If you allowed one minute for each artifact, it would take nine months to view every object in the museum. Fortunately our guide steered us to the highlights.

I enjoyed the famous royal chairs with inlaid stones, standing on top of cases piled with numerous utensils. I was intrigued with the sculpture of the scribes, bare-chested with a tablet of writing, representing learning. They appeared humble in their dress, but wielded great power. Stephen later bought a small figurine of a scribe as a memento of our trip.

With little focus lighting, precious objects were left to natural light and deep shadows reminding me of a neglected burial. Someone once described this museum as a warehouse, and it did resemble a cavernous building with piled items scattered here and there. Few traces could be found of ambitious housekeeping.

As we rambled about, I noticed four alabaster jars sitting alongside most of the mummies. These jars were often carved in the shape a monkey, dog or cow. I later found out that the jars contained the innards of the mummified person.

Without question, the King Tutankhamen exhibitions were the most spectacular! Thieves had not robbed his grave, so it was found fully intact during excavation. The precious items were dazzling in both number and superb workmanship, ranging in size from the minute to life size figures. In the small room, the bright lights sparkled on the metal and jewels. The showpiece was the funerary mask made of solid gold. The guide grew impatient as I loitered over the exquisite jewelry pieces, and kept waving me on to join the rest of the group.

Walking through the rooms of Egyptian artifacts, reminded me of when my husband, Stephen, proposed marriage. The day after he popped the question, I attended an Egyptian exhibition. Everyone kept asking to see my husband's idea of a wedding ring, not a diamond set on a gold band, but a bread twist! I confess that I saw everything that day through starry-eyes.

Lunch was at a Giza restaurant in creamy orange decor. The walls defied any thought of a right angle. By the time we finished our appetizers--round pita bread served with an assortment of ground chickpeas, eggplant, and sesame paste, I was so full that I don't recall the rest of the menu.

Barren land surrounds the area immediately around the Great Pyramids, but city buildings have encroached to the border. The contrast was stark between open rocky fields, and houses piled on top of each other. From the Great Pyramid we could see a long valley with 80 pyramids running down the length like volcanic necks jutting upward on a fault line.

Some expressed disappointment standing below the Great Pyramid, that it looked so small. I felt nothing of the kind. I was overwhelmed at the immensity of the largest stone structure in the world. No mortar was used, and no razor blade could pass between the well-fitted stones. If you took all the stones from the Great Pyramid, you could build a large wall around Europe and still have boulders left over, that's how massive it is.

The gaily decorated camels with their riders at the base of the Pyramid were a classic tourist trap, but the pyramids would have been bereft of their magic without them. I passed on riding the dromedary, but managed to take a half a roll of photographs of the camels with the pyramids in the background.

The pyramid sides appearing a straight line from a distance were actually a series of small steps. It was quite an engineering feat. I tried picturing the slaves pushing and pulling these enormous stones on rolling lumbers, laying each timber down in the front and lifting the rear one. Add an uphill grade and I began to understand why it took 20 years to build a pyramid. My lack of engineering background also made me wonder how that much rock piled in one place could still have open chambers inside.

My son and I dashed into a nearby pyramid thinking we might rediscover some marvelous treasure, or secret passageway. I could not stand upright in the pyramid, and felt sorry for the taller men. The tomb was narrow, stuffy, and claustrophobic--designed for the dead, not the living. After we made our way back outside I heaved a sigh of relief to breathe fresh air once again.

The Great Sphinx is often thought to be as large as the pyramids. It isn't. It's about the size of a two-story house. To get the optimal view of the Sphinx it should be viewed from below, but we saw it almost eye to eye from the visitor's platform. We arrived just before closing and got the token tourist picture of the largest of the three sphinxes we saw on our trip.

A German professor who lived in Cairo joined us for parts of the tour. "I enjoy driving the streets in Cairo," commented the tall slender German professor of literature.

I stammered, "You mean the noisy, polluted, jammed streets of Cairo?"

He nodded. Although the professor appeared quite sane, all I could do was stare at him in disbelief. This city had one of the worst pollution problems I'd ever experienced, a stark contrast from the glittering Cairo of the night.

SAQQARA/MEMPHIS

The first large stone pyramid was built in Saqqara, the Pyramid of Zosa, 14 miles outside of Cairo. It is distinctive because of the visible steps forming the pyramid, rather than the straight angled line we were used to seeing. Our family's Christmas photograph that year was in front of the Zosa Pyramid complete with safari headgear. Looking further down the valley we saw several other pyramids that had not been designed as well and had collapsed. Even farther away, we saw a misshapen pyramid. The angle had been changed in the middle of construction making it appear lopsided. The landscape was an open yellow plain of sand with only pyramids growing, nary a single plant or tree.

By now we were getting better acquainted with Richard and his wife, Wii. Although Richard had visited Egypt once before he still continued to photograph everything he saw. He was serious about recording his trip with his video camera, and a still camera. At every stop we waited patiently for him to shoot a still picture followed by a video. Later he kindly shared some of the photographs with us.

Many times we passively followed our guide, not certain what we were meant to see. At one point we entered a square earth-colored house. On the walls were delicately drawn geese in a marsh bank, some swimming, some wading on the bank. The drawings felt fluid and contemporary; not stiff or ancient. They thoroughly captivated me. It's ironic the art that touched me most was small and delicate, not the grand engineering feats.

During college I enrolled in an art history class. Egyptian art was one of my favorite periods, because of the stylized figures and bright colors. The one lesson I never forgot: a figure faces sideways revealing a profile, but the eye always faces towards you.

The only Memphis I previously knew was located in Tennessee. Finally I learned that the American town had been named after an Egyptian city. The second largest sphinx was located in Egypt's old capital city, Memphis. Considerably smaller than the one at Giza, this sphinx reminded me of a large-sized lion. The most impressive object at the site was the reclining figure of Ramses II believed to be the pharaoh that chased Moses and the Hebrew slaves into the Red Sea. His statue in Memphis remains but the original city itself had all but vanished. He loved to build monuments to himself and we saw many named after him.

One particular night we enjoyed a sit down dinner. Earlier in the day at an open air book sale, I had found and purchased a lovely Koran in Arabic, bound in faux leather with gold lettering. At the dinner I was showing everyone at the table my bound book. My husband nudged me to look over my shoulder. The waiter was mesmerized looking at my book.

In broken English, he asked, "Do you like this book?"

I replied, "Yes, but I cannot read Arabic."

He repeated, "It is a good book. It is a good book!" He seemed pleased that I owned my own Koran. I was a bit startled. It was a graphic reminder to revere all scriptures!

THE CITADEL, MOSQUE, AND MARKET PLACE

Babe-Gadid, also known as the Citadel, was situated on a high bluff overlooking Cairo. The view from the Citadel was not memorable since the city was enveloped in a brown smog. Still we could admire the grounds. The intricate scrollwork cast shimmering shadows on the ground and the fountain in the middle of the courtyard trickled merrily down. The magical elements of water, delicate filigree, and plants all were here. A large clock in the patio was a gift from Louis Philippe of France in exchange for the obelisk that now sits at Place de la Concorde in Paris. There was serenity here, away from the noise of the pressing crowds in the streets. The sound of trickling water, the lights dancing through the lacy screens, and a sense of completeness made me linger.

A television special was being filmed in front of the Citadel. A famous male singer stood on the top of a large white truck belting out his songs with the famous structure in the background. I got his photo but not his name.

Next to the Citadel stands Al-Azhar, an enormous mosque built before the advent of cranes and hoists. I especially remembered its plush oriental carpets with their rich deep reds and blacks. The mosque seemed huge and daunting, but too harried with tourists to allow much spiritual reflection. February was the high tourist season in Egypt.

The tour guides were almost as interesting as the tourists. Both male and female guides dressed in western clothing. Few wore the long traditional robes. There were no name tags. Not extroverts, they seemed more reserved. They often acknowledged each other and would throw out some phrase in Arabic, followed by laughter. They felt secure assuming that none of us understood their comments. On this tour it felt we played musical chairs with them. We were deftly handed off from one guide to another from place to place, and did not get well acquainted with any guide in particular. It generally takes several days for the artificial formalities to drop before becoming comfortable, so we admired our guides from a detached distance.

It was 70 degrees and we stood around in our shirts and shorts. All our native Egyptian guides wore full winter coats while they led their tours. They told us it was their winter season. I wondered what their summer seasons were like. On second thought, no, I didn't want to know.

At the Khan el-Khalili, or bazaar, we looked more than we bought. There were simply too many things to see in too short a time. Merchants barked out greetings to view their wares. I loved the pungence of a bazaar, the varied humanity and exotic trinkets. In the crush, I broke down my resolve and purchased a glass perfume bottle in the shape of a camel.

Every tourist should be warned of the obligatory shopping trips made by organized tour groups to pre-arranged vendors. Our visit to this papyrus store, however, was not entirely in vain. We learned how papyrus was made. Workers soak the papyrus reed for several days and then press the rods together under a heavy weight until dried. The plant's natural glue holds the pieces together. The crown of the reed was symbolic of the Nile, and I later used this motif in a mural I painted for a children's library.

ASWAN

I am a night owl, not a morning lark. So I can hardly believe that I got up at three in the morning for a flight to Aswan. It was worth it, though.

From a smaller plane you can see more of the land. Only a fringe of green grew along the Nile. "Desert" is the best description of what we saw all around us. A vastness of flat sand extended in every direction like melted caramel with little nubs poking upward. If there were villages below, they blended into the terrain, and appeared invisible to us. The morning shadows quickly disappeared.

As we neared Aswan, we saw the water sparkling behind two dams, like gems dancing in front of a strobe light. It was such a welcome sight after the dry desert. The first dam was the project of Abdel Nasser, former President of the country who tried to modernize Egypt. The second dam appeared merely as another retaining wall surrounded by a lake of shimmering water.

I must confess that I get Upper and Lower Egypt confused. In the United States the major rivers runs north to south. The Nile River runs south to north, so the Upper part is nearer the source, near Aswan. Lower Egypt is considered closer to Cairo. We were now in Upper Egypt.

Our local tour guide collected all of us from the airport and took us on a short ride to the edge of the Aswan reservoir. A little dinghy, or small boat, took us to an island called Philae. When the Aswan Dam was built, the temple slowly flooded. So stone by stone, the temple was relocated to a higher neighboring island. By the time the last stone was removed, the reservoir waters reached the workers' knees.

This island was gorgeous! It was surrounded by deep sapphire water enlivened with green plants, and topped with a temple whose rustic colored stones contrasted with the blue water. The temple was essentially one long rectangle with large pillars flanking the sides. Small by comparison to some other Egyptian temples, the artwork was exquisite especially of the wide female faces on the top facades.

In the afternoon we rode on a *Felucca* or Egyptian sailboat with its distinctive triangular sail. Our pilot spoke no English. He had a light tawny complexion, not a burnt but a rich amber from sitting in the sun. On top of his head was wound a turban of white cloth. After a few minutes on the water, the lines on his face relaxed and his lips bowed upward in a slight smile. He was at home on the water.

The breeze sifted through my hair. The sun lowered itself on the horizon and its rays colored everything a golden hue with long azure shadows. We tacked our way around Elephantine Island and saw the mosque where the Shiite founder, Ali, Muhammad's cousin and son-in-law, was buried. We walked through Lord Kitchener's botanical gardens and saw plants new to us. It was a long day so we were numb by now. Sleep came quickly that night.

What I do for the sake of travel! The next day we again flew out early to Abu Simbel. As Lake Nasser was rising behind the dam, the government rescued the famous Ramses II Temple. The United States even helped with the financing. The terrain reminded me of Lake Powell in Utah with its dry reddish barren landscape. We walked to the edge of the reservoir and the guide pointed below. "That's where Abu Simbel used to be, now completely under water."

The cutting marks for removal were obvious as we looked at these giant figures carved out of stone, stoically rising three stories above us. It did not take much imagination, however, to blend those lines with the headdresses, protruding beards, and enormous hands and feet. The sheer size made us feel immediately insignificant.

As we entered the corridor, it took our breath away to be in the hallway flanked on each side with mammoth Ramses II sculptures and four Osiris statues. Lights swam in a gentle darkness, creating a respectful atmosphere. Every inch of wall space was decorated with stories and conquests in Egyptian hieroglyphics. The holy of holies was at the end of the long corridor. We automatically became reverent as if our souls knew we were in the presence of kings. We intuitively sensed a power but could not define it. We had to content ourselves only with what we saw, not fully understanding with our minds, the events that had occurred in front of these statues. The artwork stands alone as a tribute to the craftsmanship of the early Egyptians.

Richard, our videographer and photographer, was light-skinned and forever being mistaken as a native Egyptian. He said being in Egypt felt like coming home. Another fellow African American and Richard sang together on an earlier trip to Egypt. They coined themselves, "The Nubie Brothers" a pun on the Doobie Brothers.

Nubia was a land south of Egypt that we knew very little about, so we thought we'd bone up a little by visiting the new and well-done Nubian Museum. Our eyes were opened to its history and lifestyle. Their people were darker complexioned and very handsome. Little has seemingly changed. The striking costume worn years ago by native women is still worn today, consisting of a colorful cloth covered over by a sheerer black lace-like dress.

Here we also acquired the taste for *karkadeh*, a dried hibiscus flower drink loaded with sugar. It not only had a rich and full taste, but was supposed to help lower blood pressure. When we returned home, much to my delight, I found the dried hibiscus flower in a local health store.

On our last evening in Upper Egypt we walked through the marketplace. The streets were teeming with people, and bright lights strung on overhead wires lit our path. I am always attracted to the spice tables with their mounds of colorful and scented condiments. I purchased some saffron for my dear friend, Maria, who often yellows her rice for Mexican dishes. Booths overflowed with carved figurines, glass perfume bottles, woven shirts, t-shirts, stuffed leather camels, and a myriad of clutter. After a while, I began to weary of the overly aggressive salesmen who would not take "no" for an answer. They operated like a relay team. As soon as one salesman wearied, a second came and then a third, following us to three or four booths before giving up. While most salesmen acknowledge you in bored tones, during this trip these salesmen were the most energetic.

Somewhere I learned that the word for "no" in Arabic is *la*. So I used *la* liberally when accosted by an aggressive salesman. The vendor would stop, cock his head sideways, and have a puzzled look on his face. I figured I was getting my message through clearly. After using it for several days, my husband informed me that *la* was a vulgar swear word in Arabic. Oh, well, so much for attempted communication in another language.

FLOATING DOWN THE NILE

It was time to move from the hotel to our ship. At every place Richard faithfully pulled along two large suitcases that belonged to his wife plus his own luggage and his photography equipment. Someone should have taken his picture of him being an overloaded bellboy.

At this point we began the water portion of our trip to Lower Egypt. We sat on the top deck of the cruise ship, more like our ferryboat. The wind was very cold, since it was winter, so it was difficult to stand on deck for long without a jacket.

It was easy to imagine Pharaohs gliding up and down the Nile. Not much had changed in thousands of years. The green fertile fields on each side of the river fascinated me ending abruptly, and the sands of the desert beginning. The contrast was so stark, it was as though someone had taken a knife and neatly sliced the field from the desert. We noted very little mechanized farming on the shore. Nearly everyone performed manual labor. A water buffalo, a donkey, and occasionally a camel pulled a hand plow. The farmer behind the animal was lifted from medieval books.

We passed another boat going upstream. I wished I'd had my camera. On the upper deck an old Egyptian, weathered by the sun, dressed in his turban and long flowing robes, smiled and bowed. On the deck directly below an ample blond European in a hot pink bathing suit with her abundant cleavage spilling over, also waved at us. Neither was aware of the other. Definitely a study in contrasts!

My husband said he heard the engines knocking all night, so he didn't sleep well on the ferry. I simply rolled over onto my good ear and heard no noise. I was so thoroughly exhausted I could have slept through a hurricane.

Omar was a supervisor of the bellhops on our boat. Stationed on the lower deck, he was always patient, even though there were times it must have been wearisome hearing the same questions over and over. I thought him the handsome Egyptian with a golden tan complexion, white hair, a Roman nose, and always an elegant *jalaba* or flowing robe. He had a melodious voice. He had been schooled in the art of hospitality, as was the custom in the Arabic world. Even when he was tired, he would be gracious at my attempts at Arabic hello, "*Salaam, Aleikum.*"

THE MUMMIFIED CROCODILE

Our first stop on the river in the morning was at Kom Ombo before other tourists arrived. For a few minutes we had the marvelous temple all to ourselves. The roof had long since caved in, but one pillar the width of three encircling men stood guard. The shrubbery around the temple was sparse. Splotches of paint remained on the walls, suggesting that most Egyptian ruins were originally very colorful. A remarkably accurate Egyptian calendar told the river people when to plant, when to expect floods, and when to harvest. Several other statues revealed Roman occupation. In a small house next to the temple were several mummified crocodiles honoring the god, Sobek. They were preserved as if they had been stuffed last month.

In an earthquake in 1992, two stones from the restoration work fell. All the original stones built thousands of years before stayed in place, confirming the excellent engineering of the early Egyptians. Embedded in the stone were wooden beams from 2000 B.C—well-preserved just a few feet away from the mighty Nile.

EDFU

Our next stop on the Nile was Edfu. I felt we were on some movie set as hired extras. Our entire group rented horsedrawn carriages and clopped through town to Horus' Temple, the largest after Luxor. Horus was the god often represented as a falcon or hawk. The temple walls were tall and smooth, tilted towards the center. The temple was covered in sand until the 1860s. I guess you could say history can easily be buried.

Throughout the ruins, the Christian Coptic had chiseled many of the Egyptian faces believing the worship of pagan gods as a desecration. They attempted to eradicate what they could with a chisel and a hammer. Fortunately the Coptics only chipped the faces, not the stories carved into the walls. I wonder how many of these tales could have reached us if there had been no written language.

LOCKS ON THE NILE

Back on board our ship in the evening, our waiters all dressed in Nubian costumes and provided us with a fun evening. Each wore a tall round hat like a fez, colorfully embroidered vest and billowy pants. As the drums and flute played, I got up and attempted a few dances. After a couple of numbers, I left the party because I was intrigued to see the river locks! It was late evening before we entered the narrow channel and dropped the 10 feet from the upper to the lower Nile, a smaller version of the Panama or Suez Canals. The only sounds I heard were water streaming by, an occasional voice in the dark, and the motors of the ferry slowly churning us north.

WEST BANK AT LUXOR

We arrived at Luxor at night, and didn't realize that the boats were locked up four or five abreast at the dock. In the morning we had to walk through the decks of each boat to reach the shore. Each décor was slightly different than the last--totally red, or velvety green with gold ornaments. It was like moving through a boat display for free.

Our first day at Luxor took us to the drier west side of the river, where the Valley of the Kings, the Valley of Nobles and Valley of the Queens were located. Over 700 burial sites were yet to be excavated. So a couple of lifetimes of digs remain for the serious archaeologist.

One could easily spend a millennium wandering from tomb to tomb. Fortunately our woman guide highlighted the best ones for us. She led us to only three tombs, but each had a distinctive importance. Their floor plans were all one long corridor with side rooms. One in particular was Seti No. 15. The colorful hiero-glyphics still had much of the original paint on the walls.

The Tomb of Nefertari, the one-eyed queen, cost a $100 to visit, probably to limit the number of persons entering. Such simple things as perspiration can affect the delicate balance of these tombs.

Queen Hatsheptsut's Temple was striking against the Theban Hills. One of the few female pharaohs, the queen dressed as a man and even wore a false beard to add to her power. Hundreds of Egyptian children were visiting the temple that day becoming as much a tourist attraction as the site. Dressed in their Sunday fin-est, they presented a rainbow of western style clothing, matching socks and polished shoes. They readily smiled for our cameras.

It was only February, yet when we finished our tour, I was hot. The hills were unmercifully warm. A word to the wise, go to Egypt during the winter!

EAST BANK OF LUXOR

The next day was spent visiting the two major sites on the east side of the Nile, the Temple of Luxor and Karnak. I am reminded of Karen, who joined our group at Luxor with her parents. A political appointee at the ripe old age of 38, she now owned her own consulting company giving advice to govern-ments. She talked with a Texas swagger. To lend credence to her successful career, her father bragged that she owned a house in an exclusive area of Washington, D.C. Karen related a daring tale that we half-believed since it was so incredible. She told of going to an African country and candidly telling the king something that could have had her beheaded. Her father had accompanied her and admitted he was terrified for the life of his daughter. It was a tense moment as the king weighed how he should respond.

Fortunately the monarch had enough diplomatic sense to laugh at her little impropriety, and she lived to share the tale with us.

The Temple of Luxor was surrounded by the modern city. A few years earlier shanties covered the original foundation. When the restoration groups came in, they had to tear down the make-shift neighborhoods. Scholars are finding that this temple was probably connected to Karnak, several kilometers to the north by more than 500 small sphinxes. An interesting addition is a mosque over the pharaonic temple. One of the original pillars at the entrance now stands in Paris, France.

This impressive temple was built by Ramses II, the prolific builder. Enormous pylons were carved with scenes of the pharaoh's military triumphs. The entrance was originally flanked by six colossal statues of the ruler, but only two survived. In the temple are other tall pillars with papyrus capital columns. Some Roman stuccoes can be seen above the Egyptian carvings. For 132 centuries, successive pharaohs added to the compound ever enlarging the space.

We walked the long ramp to the last temple at Karnak. As I rounded a corner I involuntarily uttered, "Wow!" It was one of those moments that truly reminded me why Egypt stands as a world destination. Filled with 134 enormous columns carved with exquisite designs, the Great Hypostyle Hall in Amon-Re was breathtaking! To circle each pillar would take the arm lengths of at least four large men. Standing under them I was like a tiny mushroom in a forest of giant sequoias. The pillars soared upward to 80 feet covered with inscriptions of battles. The northern half had raised relief while the southern had sunken relief. Pharaoh Seti I, Ramses father was thought to have begun the building with Ramses continuing to make additions to the sprawling temple.

Words fail to describe the grandeur and scope of this 100 acre Temple. What amazed me was who envisioned such a design, alone to possess the power and resources to create it? We were so totally taken by it that we decided to return for the Light and Sound Show that evening.

As we entered at dusk, it seemed the sphinxes bowed to us. We walked through the columns under a full moon peeking between the stones. The spirits of long ago were invited to awaken. They aroused an ancient swelling within our souls. It was as if we became a part of the heart of Karnak!

On deep reflection, Egypt had become a part of us, changing forever how we regarded the Nile and its people. Not only had we admired its enduring monuments, but we also felt its vital pulse, an intangible, but powerful force rising up from the crystalline sands to encircle us.

Tunisia

April 2000

Tunisia is a land of contrast, long history and obscurity for the Westerner. It is a land where camels are ridden. Dates, olives and *harissa* are eaten over conversations of Arabic and French. All the houses are whitewashed and most windows and doors are painted in the most beautiful sky blue, making photographic moments everywhere. The highest buildings were no more than two stories tall. Occasionally we saw a dome of a mosque rising above the flat roofs. Shepherds tended their flocks under spreading date palms. Prickly pear cacti were planted for use as fences and olive trees stretched as far as the eye could see.

Europeans flock to Tunisia's shores, capitalizing on its excellent weather and fine beaches. We landed in this northern African country at Monastir. The Tunisians did not wear long flowing robes like those we saw in Egypt, but on closer inspection we noted that their trousers had ribbed designs and the shoes were distinctly Tunisian with side seams tapering to a pointed toe.

Someday I might be able to write a discourse on hats. The cowboy has his Stetson. The Brit his bowler. The Jew his yarmulke. For the Tunisian it was a maroon-colored wool cylinder with a long black tassel called a Fez.

SALAAM

I wanted a trip that would show me the character of the land and a glimpse of her people. So I took the "Rundreiser," (literally "round trip" in German) with a German-based travel company, for one week travelling an elliptical path up and down the length of the country. The affordable package included room and board, plus airfare and guide. The down side was dates were fixed, so Stephen could not come. I went solo.

My reservation packet included a lovely pamphlet that highlighted the country, listed precautions, and included a full foldout map. There was one slight problem: everything was in German. Fortunately our tour guide spoke English, and made sure I understood the time and location of meetings. I was the tour's only American with my bilingual dictionary and a good travel guide. If I couldn't understand what I was seeing in German, I could read about it in English. Of the three million tourists that visit Tunisia each year, only 50,000 are Americans.

Tunisians are a handsome blend of European, African, and Arabian heritages with skin tones ranging the entire palette from pale yellow to dark brown. Children grow up speaking Arabic, but are taught French in school. Many later learn German and English as well. Nearly everyone affiliated with the Tunisian travel industry spoke excellent English.

ROMAN TUNISIA

The Romans occupied much of Tunisia and left impressive remains. The Roman amphitheater located in El Djem was spectacular--slightly smaller but better preserved than the Colosseum in Rome. El Djem, reputed to be the sixth largest amphitheater in existence, could sit 30,000 spectators. We also toured Sbeitla, an entire city of Roman ruins, including an arch built by Diocletian, baths, theater, and a forum. There was a strange quiet to the place with only the wind whipping an occasional gust. We were all momentarily suspended in time, located neither in ancient or modern--just there. As I gazed down the wide sloping hill, I mused about history. The Roman conquerors brought many of their own customs but allowed local cultures to thrive side by side. This allowed a loose federation to co-exist, but all ultimately paid homage to Rome.

STAR WARS

On our journey southward we stopped inland at Matmata. This region inspired much of the design of the Star Wars films. The sunken house of Luke Skywalker's uncle's was a Berber-styled home. By burrowing under the ground, the Berbers were able to escape the wretched heat of summer. Over 700 such homes were in the region. The Star Wars' film showed little people with flashing eyes, the Jawas. The Jawas were merely wearing Berber coats with hoods on them. I thought that the filmmakers were totally original, instead they merely adapted what they saw.

If you took the American southwest, changed cedar trees to olive groves, sprinkled palm trees for cottonwoods and switched Navajo Indians for Berbers you'd have Tunisia. I loved driving by a Berber house with two camels parked in front instead of a pickup.

We lunched in a Berber restaurant. Our meal began with "brik" a pastry taco filled in the center with egg, onion, and cheese. The main course of lamb's meat with couscous was especially delicious. Tunisians eat lots of vegetables. They also love their food so hot that foreigners taste only fire. *Harissa* was a condiment of ground red peppers. The Tunisians toned down their food for tourists. To wash away any remaining chile taste, we sipped their national drink of a stout mint tea.

I met a trio of lean French cyclists, perhaps in their sixties, biking their way across Tunisia on a 10 day trek. Speaking French made it easier for them to get around, but I still admired their spunk in undertaking such a challenge.

ISLE OF DJERBA

Djerba was the island where the famed Ulysses met the lotus eaters. Try as I might, I could not see one lotus. The island was a flat ancient land with thin desert vegetation and sparsely populated. One visible Roman remnant was a stone road still in usable condition.

That evening we experienced one of Tunisia's rare rainstorms. The northern half of the country receives about 24 inches of rain but moving south moisture dries up leaving less than eight inches a year. The rain washed the sky, leaving it brilliantly clear the next day.

THE SAHARA DESERT

Our hotel in Douz was the last outpost before the great Sahara Desert. Gazing out my window, I saw camel drivers giving rides to tourists and dashed to join them for a slow hour's ride. I felt like Lawrence of Arabia astride a camel with a long cloth wrapped around my head. As we inched up the hill I snapped a photograph of a little mosque surrounded by nothing but sand. On closer inspection it turned out to be a movie set. Tunisia is a popular filmmaking site.

The camel is such an amazing animal. It can go for days without water, but when thirsty consumes many gallons at a gulp. Even more amazing was its obedience. The camel driver simply puts the camel's lead rope under a walking stick, and the camel stays put. I was told that training begins when they are but a baby, and the lesson remains fixed in the adult camel's brain. The action was symbolic. The camel was so much larger than the stick, and could easily wander away, yet its training was thoroughly ingrained.

The feet of the camel were so interesting--the pads flatten out on the sand as they walk to prevent their feet from sinking into the sand. The camel's rocking motion took getting used to, but soon my body was in rhythmic sway with the camel. However, I was relieved not to be traveling 30 or 60 days on the back of a dromedary.

Our next stop in Douz was the Thursday marketplace. It was a large courtyard surrounded on three sides by one-story sand colored adobe buildings. A few large trees gave much needed shade. Mounds of carved stones boxes, of every size, shape and color as well as necklaces and clothing were heaped on the tables. Men wearing loose flowing robes and some in western trousers hunkered over games of dominos or drank mint tea at the café. At another booth selling farm tools, I saw a hoe with handles only a foot long. Using such farming implements would require a strong back. I wanted to buy a wool coat that resembled the Star Wars Jawa, but resisted. The market seemed more like a community gathering than just a place of commerce.

I was correct in assuming that the market was a weekly social event. The marketplace was abandoned the next day, the courtyard empty except for one man reclining under a tree. Outside on the street a lone man in long robes leaned against the building, perhaps reliving the conversations of the previous day. I counted no more than three people where there had been hundreds the day before.

In the late afternoon, after the strongest heat of the day subsided, we took four-wheel jeeps into the Sahara, jostling over miles of sand. Fortunately our driver knew where he was going, because there were absolutely no road signs and nary a tree to guide the way. We drove over mounds in the jeep. Finally when we stopped, and stepped out, we sank eight to ten inches. Saharan sand was very fine, yet did not cling to our shoes and clothing. My eyes caught a distinctive track that ended with a large black beetle making its way across the waste. How incredible in the middle of this dry desert, there was life trudging along. A desert is a miraculous place. At first glance we think nothing can live or thrive in this barren sandbox but we are always pleasantly surprised.

We stopped to inspect the home of a Bedouin family. Their tent was made of dark, heavy woven wool draped over poles. The inside of the tent was cool but flies were abundant. Trunks and blankets were neatly tucked against the back of the tent. We politely waited while the wife finished her prayers. She was sunburned and likely much younger than she appeared. What was most amazing to me was her isolation from anything that resembled modern civilization as we knew it. It had taken us over an hour to reach their home in a jeep. We wondered how long it would take the woman to walk or ride an animal to her closest neighbor or town.

The low light of the setting sun cast a marvelous powder blue shadow over the dunes. It was truly an ocean of ripples and tides of crystal grains sculpted by the wind. Our guide reclined on a dune and shared how he loved the desert. He asked if we felt the peace of the desert where the only sound to be heard was the faint whistle of wind. Our guide found beauty where we thought there was only desolation. I felt myself slowing down and trying to rid my brain of the stereotype of a desert being an arid place. We sat down and the calming presence of the desert spirit inched its way into our being. No one spoke. It was only through silence that we could begin to connect. A warmth began in my chest and slowly filled my entire body to the ends of my fingers and toes. I could think of nothing else but how the white sand was enveloped by the shadows of the sky. Time was suspended. After half an hour, our guide sighed and signaled us back into our jeeps.

ATLAS MOUNTAINS

We crossed the great dry salt lake called Chott el Djerid, once part of the Mediterranean Sea. Arriving in Tozeur, we visited a small museum of Tunisian life built by the late President Bourguiba (1957-1987). It was not unusual to see his name. Nearly every town had a Bourguiba street named after this most influential first president. Habib Bourguiba introduced many pro-Western reforms during his presidency including making education a high priority. He supported women's rights and other social changes that transformed Tunisian society.

We spent the night in Nefta. Man-made wells brought enough water to irrigate the 200,000 palm trees crowded into this narrow valley. I had never seen so many trees growing so closely together. Tunisia had great contrasts—one moment you were standing on barren brown sand, the next you were surrounded by abundant green vegetation.

Again we went four-wheeling towards the Atlas Mountains. This parched range stretches across the southern border of Algeria and Morocco and separates the Mediterranean from the Sahara

Desert. Atlas is a name I remember because of the peculiar curly haired lion from this region. The large cat appear in a painting by Peter Paul Rubens called *Daniel in the Lion's Den.* The painting was a favorite of mine when I was a docent leading children's tours through the Washington D.C National Gallery of Art. I never dreamed I would actually visit the Atlas Mountains!

COMPLETING THE CIRCLE

In one day we drove from the waterless dunes of the Sahara to the lush vegetation of the Mediterranean coast making several stops along the way. Our first stop was Kairouan, the fourth most holy city in all of Islam, and the most holy of cities in Tunisia. We toured only the outside of the Great Mosque, since the interior was closed to non-believers. All we really saw was the sandy colored minaret.

The best Tunisian carpets are made in Kairouan, so we made the perfunctory visit to a rug shop. After the effusive welcome and cup of mint tea, the bearded salesman in long robes and his helper in plainer robes lay carpet upon carpet until there was a pile a yard high. Most carpets were made of wool, but there were a few silk ones. Then the salesman teased potential buyers as the helpers began rolling up the carpets. It was a show to watch as these salesmen plied their charisma and wit. The carpets were gorgeous costing thousands of dollars, not for the budget traveler.

Tunis has a large well-preserved medina, the old walled city. One resident told me there were over 200 small streets in the old part of town that allowed you to discover something new every time you visited. What a delight to enter in the morning before many of the shops were open. The quiet allowed us to feel the stones polished by human footprints, to be taken to the top of the roof to view Tunis through arches of mosaic tile, to meet people willing to tell you about the Berber women who hand-rolled flower essence, to watch the street of barbers cutting hair, and to glance at the veiled women patiently waiting for the stores to open. I felt myself transported to another era.

How I longed for more time in Tunis' medina. One of the frustrations of an organized tour is conforming to a schedule, and not always having enough time to explore and wander at will.

CARTHAGE

We drove by an American cemetery located in Carthage--a pivotal battleground during World War II. I silently paid homage to these brave soldiers. We ended up at a field overgrown with weeds which contained many old stela--a reminder that the Punics had also lived here. These people believed in the human sacrifice of firstborn children. Boys and girls between the ages of 1 to 12 years were strangled to death before being sacrificed. The Punics were later absorbed by the Romans and nearly forgotten.

Our final stop was at Sidi Bou Said. This picturesque town was perhaps the most celebrated by artists and writers. If a travel brochure featured a town with whitewashed walls and blue window trim representing Tunisia, it was probably Sidi Bou Said. I can still picture the square-topped houses perched on the side of the hill marching neatly into the deep blue Mediterranean.

RUNDREISER

I saw nearly every inhabited corner and gained a greater understanding of Tunisia. It is a well-kept secret, at least for most westerners. It is exotic, not overcrowded with tourists, and affordable. Most of all, it satiated my wanderlust for at least a month! I managed to memorize the entire Arabic alphabet and read some simple words by week's end. Though I forgot the alphabet by the next week, I still remember the rich memories of Tunisia.

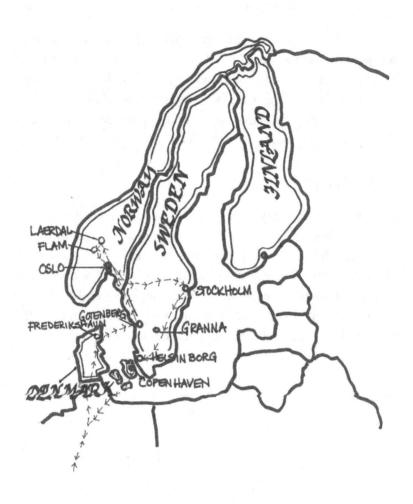

Scandinavia
Sweden, Norway, Denmark

June 2000

ON TO OSLO, NORWAY

Barbro is my friend from Stockholm. My husband's family has Danish blood. All the Hansens, Johnsons, Peterson, Jensens, and Larsens that I grew up with, names ending with a "son" or "sen" had their origins in Scandinavia. So for me it was a natural step to visit these northern countries.

We took the ferry across the Baltic Sea to Gotenberg, Sweden. For most Americans, Gotenberg was the place to pick up a new Volvo car. The town was meaningful for me because I had met two tall handsome men from this western Swedish town on my first trip to Europe. They gave my friend and me a small glimpse into European lifestyle. We lost track of them, but I remembered the name of their home.

Lots and lots of wooded acres lined the roads. The highways connecting major cities were surprisingly only two lanes, which made driving slow. We noticed that everyone drove with their headlights on, a law in a country where there was more darkness than light during the winter.

We arrived in the early evening in Oslo, a capital city full of islands, reminding us of Vancouver, British Columbia. Stephen and I hopped onto the subway and within three stops were in the heart of the city. We wandered down to the wharf, near the famed city hall where the annual Nobel Peace Prize ceremony is held. Only one prize is given in Norway. The other prizes are awarded in Sweden.

Our tour included a visit to the top of a world famous ski jump. As we looked down the terrifying long slide, we wondered if courage or insanity drove people to leap off the track. The reward for being at the top was a spectacular view of Oslo. Looking over the city, I laughed seeing grass growing out of the sod roofs on the houses.

We stopped at the Viking Museum and saw genuine Viking ships. I stood in amazement picturing these hardy sailors crossing the ocean in an open boat not much larger than an oversized rowboat with sun and rain pounding on their heads. Storm waves could easily engulf the boat. Hardy, I suspect, is a weak word to describe these seafarers. Other relics included ornately carved wagons, chests, and hand implements. The primitive urge to beautify manifests itself even in everyday objects.

When we were on our own, Steve and I spent time in the Nasjonalgalleriet where the famed Edvard Munch's paintings were housed. I could not resist having my photograph taken next to his most famous painting, "The Scream," with my hands cupping my head and my mouth open mimicking the Screamer. I was surprised that there was no cordon or security around this fabled painting. Later this painting as well as several others were stolen and recovered.

The majority of people were Norwegians, tall with striking blue eyes and blond hair--a handsome people. But sprinkled in between were other nationalities. Bolivian street singers played their reed flutes and drums. Pakistani businessmen ran shops. I wondered how far these folks had travelled to come to Oslo. What made people like these uproot from their homes and move halfway around the world?

ON TO THE FJORDS

The word "smorgasbord," sandwich table, came to us from this region of the world. Even for breakfast in Norway cold cuts, various hard breads, fruits, fish, and pickled vegetables were set out in the morning. Stuffing ourselves with all this delicious food kept us sated far into the afternoon.

On the curving road to the Sognefjord, we found ourselves leaning to the left and then to the right as the bus swayed like a ship through a storm. Fortunately no one got seasick. It was a drizzly day and I wondered with no central heating how these northern folks kept warm and dry. Perhaps they didn't. We passed the oldest wooden church in Norway, Borgund Stavkyrkje. The wooden shingles on steep layered roofs formed a picturesque covering over the wooden domes.

At the beginning of the longest and deepest fjords in Norway, was located Laerdal, a cozy town. We learned that this street was listed on the national register of historic districts especially a colorful winding street fringed with quaint houses adorned with lacy latticework. I snapped a photo of red, blue, and yellow houses reflected in the still water, the light in the far north softening all sharp edges.

Of all the days we needed sunshine it was our day on the fjord. We got it! I'm not Irish, but I claim adoption of their luck! The sun usually shines wherever I go. Although sunny it was still chilly on deck of the hydrofoil ferry, but we braved the winds for the unobstructed view. The sky was crisp and clear, smelling clean, not salty. The boat skimmed the deep ultramarine blue water. Towering mountain slopes plunged into the waters on all sides of us. This was indeed a rare view of nature in pristine condition.

Two hours later we left the ferry and took the Flam Line, a narrow-gauge train. We kept darting from side to side snapping photographs of spectacular waterfall after waterfall. The train stopped at the largest fall, allowing us to photograph the legendary female "troll" who led men to their deaths. In reality, I think she was a college student earning her summer keep.

At the end of the 40 minute ride was Gol, a stop where we left the train and basked in the warm sun. We walked down a hill and saw a group of preschoolers playing under melting glaciers in the soggy soil, while their teachers sunbathed. It was one of those memorable moments where sun, mountain air, and vistas come together filtering into our brain and forever remaining lodged as a pleasant memory. If we visit Norway again, it will be to see the fjords.

SWEDEN

Not many Westerners can say they drove from Norway to Sweden! And with good reason, since it's a long, monotonous haul past unending forests and lakes. Finally we reached the outskirts of Stockholm where Alfred Nobel was born, the chemist who discovered dynamite. After he was criticized for an invention that blew up and killed people, he pledged his wealth toward the betterment of humanity. Nobel prizes in science, medicine, literature and peace are awarded--some of the most prestigious awards in the world accompanied by a sizable monetary gift.

STOCKHOLM

Stockholm was the largest of the three Scandinavian capitals on our trip made of more than a dozen islands connected by bridges or ferries. After pondering our guidebook, we realized there was simply too much to see in one short morning--but it didn't stop us from trying.

We took a small ferry from our hotel to Skansen, one of the earliest open air museums in the world. Williamsburg, Virginia, is an example of an American open air museum. We wandered Skansen viewing regional houses, mostly made of wood, much like our American log cabins.

We spoke with an attractive but tired young woman who wore a wreath of fresh flowers on her head and carried decorative streamers of natural fibers and dried flowers. She told us she was returning home from a Midsummer's Eve party that had lasted all night. This celebration marked the longest day of the year when the sunlight literally never left the sky.

Next we high-tailed it to Stockholm's number one tourist site, the VASA--a war ship that sank on its maiden voyage, less than a nautical mile from its launch. Because it was top heavy, full of ornamentation and turrets, it never made it out of the bay. Four hundred years later the Vasa was recovered and restored, a marvelous craft made of carved wood 230 feet long and 172 feet high. We could have spent all morning seeing films and inspecting the enormous ship in the building designed especially for it. The VASA became Stephen's favorite.

My husband kindly accompanied me to the Junibacken, a little museum based upon Astrid Lindgren's book, *Pippi Longstocking*--a childhood favorite of mine. A short train ride led us through the various episodes in Pippi's life. I was delighted to relive my childhood book.

In the Nordiska Museet, Sweden's largest museum, was a small section dedicated to Swedish cultural history. Lovely dioramas tracked birth, courtship, holidays, and finally death. Many of the traditions felt familiar to me. They have probably been absorbed into our American way of life when many Swedes immigrated. When a man goes courting and is intent on marrying a young lady he gives his Love Spoons, carved wooden spoons, as part of the strict courtship ritual, as they do in Wales.

I was amazed we crammed all of this into one morning! Fortunately everything was located close together. We were also becoming veteran museum goers, and knew how to move swiftly through an exhibition.

In afternoon we headed to Denmark. But first our group stopped by Granna, a little village on a large picturesque lake. Its claim to fame is as the home of *polkagris* meaning "polka pig," peppermint candy canes. Naturally we purchased the sweet delectable.

When asked how the local residents put up with all these tourists, a kind Swedish gentleman got a twinkle in his eye and answered, "The season lasts only two months," and kept walking.

DENMARK

We ferried the narrow crossing in less than an hour to Helsingo, the narrowest point from the Baltic to the North Sea. In olden times charges were levied on sea traffic making a goodly fortune for the royalty who collected it. Nearby was the Elsinore Castle made famous in Shakespeare's *Hamlet*. The castle stood on level ground, not on a high cliff that I often envisioned. Although Shakespeare never visited Elsinore, he did capture its dark mystique.

We had a quick city tour of Copenhagen, first visiting the famous Little Mermaid perched on her rock in the bay at Langelinie. The bronze was only four feet tall, much smaller than her larger-than-life reputation. The Dutch were the major architects for this city and their influence reminded us of Holland. On our own we went to the National Museet with its excellent Viking artifacts of runic stones, cups, carved chests, jewelry and a bronze chariot excavated from burial mounds.

We stopped at a museum featuring Denmark's most noted sculptor, Bertel Thorvaldsen, 1770-1844. He is claimed by the Danish although he lived most of his time in Italy working for the popes. We were pleasantly surprised to find out that Thorvaldsen created the Christus popularized by the Spanish Lladro Ceramic Company. His sculpture work was both monumental as well as exquisite showing carved stone as soft as velvet.

Our dinner of smoked salmon was made more interesting by our table partner who joined us wearing a cowboy hat and boots. From Oklahoma he was now working on natural gas and oil lines in Norway. A skilled salesman he convinced us that when we retire we should raise buffalo instead of sheep. An ever flowing fountain of ideas and information he was the epitome of an American cowboy.

It was high school graduation time in Copenhagen. The graduates sported tiny sailor hats. Young men in large open trucks rode up and down the streets yelling and screaming at the populace. It was a merry time!

A large marching band led us under twinkling lights into Tivoli Gardens, the first amusement park in the world located in downtown Copenhagen. We enjoyed seeing pavilions with orchestras, numerous restaurants, and carnival rides. The storybook ride featuring Hans Christian Anderson's fairytales was not busy so the attendant offered us a second ride for free! Anderson wrote over 170 tales including The Princess and the Pea, The Little Mermaid, and The Ugly Duckling.

SCANDINAVIA

All the cultural awareness books emphatically state how much the Norwegians, the Swedes and the Danish appreciate it when you recognize them as individual countries, not as a lump. After this trip, we did better at noting the differences.

Norway had its fabulous fiords and natural beauty. Even though all the countries had Vikings, I associate the tribe with this country. Sweden had its Vasa Ship, love spoons, and striped candy canes. Denmark had her Tivoli Gardens, the Little Mermaid and the original Christus statue.

Now I'll lump them together again. The people put us all to shame since they spoke English almost better than we did. They ate herring in any form, raw or cooked. The rural lands were pristine and heavily wooded, but roadways were not always well developed. I will go again, but next time, I'll fly!

Kiev, Ukraine
Mother Of All Russian Cities

July 2000

Foul-ups can sometimes be an opportunity in disguise. Because the airline bumped us off a flight from Tel Aviv, Israel, we ended up with two free passes to anywhere the company flew. We selected Kiev, Ukraine, partly because it was an exotic place and partly because we had acquaintances living there. To celebrate our American Independence Day, we climbed aboard an airbus and headed to Kiev (Kyiv in Ukrainian) for a long weekend.

SAFE ARRIVAL

In two short hours directly from Frankfurt, we landed in Kiev. "My," I thought, "that was easy." Fortunately our luggage arrived complete with our gifts. We brought them to sweeten our reception--perfumes were a favorite and my friend, Svetlana, specifically asked for a clothing rack. By the time I had purchased all the gifts, I could have paid for several nights in a hotel, but I would rather have been with my friends.

As we passed the airport's final checkout, we saw Svetlana frantically waving for us to follow her on a dead run. "Hurry, we need to catch the bus!" she shouted over the crowds rushing towards the street. We ran as fast as our legs could take us jostling our luggage and packages and boarded a 1950s bus with its fading paint and rounded edges.

"Hello! I am so glad we got on this bus!" panted Svetlana. "We would have had to wait another 30 minutes for the next bus into town!" I quickly introduced my husband to Svetlana, and we all laughed at our hurried beginnings.

How did I meet Svetlana? She came as a translator for the Ukrainian military delegation to Ramstein, Germany. I had the opportunity to host her and another translator, Iryna, during their visit. We maintained our friendship via email. I noticed how much her English had improved working with Americans.

The bus ride took us past forests on the flat east side of the Dneiper River. Upon crossing the river, we were greeted by an enormous 72 meter (216 feet) tall silver statue called 'Defense of the Motherland'—a Russian monument of a woman holding a sword. Our bus curved its way up the hilly west side of the river to the city proper. Our first impressions of Kiev were positive--well laid out, the general appearance of cleanliness with wide streets. Monumental buildings and statues of heroes were scattered everywhere.

We disembarked on a busy street and dragged our luggage to a Soviet-era high- rise. We were in the heart of the embassy area, yet, the peeling paint marked all the apartment buildings around us. Because of the deteriorated conditions, Svetlana confessed that only three years ago she would have been embarrassed to host a westerner in Kiev. Things had markedly improved, although the economy was still sluggish.

Svetlana introduced us to her mother who was a professor of philosophy at a nearby university. She had a round face framed by bleached blonde hair and stood about five feet four. Her intense light blue eyes shone with intelligence. Svetlana was also the same height as her mother, with dark brown hair and resplendent large dark eyes. We also met her brother, Nikita, who had just graduated from the English language university. His 6'2" frame filled the entire doorway.

All the young people knew that speaking English was the way to forge ahead in Ukraine. The traditional jobs do not pay enough, only a few hundred dollars a month. However, with a job in the international sector, a Ukrainian could begin to prosper. The family all spoke some English.

We were delighted with their cozy apartment--two bedrooms, a bathroom, and a toilet room, a kitchen, and a living room with a balcony. The twelve-foot ceilings gave a spacious feel to the quarters. We unpacked our baggage in the living room where we would sleep on a comfortable fold-down sofa.

Soon we were all off to an art exhibit. The crazy taxi ride took us through twists and turns on wide tree-lined boulevards to the office building where the exhibition was held. Svetlana settled the bill with the taxi driver for one dollar. We met up with Iryna, our mutual friend, and her new husband, Dima, who were obviously still newlyweds by their dreamy-eyed gazes at each other.

The art exhibit consisted of drawings of the Himalayas by a famous Russian artist whose name eludes me. Since it was Saturday afternoon and admission was free, the small gallery was filled with people. The pictures were small and pleasant to look at but nothing innovative. We returned to the apartment.

Our first meal was typical Ukrainian food made by Svetlana's mother. Tomatoes tasted like tomatoes, firm, red, and ripened on the vine. Also included were a flavorful cabbage salad, a cottage cheese salad with eggs mixed with fresh dill and mayonnaise, rich glutinous bread, and boiled potatoes seasoned with fresh dill. The freshness without preservatives was obvious to our taste buds and everything settled well on our stomachs that night.

TOURIST KYIV

We zonked out on the fold-down bed till morning. Soon it was time for a filling and delicious breakfast. It consisted of white rice mixed with currant berries and peanuts, tomatoes stuffed with mayonnaise, and boiled zucchini in a tomato sauce with bread. We drank compote made of boiled fruit with sugar. Although we were not accustomed to such a breakfast it was tasty.

Our first stop of the day was at the Golden Gate, Zoloty Vorota. In medieval times, a complete stone wall encircled the city. The way in and out of the city was through this gate where a toll was exacted, thus the name "golden." The structure has been skillfully restored standing three stories tall. From the top of the gate we took in a lovely view of the city. At the base of the gate was a highly, stylized statue of the founder of Kiev, Volodymyr.

One of the most popular orchestral pieces rendered by American high school bands is "The Great Gates of Kiev" from the "Pictures at an Exhibition" piano suite by Mussorgsky. He was a Ukrainian composer. Stephen quietly hummed the parts he could remember in homage.

Across the street was a miniature blue and yellow tanker truck. It was a vendor truck where they sold a national drink called *kvas,* a nonalcoholic drink distilled from wheat with a flavor akin to beer. Of course, I had to try it. After a couple of sips of the clear golden liquor, I concluded it was an acquired taste and passed the glass to my hostess.

Stephen thought he had attained ultimate status when native Ukrainians stopped him in the streets and asked him for directions. He blended in with the crowd. Ukrainians have been invaded from both east and west, and are a mixture of many races from blond blue-eyed Europeans to the darker Asiatic features with high cheekbones and almond eyes.

Kiev was almost totally destroyed by the Mongols in the 13th century and many buildings lay abandoned for several hundred years. The people steadfastly restored their beloved city including St. Sophia Church, one of the biggest tourist attractions. The church complex was built in 1017, not only as a religious and political center but also as one of the first schools and libraries in the region of Kiefvan Rus. The main cathedral was spectacular although not long in the conventional sense but rather shortened, almost square in shape. The mosaic in the central apse holds a picture of the Virgin and the altar piece was gilded in gold. Walking beneath the pillars you could sense antiquity. The sepulcher of the famous king, Yaroslav the Wise, 976-1054, was there. One of the cleverest things this king did was to marry his daughters to the kings of Norway, France, and Hungary, building strong diplomatic ties.

My Ukrainian friends complained that the admission to museums and events was so much higher for tourists than for the natives. It was maddening until we remembered that the average income in Ukraine was $100-$300 per month. I did not mind paying three dollars to see a national treasure.

In the garden of St. Sophia's, we spied a musician in a full-sleeved shirt. He was playing a large six to seven stringed Ukrainian instrument called a *kobza,* similar to a guitar with intricately inlaid wood designs. The sound reminded me of my elementary school autoharp. Art students were scattered about watercoloring excellent renditions of the church.

We paused at another imposing statue of Volodymyr, founder of Kiev which stood on a jagged rock base located on a spacious plaza—a famous landmark of this city. Then we saw the onion domes of St. Andrew's Church, recently painted so that the gold gleamed. Rastrelli, the famous Russian architect born in Italy, designed this church in late baroque style as well as many of the buildings further north in St. Petersburg.

We slipped past the History Museum to Andriyivsky Uzviz, or the Street of Artists. Oil paintings, crafts, and Ukrainian handiwork vendors were shoulder to shoulder down the winding hill. It took us several hours to meander through the many booths, and eye the various crafts. We saw the Ukrainian version of a bagpipe player, several pipes hanging from a white furry square bag, but he wore no tartan kilt. His outfit was a peasant linen shirt and dark brown homespun pants not quite as colorful as his Scottish cousin's. This was a reminder that bagpipes were not the exclusive domain of one group.

We walked by Red University which got its name when Tsar Nicholas I painted the building blood red in response to student protests against mandatory conscription into his army. Its real name was Shevchenko University in honor of the country's most famous writer. Taras Hryhorovych Shevchenko, (1814-1861), poet, artist, and humanist, is considered to be the founder of modern Ukrainian literature.

When we returned to the apartment, Nikita, Svetlana's brother had just returned from visiting their grandmother in the country. He had lugged an enormous basket of black currants home. The mom quickly set about making steamed currant dumplings with cottage cheese topped with their version of sour cream. The other dumplings included cottage cheese with honey. They were absolutely decadent because freshness added zest to any dish, and also everything was naturally sweet, not heavily sugared. We ate too many for our own good and had to unfasten our belts.

After recovering enough to walk, we ambled off to a concert in the local Catholic Church. A strong mezzo-soprano and a wiry organ player alternated musical performances. The opera season had ended, our friends explained, else they would have taken us to the grand opera house underscoring how important cultural events are to this society.

We Americans have grown up with the conception that everything on the other side of the Iron Curtain was gray and oppressive. Yet, in many respects their educational system surpassed ours as evidenced by the Russians putting the first satellite into space. Their classical culture thrived in music and dance. Cultural events were integrated into their daily lives since television was not widespread.

BEET SOUP

Did you know that Borsht, beet soup, was not a Russian dish but Ukrainian? We ate this delicious red soup with potatoes and cabbage topped with a dollop of white sour cream. The bread accompanying it was full-bodied and tasty. For dessert we drank hot, white chocolate.

Nikita was our guide today. He matter-of-factly asked if we wanted to ride a taxi or walk to the Caves Monastery. We all agreed that walking was better and that we would take a taxi home. Only we forgot to ask how far it was, and he forgot to tell us. It was several hours away, so we can claim we saw much of Kiev on foot.

We passed the Horodetsky House, built by a cement company owner after his only daughter died. The top of the roof was filled with animals made of cement. The national president's office was located across the street and I wondered what the leader thought each day as he looked out the window to see these animals, both real and fantasy.

Finally we reached our destination--the Pecherski Lavra, or Caves Monastery--the number one sight in the city. The name came from the subterranean caves crisscrossing underneath the complex. Nestled next to the river, the Monastery was a breathtaking sight with its numerous gold onion domes and turreted buildings. Once inside the gated compound, we found many smaller museums worthy of a visit.

First we climbed the hundreds of stairs to the bell tower and were rewarded with a commanding vista of Kiev and the Dneiper River. From this vantage point we saw Kiev as a city filled with parks and statues. Winston Churchill said whenever he came to a city for the first time, he went to the highest point in the town to gain an orientation. It made sense.

Our favorite was the miniature museum, where Nikolai Syadristy made a hobby of creating microscopic sculptures. The details were so tiny that we had to use a magnifying glass to view everything. One interesting piece was a hair follicle that had been polished to a clear sheen. Inserted into it was a small painted rose. I wondered how anyone could work with skillful precision on such tiny pieces.

Another folk museum showed the regional costumes of the country as well as the world-renowned Ukrainian folk Easter eggs, *pysanky*, with their complex designs. The eggs were often dyed black with contrasting geometric colored designs covering the entire surface. We paid to enter the complex, and then we paid again to see the smaller museums, but they were well worth the extra change.

The day we selected to go to the Monastery coincided with one of four major worship days, St. Tillaman. The Monastery was packed with pilgrims waiting patiently under the blazing sun to enter into the little caves. We decided to forgo the four hour wait. Nikita took us to an underground burial site where famous mummified priests were buried. We lit a beeswax candle and walked through the maze of tunnels with hundreds of other people. The air was so stuffy at times for lack of enough oxygen. People would stop and kiss the top of the various coffins. I passed, not knowing how many germs were lurking on the glass. At one point a gust of wind roared through and blew out everyone's candle. An echoing "oohhhh" ran through the crowd. Then folks grabbed for their matches and relit their candles.

Nikita whispered, "Priests would often come down into the tunnel to meditate." I guess it would be quiet down there if there weren't hundreds of pilgrims. But personally I found the tunnels claustrophobic and had difficulty thinking about meditating. I'd rather be on the river in the sunshine breathing fresh air while collecting my thoughts.

The Caves reminded me not of the 21st century but an earlier Russian era because of the orthodox priests in their black robes, the humble look of the many peasants standing patiently in line, and the walls blackened with age. The covered walkways creaked underneath our feet and wooden lintels were smoothed and worn by many hands rubbing them. The sun shone warmly today, but I also wondered if a cold blustery snowstorm might have been a more accurate portrayal.

We spent several hours at the Caves before we decided to return home by taxi. As we rushed by office buildings, Nikita pointed out that Dell Computers purchased a lovely building on one of the best streets in Kiev, but that renovations had stalled. He did not know why--perhaps it was because the company had not found the right person to bribe or the bribe was not large enough. Ukraine was a country rich in natural resources and had a well-educated workforce, yet the economy was having difficulty moving forward. Old skeletons from Soviet era days may still be haunting the movement towards reform.

Ukraine was sputtering towards capitalism but keeping one foot in the old communist system. The examples were all around us. We saw a sleek young lady heavily made up wearing a very short skirt walking next to a plump older woman with teeth missing and her head tied in a scarf. Vendors on the streets and in the subway sold the latest pirated western CD's and software. Classical books sat unsold on bookstore shelves. Many buildings were still a drab gray. Prices for lunch were $15 or more. How could the average Ukrainian afford it?

INDEPENDENCE DAY--JULY 4TH

We began our American Independence Day with a bowl of porridge, much like our version of cracked wheat or barley. We finished up leftovers from yesterday's breakfast of potato salad and coleslaw. The food was always fresh and tasty although not customary to our palates.

Svetlana's mother had the day off and Nikita was able to join us. We boarded a bus for our hour ride south of Kiev to the Folk Architecture and Rural Life Museum called Pirogovo. Located on 150 hectares approximately 375 acres, the open-air museum contains over 200 examples of typical Ukrainian buildings. Folk costumes, fabrics and carpets and housewares were set out as they would have been in a peasant home. Windmills that once dotted the old wheat fields of the steppes were brought to this location. Churches, farms, flower and vegetable gardens gave us a feeling of rural Ukraine. The most unusual structures in the park were the hollowed logs used for beehives. They looked like little homes for gnomes.

Stephen privately confessed he had seen too many open-air museums although he never appeared to be bored. On the other hand I was ready to keep seeing everything on the list of things to do. I guess it's something I was born with--an insatiable curiosity about different people and places. A high school classmate of mine had married and reared her family while living in the same home for 30 years. She and her husband played horseshoes, worked in their garden and were perfectly content with their lives. I couldn't help but draw a stark contrast between her life and mine. In some ways I envied her "stability" and ability to put down roots. My life was harnessed to wings, however, and I fluttered around the world.

Svetlana's mother packed a lunch so we ate our midday meal on a blanket surrounded by greenery. It is difficult to carry on a conversation when only one other person spoke fluent English. So we simply sat, smiled a lot and focused on eating.

Svetlana's mother suddenly gave a little shriek of delight. She pointed to some little white flowers outside the park that looked like miniature daisies and dashed over to them. She began grabbing an armful and gave me one bunch. I couldn't figure out why she thought the flowers were worth the effort being so small, but I politely accepted. I later learned that the bunch was chamomile used in making tea.

To thank the family for their hospitality we offered to take them out to a restaurant on our last evening. They politely declined saying they felt eating at home would be better. We were in no position to argue so we offered at least to pay for the food that would be prepared. I trotted off to the market with Mom.

We rode down the elevator and walked to a store a few doors away. We entered a large room painted lime green and lined with shelves all behind the counter; there were no open shelves. We had to get the attention of a clerk, point to the item on the wall and then the clerk placed the items in our pile on the counter. This went on for about ten minutes. Finally Mom decided we had all we needed including a delicious national pastry with lots of meringue on it. I paid for the groceries.

It was too easy for me to criticize the seemingly inefficient system of shopping. I repeated to myself, "Just because it's different, doesn't make it bad!" Fortunately there were only a few people in the store, so our service was relatively speedy. Once in Moscow I recalled a clerk screaming at the top of her lungs at some poor customer because he wasn't making his selections fast enough.

The meal that night was delicious with gravy pork tenderloin, fresh boiled potatoes, and coleslaw ending with the meringue dessert which literally melted in my mouth. I agreed that dining at home was better than in some noisy restaurant!

FIT TO TOUR

Svetlana said that we saw more than the average American visitor because many of the Americans she translated for stopped more frequently to take breaks. She found us to be ardent tourists, seeing as much as we could as hard and fast as we could. We hit every major highlight in Kiev listed in our tourist book.

According to Stephen Ukraine was like Kansas with its vast open farmlands and rich fertile soil. During Soviet times Ukraine was called the Breadbasket growing wheat and other staples. Her people seemed friendly and warm. Underneath the cultural and language differences there was a basic goodness.

It was a nice compliment when Svetlana's mother said we should have stayed longer. I replied that it was better she say that than ask when we were leaving! We all laughed! We were so fortunate to have seen Kiev, the Mother of all Russian/Slav Cities from such a personal point of view!

The Emerald Isle-Ireland

August 2000

The Emerald Isle has a spirit that rises above the green bogs and velvet hills like wisps of smoke that gently wrap around the heart and haunt your soul. Long soft shadows created a setting that made leprechauns and fairies almost believable. Dark stone fences contrasted with the verdant grass speckled with sheep.

Cliffs plunged into the sea. Some things cannot be described in words. They must be felt to be understood. Ireland is such a place.

About five million Irish live in Ireland today. It was interesting that the successive waves of emigration created a larger populace abroad than what remained. Descendants tend to have a yearning to learn more of their ancestral home. Americans in Ireland were a common sight. Beyond kissing the Blarney Stone, sipping Guinness in a local pub, or wandering through ruined castles, there remains a longing to connect to a proud heritage. Although we are not of Irish descent, the tug was still strong for us to visit The Emerald Isle.

BEING THERE

We had seven days. Our rental car was reserved but we had no room reservations since friends told us we could manage with bed and breakfasts in Ireland. They were right that there were many lodgings along the road. Armed with our map and a couple of good tour books, we flipped a coin which landed on tails so we headed north, eventually making a clockwise route of the Republic of Ireland.

Our first night was at the remote farmyard of Mary and Michael, an Irish farming family who extended us a wonderful welcome. Their yellow plastered home was surrounded by a small courtyard with the closest neighbor ten miles down the road. With unusual energy and good cheer, Michael, with his bald head and slightly askew ears, delighted us with his strong Irish brogue. Mary, a stout redhead, and equally energetic person, made all the food herself, including the sausage we ate.

A hearty Irish breakfast began with cold cereal followed by fried eggs, sausage, Irish bacon like our ham, a fried tomato and black pudding. Black pudding also called blood sausage is made of curdled and boiled pig blood, mixed with chunks of pork fat and spices in a sausage casing. It tastes like preserved meat with a grainy texture. Occasionally fried potatoes and soda bread toast were included. A friendly reception and full stomachs were an auspicious beginning.

GALWAY AND CONNEMARRA

Ireland's natural beauty is a magnet for travelers. The rolling hills carpeted by intense lime-green fields were sectioned by rock walls. Tiny white sheep dotted the landscape. The ever-changing weather created a kaleidoscope of light from dull gray to a dappled light to brilliant sunshine. Wildflowers lined the roads. Enormous hydrangeas filled gardens with their bright pinks, azures, and purples. Flower boxes abounded with a multitude of blooms. I was surprised to see large yucca plants, which I associate with desert terrain. The Gulf Stream kept the temperatures moderate, even though Ireland was far north of the equator.

One should plan to experience all four seasons in a single day in Ireland, in order to avoid disappointments caused by weather. Our attempt to visit one of the major sights, the Cliffs of Moher, left us hearing rather than seeing the ocean roar through heavy fog. We debated waiting several hours for the mist to lift, but decided to move on. Postcards helped us to "see" what we had missed.

A word must be mentioned about Irish roads. The main highways are surfaced and have good signs, however, they are only two very narrow lanes. On country roads, the width was scarcely enough for one and a half cars. A journey that would take a few minutes on a major four-or six-lane highway required nearly two hours. Added to this was the challenge of sharing the road with other cars, trucks, tourist buses, cyclists, and sheep. One learns to slow down.

Galway was one of the fastest growing cities in Ireland. Rolling in for a quick lunch was like going to any major American city with McDonalds, computer stores, and huge garden shops. All of Ireland was experiencing resurgence in growth of 25 percent per year. My sincere hope was that the growth was carefully planned so that the Irish ambiance would not be lost.

How odd it seems that British kings banished the Irish people to the far corners of the island, thinking those lands wild and uninhabitable. Now these are the very places that draw tourists reveling in the unblemished wilderness. At Connemara bald mountains sank to soggy bogs where strange brown piles of earth turned out to be peat used for heating homes. Upon closer inspection we saw traces of handheld shovels used to retrieve the peat, making neat squares in the ground. There was no one around, but simply a shovel protruding from the ground.

The crowning site was Kylemore Abbey, which was a misnomer to me, since it resembled an ornate castle with jutting square towers topped by crenellated ridges sitting at the edge of a lake. A wealthy couple honeymooning in the region fell in love with the countryside and built the castle in Connemara. Today it is an international girls' boarding school, drawing from families across Europe. They school offered tours, and our lovely young hostess was from the French region of Lyon.

We opted not to go to Northern Ireland because of lack of time. Later we heard reports of bombings and were happy with our decision. Instead we headed east towards Dublin. As the string of holiday cars began backing up, we stopped and found a lovely B&B—the beauty of impromptu bed and breakfast is not to be stuck in a traffic jam!

Our host appeared to be a single man. We never saw a woman in the house. He was in his late fifties, tall with a shiny bald pate, and he wore a gray cardigan. His house was rather modest with outdated furniture, not something that would normally tantalize patrons. But the home was located right off the highway supporting the old business adage that location is everything. He was a rather shy host, and had minimal interaction with his guests, setting the breakfast table and vanishing from sight until cleanup. Some B&B owners sit and chat away during breakfast to learn more about their guests. Perhaps our proprietor wanted to give us space, or felt his job was begrudgingly tedious. We'll never know.

THE LAKELANDS

Central Ireland is sprinkled with lovely lakes. We stopped at a small puddle and watched the sun set. Sitting close to us was a foursome of young French cyclists from Breton who were camping out; in fact, we saw many cyclists crossing Ireland. We chatted with them, but they were obviously uncomfortable speaking English so the conversation was brief.

Working from our map, our next historic site at the bend of the River Shannon was Clonmacnois, an impressive monastic site established by St. Ciaran. This was the most important Celtic site throughout Europe during the sixth century for art and learning with many famous manuscripts produced here including the Book of Dun Cow. There are two complete High Crosses located here. Celtic crosses have two crosspieces, but at the junction is usually a decorated circle.

Who were the Celts? They originally came from Bavaria and Bohemia, then spread throughout Europe and westward. The Celts were said to be a rather striking people, tall and fair-skinned, with blond or reddish hair. They were proud, brave, quick to defend their honor, and warlike in spirit. Celtic customs and traditions survived relatively intact to the fifth century, because Ireland was the farthest west of the British Isles and was never part of the Roman Empire. Only in the eighth century did the Vikings raid.

I learned that the word, *hillbilly*, originated in Ireland. When England was at civil war during the 17th century, the followers of William III were called "Billies," an abbreviation of William. The southern Irish Catholics and supporters of James II referred to these northern Protestant supporters of King Williams as "Hill-Billies" and "Billy Boys." When they moved to America and moved to the frontier areas of the Appalachian Mountains, the name *hillbillies* stuck.

BOOK OF KELLS

We arrived in Dublin on Monday when museums are closed so we missed the National Museum. However, we did get to visit Trinity College that proved to be the highlight of Dublin. This stately university housed the famous Irish Book of Kells, a manuscript created by monks in the 9th century considered the pinnacle of Insular Illumination and one of Ireland's finest national treasures. The elaborate artwork included figures of humans, animals and mythical beasts intertwined with vibrant colors. The calligraphy was written on 185 calfskins used to create the vellum since paper as we did not exist.

In the book *How the Irish Saved Civilization*, Thomas Cahill explains how diligent monks copied manuscripts from the Greeks and Romans, preserving them, while the Barbarians destroyed the originals. Western civilization would never have inherited the classics had they not been preserved in Ireland.

We meandered upstairs to the Long Library, where over 200,000 volumes of dusty leather-bound books were shelved. Tall wooden planks hovering thirty feet above us were jam-packed. Scents of old leather mingled with aged wood. At the end of each shelf was the marble bust of a famous philosopher, Socrates, Plato, and Aristotle. I am certain this was the prototype for many libraries in the world. I couldn't help but feel I was in the presence of great learning.

Dublin was an attractive city. I wondered if there was a zoning law since most of the square buildings never rose more than four stories. We ate "genuine Irish stew" or so the sign over the restaurant bragged. We quickly tired of the traffic and noise, however, and headed south.

Passing a Dell Computer company building, we were reminded that Ireland was number two in software exports in the world. Many American companies were moving to Ireland because of the tax incentives and an English speaking workforce. My mother's neighbor lost her job when her employer moved to Ireland. The company had offered to move her across the Atlantic Ocean but she declined.

POWERSCOURT

We kept driving south until late afternoon, then began looking for our night's lodging. It was like playing Russian roulette to find a decently priced bed and breakfast—luck of the draw. If we began early in the evening our chances increased of finding great quality with reasonable prices. The bed and breakfast we found for the night offered a panoramic view of the valley below. Our hosts were a young couple in their thirties. The father had a full beard and a bit of a belly from too much Irish malt. The mother was a blond, robust woman with two small children tagging behind her. The house was so new that construction equipment still lay about, but the couple was already boarding visitors to cover their cost of the mortgage.

Outside the bed and breakfast I sat on a park bench under an umbrella during a light drizzle. I could not inhale enough of green Ireland with both my lungs and mind. Below me was the valley where one of the famous gardens in Ireland was located, Powerscourt.

Located on the side of Great Sugar Loaf Mountain, The Garden of Powerscourt was purported to showcase the most striking landscape in Ireland so we decided to venture over. The gardens began with a classical formal Italian landscape in the center guarded by two winged horses, a staircase descended to small lakes and a fountain was flanked by a walled garden with roses and herbaceous plants. It included other gardens including a small Japanese garden spread out in concentric paths, and the

Dolphin Pond. It was said that the owner suffering from severe gout would tote his bottle of sherry when supervising work on the garden. When the bottle was empty, work ceased for the day.

GLENDOLOUGH

My husband spotted Glendolough on the map and wanted to stop there, only a short distance from Powerscourt. However, the short distance turned into a two-hour trip as narrowing country roads limited our speed to 40 mph maximum.

We arrived to gaze upon two lakes rimmed by purple mountains with traces of snow forming a box canyon. Evergreens dotted the hillsides. We understood why Kevin the Monk made this secluded valley his home. Kevin was born into a royal house but rejected his life to become a hermit. He established a monastic Catholic order in the 6th century that flourished for over 600 years. One legend is that a woman followed him and he dreamed that she stood between him and Heaven. When he awoke he found her beside him, so he pushed her out of the cave and she fell down to the river 90 feet below. Another legend says that he had a fight with a powerful witch and in the battle she fell unconscious into the lake. It is a tangle of tales that added interesting notes to his mystique.

Round towers 30 feet tall were historic sentinels of the Irish monastic period. Houses also consisted of piled rocks topped by thatched roofs. The stone structures appeared to be loose dark rocks balancing on top of each other. If mortar was used, it was not visible. Stephen felt he could spend the rest of our vacation here. I nudged him onward.

KILKENNY

The prefix "kil" means anything associated with a church. The town of Kilkenny was colorful with brightly painted storefronts, the stone ruins of an old church, and the River Nore. The tour of Kilkenny Castle was enjoyable. When major restoration was done several years ago, they ordered carpets for the formal parlor from the company that made the original rugs. Measurements did not need to be taken again, since the company still had its records from over 150 years ago--incredible bookkeeping!

We found the Hannahs' farm where we stayed for the night. As we emerged from of our car, a bird cawed. Our tall host, Sean, was standing outside and asked, "Do yew know what kind of bird that was?"

"Ah, duck?" I guessed.

"Nah," my husband said. "Even I can tell it's a crow."

Sean laughed that a city girl could not tell the difference between a duck and a crow. He was a retired fireman who had kept his body lean and in shape. He excused himself since he was calling the numbers for the local bingo game. All proceeds paid the insurance for the town hall. Had we not been so exhausted we might have joined them for a personal glimpse of Irish pastimes.

WATERFORD/BLARNEY

Everyone raves about Waterford Irish crystal. We learned that a Czech master taught the Irish the art of engraving the exceptional quality crystal after WWII. The company rejects nearly twenty percent of the first glass blown. The next cycle results in a 15 percent rejection and on down the line. It takes five years to learn to cut the crystal and three more years to become a master. When I asked how much the engravers earned, the guide said she did not know but that the craftsmen were paid by the piece and by other formulas, in other words she didn't know or wasn't telling. The job was handed down from father to son so the pay could not be too bad. We indulged in a small crystal bowl and had it engraved with "Happy Anniversary!"

From Waterford we headed to Cork, where we hoped to find the Blarney Stone. I mention hope, because we were not clear where the stone actually stood. Through a series of guesses, we ended up at Blarney Castle. We stood in a long line slowly climbing the 127 steps to the top of the tower. I was pleasantly surprised that we were the only foreigners, everyone else in line was from that region. To kiss the stone, you lie down, lean backwards and kiss it upside down since there is a wide gap between the walkway and the wall. It was a tad scary since you were so high. A nice man made sure I had a firm grasp. The folks there promised they clean the stone often so as not to pass on ailments, although no one scrubbed while we were there.

There s a stone there
That whoever kisses,
Oh, he never misses
To grow eloquent....
By Francis Sylvester Mahony
19th century

By kissing the stone one becomes endowed with the "gift of gab." The saying, "He's full of Blarney" or full of hot air originated with Cormac MacCarthy, owner of the castle, who was to surrender his fortress to Queen Elizabeth I as proof of his loyalty. Something always happened at the last minute to prevent the actual transfer. He kept the Queen dangling with glib humor and promises until she exclaimed, "Blarney, Blarney! What he says he does not mean!" Kissing the Blarney Stone worked on my husband! He carried on lengthy conversations with everyone we met from then on.

The evening dinner was in the local pub, the highly rated Blairs Inn. It was a long white plastered two-story bungalow with flowering window boxes. As we entered the dark interior, men talking in Irish brogue were winding down for the evening. The warm wood fire crackled in the cozy fireplace. It wasn't a movie scene, but was a genuine Irish meeting place. We scooted to the back where we indulged in some delicious Irish meat and potatoes.

We stayed the evening at the Hannons' Bed and Breakfast atop a hill with an acre for their home and an acre for their horse. He was a retired major in the Irish army. We nestled ourselves on their back patio with our hosts and watched the sun set.

"Aye, my assignments have been pretty much in the British Isles," Major Hannon confided.

"My goodness, that was a lucky turn of events. We have fortunately and unfortunately been transferred often and far and wide. It is a blessing and a curse in the same breath," my husband responded.

"We've loved living in various parts of the world and made friends wherever we've been," I chimed. "But it's the moving that drives us a bit crazy."

We were bedding down in a lovely Irish home for a most reasonable sum. I thought briefly of military neighbors in Germany. He was a rank lower than my husband and did not bring home as big a paycheck. Yet during their vacation in Ireland, they blew hundreds of dollars staying one night in a famous resort just so they could tell their friends. I could have paid for an entire vacation with the same amount of money. The wife once asked me how we could afford all our travels. I gently reminded her that we lived frugally, were not paying mortgage on a vacant house in the States, drove only one old car, didn't belong to any private clubs, or subscribe to expensive phone service. It was important for her to splurge. For me, seeing the world was my goal. It's all about priorities, isn't it?

RING OF KERRY

We kept moving westward to the Ring of Kerry, a peninsula jutting out from the southwestern point of Ireland that has become a popular day trip for tourists. A local told us that we should try going clockwise around the Ring to avoid following the large tourist buses going counterclockwise. We found this good advice. When sharing the road with an oncoming bus, we either got off the road and waited, or held our breaths hoping that we both could pass since the roads were only wide enough for two cars to squeeze by. The buses made it challenging to drive, slowing our progress considerably.

The largest town in the region was Sneem, a romantic village with brightly painted buildings teeming with tourists. The two-story buildings were painted emerald, violet, pale pink, yellow and melon. The word Sneem in Irish meant "knot" and is referred to as the "Knot in the Ring."

As we headed westward, we could see the outline of the Skellig Islands. We drove westward with the Islands directly ahead of us, black pinnacles that at one time housed secluded monks. That exploratory spirit in me kept wishing I could charter a boat and ride the eight miles out to the rocks. What would it have been like to have been a monk crossing the Atlantic in rough waters, with birds crying and darting overhead, then climbing the 700 feet to the monastery in long woolen robes only to find empty rooms and vows of silence. As we rounded the bend and headed northward, a part of me yearned to explore, but I had to quell that feeling and say—"perhaps next time."

As we approached Killorglin, the Puck Fair with carnival was in progress. The main event, a show horse jumping competition, brought hundreds of people pulling trailers. A car with a loud-speaker on top went round and round through the town blaring music with occasional announcements. It took us a while to drive through the center of town because of the crowds. We would have stayed there but all the B&B's were full, and we were weary of tourists, even if we were visitors ourselves.

RING OF DINGLE

On their family's first visit to Ireland my friend, Barbara, shared that their children did not want to leave the Dingle Peninsula. It was more remote than the Ring of Kerry but had more sandy beaches and dramatic scenery. There were fewer tour buses, too. Despite the cloudy weather the scenery was spectacular.

My favorite spot on Dingle was the Dunmore Head over-looking the Blasket Islands in the Atlantic. Smooth sea green hills waded into a sapphire ocean and white foamy lace fringed the edges. The islands were craggy rocks coated with heather. Fog began rolling in enveloping everything till the islands appeared

to hover above the water. There is a spirit in this land that reso-
nated with my being. I cannot pinpoint what I felt, but it was
quiet, powerful and at hand.

While at lunch in the colorful town of Dingle, we met a lady
from Dublin.

"Hmmm, I think I'll have the lamb stew, Stephen," I said.

"That sounds good! I'll have the same," he told the waiter.

Sitting at the next table a slender fifty-something woman
with blond hair asked, "Where are you folks from?"

"We are Americans but we live in Germany," Stephen replied.

"Do you live around here?" I asked.

"No, I live in Dublin but come for my holidays and most of
my summers. I've been coming here for over 20 years."

I took a closer look at the woman and she had the markings
of an aristocrat--expensive tailored clothing, well done makeup
and a slightly arrogant demeanor.

"I bet you've enjoyed it here. We think it is so enchanting!"
I commented.

"Well, it has changed a lot and not for the better. I predict
that in ten years the peninsula will become as commercialized as
Kerry. Something I dread."

"Sorry to hear that. We hope that it will be wisely developed to keep the beauty and still allow the tourist," Stephen
commiserated.

"I do, too!" she agreed.

My friend Barbara recommended that we take the Connor
Pass over one of the highest summits in all of Ireland offering a
terrific view. Unfortunately we arrived during a rainstorm, so all
we saw were clouds and driving rain. I remember my knuckles
being white from gripping the steering wheel trying to drive down
the steep hill with an oncoming car ahead of me. I wondered
if we could manage, because the road was so narrow—allowing
only one car to pass at a time. The other driver, bless his heart,
backed his car down the hill until there was a slight indentation

in the cliff to park. I was grateful I didn't have to drive backwards uphill, knowing there was a sharp drop off into the ocean if I veered in the wrong direction.

LUCK OF THE IRISH

Somewhere on our journey we met a retired sea captain who proudly boasted that there were over 300 golf courses in Ireland.

"Do you know if anyone has played them all?" I asked curiously.

"Now, that," he said "is a good question" and he humbly walked away.

We are not golfers so we can't claim knowledge of the links in Ireland. We can assert that without a set schedule or formal tour, we saw a personal side of Ireland. The land was stunning but more importantly the ordinary Irish people we met were hospitable and cheerful.

The Irish are gifted with a little blarney, giving us blessings, curses, quotations, toasts and proverbs. Two famous Irish Blessings stand out and are shared in closing:

May God give you
For every storm a rainbow,
For every tear, a smile,
For every care, a promise,
And a blessing in each trial,
For every problem life sends,
A faithful friend to share
For every sigh, a sweet song
And an answer for each prayer.

May the road rise to meet you
May the wind be always at your back
May the sun shine warm upon your face
May the rains fall soft upon your fields
And, until we meet again,
May God hold you in the palm of His hand.

~~~~~~~~~~~~~~~~

Greece

September 2000

Greece was the birthplace of democracy, drama, history, and philosophy. Even the mighty Romans copied the art and architecture of this once thriving civilization. Today words like *sophisticated, metropolitan* and *philanthropy* had their origins here. This society touched every corner of the civilized world, so we had to travel to this ancient land to find more of our cultural origins.

On our flight we stopped in Thessaloniki in northern Greece. I immediately recognized the name from the New Testament in the Bible. From the air it looked like a lovely beach resort town. People on the plane sat politely in their seats during the stopover while some passengers left and others boarded. I asked the stewardess if I might simply walk the open ramp and touch ground in Thessaloniki. Fortunately, she agreed that my curious request was harmless, and I bounced down the metal stairs, placed my hands on my hips, and declared that I had touched *terra firma* in Thessaloniki!

It was an auspicious day to land in southern Greece—the sun was radiant and sparkled on the water. I was immediately enchanted with our bright beginnings. The Athens airport, located near the seaport town of Piraeus, had a California feel, open air restaurants, and shops along the major thoroughfares. The main streets were wide, but the side streets were narrow one-way alleys. The area was cleaner than I expected, but other Americans thought it unkempt looking.

Our tour guide met us at the airport. Her name was Helen, a dignified-looking, slender woman in her sixties, with salt and pepper hair cut in a bob. She had classic features and was a handsome woman save for a fatigued look. She had been an English teacher and fortunately her English was perfect!

Our bus driver was a tall lanky Greek with a bald suntanned head and a broad warm smile enhanced by a few missing teeth. His enthusiasm set the tone for the week! I was curious about the small planter of basil he had in his bus window but couldn't converse in Greek.

ACROPOLIS

We had nearly an entire day to ourselves before the tour began in earnest, so Stephen and I launched ourselves into a self-directed tour of Athens. Scattered throughout the downtown were remnants of antiquity. Tall columns rising over the rubble of stones reminded us of the never-ending tales of Roman, Byzantine, British and German occupations.

Our first stop was the Acropolis, literally meaning "high city." It was true. From nearly every vantage point in Athens, one saw the outcropping. Rising 512 feet above the city, this fabled cluster of ruins drew us back to the Golden Era of Greece, the 5th century B.C. It outshone its photographs.

As we climbed the hill, I was a bit afraid I would slip on the well-worn stones steps leading to the top. Time has given a yellowish sheen to the rocks making them highly polished. It was not a difficult hike, but much steeper than at first glance.

To merely walk the high heights was not enough. I wanted the rocks to talk about all they had witnessed. Here was ancient history before our eyes and beneath our feet! I was horrified at one man's assessment of the hill years ago, "It's just a bunch of rocks!" I was shocked that he would travel so far to see so little.

One book showed photographs of today's ruins with a plastic overlay. An artist's rendition showed how each building probably appeared in its prime. This greatly helped me envision what the Hill looked like at the height of its power.

ATHENS

As we walked along, it seemed that men at every corner were flipping worry beads. These were threads of beads a few inches long that were held in the hand and flipped upward over the hand in repetitious motions. I never learned if this was merely a nervous activity or if it really relieved people of their worries.

The Acropolis had been a sanctuary limited to royalty, priests, and invited guests. The real work of living in the city had been carried out in the Agora. This section was located below the hill northwest of the Acropolis. Excavation was still going on uncovering the marketplace, schools, theaters, workshops, and houses located here during ancient times.

The Agora was now called the Plaka. Hundreds of souvenir shops filled the old rooms located on narrow streets. There was a delicious atmosphere of preserved antiquities and modern technology. Fortunately for tourists, the souvenir shops in the Plaka were open early and closed late at night for last minute purchases of sponges, t-shirts, spices, and the ubiquitous museum copies of Greek figures. Jewelry and leather items were also good purchases. I never did master the money system at 380 drachmas to a dollar, but still managed to purchase a t-shirt embroidered with the Greek alphabet.

The second most conspicuous sight in Athens was another rising hill called Likavitos standing 909 feet high, not as broad as the Acropolis, but actually taller. So we decided to amble over to it.

On our way, we saw the changing of the guards at the Tomb of the Unknown Warriors. The guards wore red shoes with black pompoms, billowing white short skirts, white leotards topped with a deep maroon embroidered vests, and fancy caps. They marched so stiff legged that my knees buckled in empathetic pain.

We made the mistake of climbing Likavitos during the heat of the day. When we reached the top we were panting for water. The natives take a siesta for a good reason during the hot summer months. We modern day people don't realize that many traditions were born of common sense.

The advertised funicular was never found, so we climbed the entire distance by foot to the lovely white church at the top, the Byzantine St. George. The view made our efforts worthwhile. We took fabulous shots of the Acropolis and had an eagle's view of the city. Then we bounded down the hill to other sites.

Most tourist haunts were located between the Acropolis and Likavitos, and we located streets easily from our map. We found the Goulandris Cycladic Museum without too much trouble. Located near the National Gardens and Parliament, this museum housed relics from the Cyclades Islands in the Aegean Sea. Many of the remnants resembled the heads found in Easter Island in the Pacific, but were much smaller. These images were thousands of years old, yet they reminded me of contemporary sculptures with a raised edge in the center of the oval representing a nose, with no eyes, ears or mouth. Perhaps some of our modern sculptors were merely imitating the Cyclades, and were not as original as we first thought.

A temporary exhibit in the museum displayed items excavated while digging the subway. It took twenty years to build because of the numerous excavations. Fabulous marble and bronze items were retrieved. The display gave us a strong sense of literally standing on eons of history.

Near the National Gardens was the rebuilt Olympic Stadium. It seemed so elegant made entirely of marble more like a palace in the shape of a long oval. The entrance was chained, so we could not wander through the seats.

We backtracked down a few streets and found a statue of Harry Truman, thirty-third President of the United States. President Truman greatly aided the Greeks after World War II by helping provide military and economic assistance. Born in Independence, my husband was pleased that another Missourian would be honored so far away from home.

The next day was the guided tour of Athens by Helen. We began with the Acropolis. The Parthenon is the central temple on the Acropolis dedicated to the Goddess Athena. She was the mythological figure that leaped out of her father's Zeus's head. Her sculpture in the Temple, now destroyed, was supposedly made of ivory and gold, and filled the entire west wall of the temple. Our plastic overlay book became helpful in picturing what the empty room was like in its prime.

The most unique figures were the six stone maidens, *caryatids*, holding up the south portico of the Erechtheion, a smaller sanctuary. Most columns run straight up and down. These were carved as figures of women. What we actually saw were the cement copies. The originals were now in the museum located on the Acropolis to protect them from decomposing. At times fumes in the city cast such a haze we could barely see from hill to hill, so the protection was a good decision.

We toured the National Archaeological Museum. So much was packed into one building! The collection from the Mycenae Kingdom that preceded the Greeks was spectacular including the gold death mask of King Agamemnon. Their jewelry was of incredible quality and design, indicating a highly cultivated society. It is not often that I dawdle over glass cases of jewelry, but I was so taken with the intricate and masterful designs that I nearly missed the bus.

In the afternoon we were left to wander on our own. We decided to check out the Museum of Greek Folk Art, but couldn't find it easily because the guide book (gasp) gave the wrong location. We arrived only ten minutes before closing and the attendant was reluctant to admit us. I must have looked so forlorn that she waved me on without charge. Stephen remained in the plaza, too embarrassed to enter. I climbed to the third story at the top and worked my way quickly down the small museum. Seeing all the regional costumes grouped together in one place, I noted a strong Persian influence in Greek dress that I had never correlated before, the turned-up pointed shoes, the gold braid on the vests, and the coins around the face of women.

We stopped for a quick snack on the plaza. My mouth dropped open. For a moment I thought I saw a living Adonis as though he had walked off his pedestal--the profile with a straight nose, the full curved lips, the piercing melancholy eyes, and the dark curly hair were all there! It was a good thing I had a husband to tether me, or else I would probably have followed him through the alleys of Athens.

CLASSICAL TOUR

After two days in Athens we headed south towards the peninsula of Peloponesia. The peninsula is held to the mainland by a narrow neck of land near Corinth. There, a deep channel has been cut allowing sea traffic to cross from the Ionian to the Aegean Sea. As we stood on the bridge looking straight down for hundreds of feet, I thought to myself: technically Peloponesia is now an island, since it is surrounded on all sides by water. But because the last body of water was a manmade channel, perhaps it is still considered a peninsula.

The Apostle Paul stayed in Corinth the longest period during his wanderings in Greece yet converted only two persons his entire stay. He published two books, I and II Corinthians, that were later added to the New Testament, writings that have kept these ancient names alive in my mind.

We passed the mountains that sheltered the city-state of Sparta, rival to Athens. They were warriors not builders or philosophers so nothing remains of this warring nation. My sixth grade teacher painted a word picture of a civilization so dedicated to war that crippled babies were simply left on the plains to die, knowing they could never become great soldiers. His lesson has stayed with me all these years.

We continued on to Mycenae where the old citadel offered a commanding view of the valley below. The area was the powerful center for the Mycean civilization, the people that preceded the Greeks. The gold masks we saw in the Athens Museum came from this burial site. The archaeologists transported the small valuables to Athens and left the burial stones. We entered through the Lion Gate, a triangular rock etched with two lions supporting the weight of the stone entrance. We scrambled around the ruins at the top of the hill trying to make sense of the civilization that inhabited it.

The rolling hillside, brown with scattered trees, reminded me of northern California and Italy with its Mediterranean climate. Another group was climbing alongside us from Italy.

"Doesn't this area remind you of Tuscany Italy?" I asked a woman standing by me.

"Yes, it really does," said the woman, "but I haven't tasted the wine yet to see if the comparison holds true on every account."

At the bottom of the hill was a burial mound made of stacked stones shaped like a beehive and covered over with dirt, the tomb of Clytemnestra, the wife of King Agamemnon. We walked inside and marveled at its roominess. This civilization built its living quarters on the top of the hill and its burial sites below. Some societies build their ceremonial sites on hills and live in the valleys. As a living person, I prefer the view from the hill--only if I don't have to walk uphill!

Then we drove a little further to tour the great theater of Epidaurus, so acoustically perfect that the actor's natural voice carried to the back sections of the huge structure. When volunteers were requested, I raised my hand and recited the first few lines from Lincoln's Gettysburg Address. The audience indicated that I was clearly heard even though I spoke in normal tones. I marveled that no electronic device was necessary to magnify the human voice. Capturing the acoustical sounds took some engineering skill. Stephen and I deduced that one reason the theater was preserved was that it was built into the side of a hill which gave it support. It's amazing that the Greeks took natural materials and fashioned them into useful purposes.

Epidaurus was also known for its medicinal cures. Modern medicine's symbol of the *cadusa*, two snakes entwined, first came from this area. The belief was that a lick from the sacred snake was purported to help heal patients.

Everything has a meaning in Greece, even the graffiti was categorized by color. Red graffiti was communist. Green represented the socialist. And blue the conservatives.

OLYMPIA

We stopped at Olympia, home of the Olympic Games. The competitions were instituted to encourage peaceful interaction between the warring city-states. Only during these ten days of competition would cities lay down their arms. However, women were banned from the games at the risk of being put to death. All contestants were naked to give freedom of movement, and to ensure that no woman could secretly compete.

The grounds were on a flat plain surrounded by hills. A hodgepodge of buildings and ruins lay scattered over the grounds. Though the columns lay scattered in pieces we could see how skillfully they had been carved and held together. I was particularly impressed with the bathtubs. Bathing was such a ritual, an ablution and perhaps a luxury in an era without hot running water.

Little has been restored, so an excellent guide is a must. Helen was splendid as her descriptions converted the tumbled pillars into the great wrestling hall, the elaborate guest rooms with ponds, the special buildings for ambassadors, and the great temple of Zeus. The smaller Temple of Hera yielded up the famous statue of Hermes with Dionysus, now in the Olympia Museum.

The stadium scarcely seemed large enough to hold 30,000 spectators, feeling more like a slight dip in the ground. There may once have been wooden benches in the stadium but they were all long decayed. The original starting line was made of marble and I made my husband pose in race position while I snapped a photograph.

We stood at the Temple of Apollo, where the Olympic Torch was first lit in 776 BC and continues to be lit every four years. The event occurs on open ground where a large magnifying glass called a parabolic mirror reflects the sun to light the Olympic torch.

How is it that this tradition of the Olympics has come down to us today? History is arbitrary in what it chooses to remember and replicate. Why were certain pagan festivals remembered and celebrated while others fell by the wayside? Why were particular legends perpetuated while others were totally forgotten? It's a curious twist in history.

We stayed in Patras that evening. My husband's colleague in Germany hailed from this bustling seaport town, so we took added interest in observing the people. Overnight ferries from Italy docked here so there was a lot of activity. The water was a gorgeous deep aquamarine and turquoise. The town seemed more European than Greek in architecture, but the people were definitely Greek in friendliness!

DELPHI

In the morning we crossed the Gulf of Corinth by ferry to the mainland. Our destination was Delphi. The bus swayed as we climbed the switchbacks up Mt. Parnassos, nearly 3,000 feet above the bay.

Delphi was the home of the Oracles, the priests and priestesses who were able to divine the future. Delphi was said to be established when two eagles landed. Another story was that sheep acted strangely whenever they came to a particular chasm in the mountain. The shepherd chasing his sheep was said to fall into divining trances.

It was the seat of a most famous temple of Apollo, where people would gather to consult an oracle. The oracles were never wrong, because they used riddles. The receiver was never quite sure of its meaning until later. The most famous was the tale told of King Croesus of Lydia who asked if he should attack the Persians. He was told, "Croesus, having crossed the Halys River will destroy a great realm." Encouraged, he crossed it only to find his own empire destroyed. He had not bothered to ask which side would be victorious.

The ancient city was the religious center of not only the Greeks but also the Romans who built many structures on the side of the hill. Going up the Sacred Way, there were numerous monuments of gratitude from cities and individuals. On a cornerstone that most tourists quickly strode past was the inscription of Socrates abolishing slavery. Helen, our guide, diligently tried to explain Socrates' significance to us wandering Americans. She told us that Socrates hated the very thought of slavery to men, slavery to mere opinions, slavery to fear, slavery to man's low desires, and slavery to high ambitions. He believed that reason could liberate human beings from these various forms of bondage.

That night we peered over the large porch of our hotel perched high above the valley and smaller barren hills, basking in a long uninterrupted moment of reflection. As the curtain of darkness slowly lowered over the valley, tiny lights twinkled in the scattered cottages, surprising us with their number. Not a word passed as the blackness enveloped us. Only when the certainty of day had vanished did we stir. A divine spirit resides in Delphi, and we felt it.

PARAKALO (Please and You're Welcome in Greek)

As our bus pulled into Athens the next day we felt a sadness that the trip was ending. Everything had cooperated splendidly-- the weather, the schedule, the guides, and the transportation. As a fitting reminder of our trip my husband insisted on purchasing for me a lovely gold necklace with tiny dolphins interspersed between Greek squares. We selected it not only for its unique design but because the dolphin was the form taken by Apollo, and we wanted to have the gods with us always.

Ours was a classical tour of Greece focused on the fabulous relics of this ancient land. As with all tours we conformed to a schedule. We were not able to shop long enough or linger over a particularly interesting sight. However, we had a knowledgeable guide who could answer questions, steer us away from possible problems, and a bus that dropped us off in front of the buildings. There were times we missed some of the accidental tourist memories. However, having someone figure out the ideal itinerary, transport and feed us, and board us in a comfortable bed in good hotels made the trip exceptionally enjoyable.

One thing I know for certain is that with each journey, regardless of how it is organized, the world becomes a little smaller as my own personal understanding grows and expands.

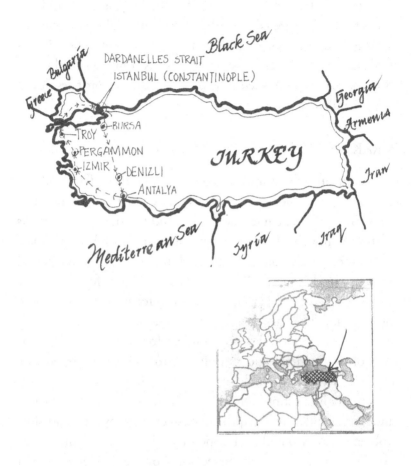

Swirling Dervishes Of Turkey
The Western Half

November 2000

Nineteen hundred and twenty-three was an auspicious year. Not only was my father born in that year, but the Turkish Republic was established. Under the leadership of Mustafa Kemal, later called Ataturk, Father of Turks, many reforms were instituted including the abolishment of the Arabic alphabet for romanized letters. This raised the literacy rate from a paltry eight percent into the 90 percentile.

This land, also called Asia Minor, straddles Europe and Asia, and her people were an exotic blend of both continents, dark-haired, dark complexioned, contrasting occasionally with green eyes.

We considered many options how best to see Turkey. My husband especially wanted to see Istanbul, so we selected a German tour that covered the western part of Turkey and included the fabled old city. The only catch was that everything would be in German. In retrospect, it turned out to be a great bonus. We were able to practice our mediocre but improving German. There were challenging moments, but nothing insurmountable and in the process our understanding of the language improved dramatically.

GUIDE OF ALL GUIDES

Orhan was our guide, a handsome man of Turkish-Bulgarian ancestry. He was in his mid-thirties, slender, six feet tall, with dark hair, and tanned complexion. He had grown up in Germany until age 12 so he spoke fluent German, and some English. We immediately took a liking to him.

Orhan was one of the best guides we have had. He was able to organize people, and watch for their individual needs. He passed around a scrapbook of regions in Turkey. A first for us was his use of visual aids. He used a little model of a rug when explaining carpets. He brought a map of Turkey to use in lecturing about the various regions of the country. He held up a real cotton plant when talking about cotton.

He was a natural born teacher. At the end of the trip he dug into his own wallet and gave all of us a good luck charm, the

Turkish blue eye, a circular orb with a white dot inside a white circle. He claimed he loved his work and his country. It showed!

IN SITU LEARNING

Our odyssey began the next morning on a bus going northwest from Anatalya following the western coastline of Turkey. Greece was across the Aegean Sea with numerous islands dotting the water like steppingstones. A sailor could easily go from island to island sailing from one land mass to another. Still I was surprised there were so many antiquities in Turkey from the Greek civilization. Somehow I had visualized a Muslim fence around Turkey. I needed to be reminded that it was Greek, long before being Turkish.

Our first stop was at Aphrodisias, home of Aphrodite, goddess of love. Some of the most extensive Greek ruins in all of Turkey were located here. Many of the sarcophagi were well preserved considering they were close to 2400 years old. The details on the scrolls, bas-reliefs, and designs were exquisitely carved into the marble. Columns were not one long solid piece, like Egyptian obelisks, but were comprised of jointed pieces, piled on top of one another and often fluted. The amphitheater was the largest in the country, almost completely intact, seating 30,000 spectators for plays, lectures and cultural events.

Next we toured Ephesus, which is ranked with Pompeii as one of the two best-preserved cities of the ancient world. Roman names overlapped with Greek since it was originally Greek, then Roman, and finally a Christian city. The Apostle Paul of New Testament fame was chased out of the city by the silversmiths who feared that his preaching against paganism would lessen the sale of their silver shrines to the Goddess Diana.

The most conspicuous landmark in Ephesus is the façade of the fabled two-story library. Only the front remains of the destroyed building. In its heyday it was a city of great learning

and I would love to have sat at the feet of their great philosophers. At one time the library housed 200,000 books made of
leather parchment. Legend says that Mark Anthony shipped
all the books to Cleopatra as a present. Unfortunately, nothing
remains today.

Ephesus was a compact city, essentially one long avenue, but
its ruins were enough to conjure visions of its original inhabitants. I remember walking down the avenue's slight incline on
large square cobblestones flanked by sculptures and memorials
centuries old. I pondered what famous Greek or Roman had also
walked on these ancient paths wearing flowing white togas. I
tried to picture women carrying fresh water heading toward the
bathhouses and people using the public restrooms complete with
running water. I swore I heard the bustle of a vibrant city.

Our bus made an unscheduled stop. Orhan, our guide, met
his father-in-law on one of the busy modern city streets. From
the bus we watched our guide kiss the older man's hand, and
touch the hand to his own forehead. Then he proceeded to kiss
both of the man's cheeks. Orhan later told us that kissing the
hand was a sign of respect, and the kisses on the cheek were signs
of affection.

The next Greek ruin we visited was Pergammon, located on a
high point overlooking a strategic valley where armies came and
went. One of Alexander the Great's generals, Lysimachus, stored
his booty here. For a period of time Pergammon was a major
power in the ancient world. The amphitheater there was as steep
as any we had seen. I get a touch of vertigo thinking about it.
All of these theaters have near-perfect acoustics. We also saw a
scrawny pomegranate, and a peppercorn tree for the first time.

Back in Germany, we visited The Gate of Pergammon in
Berlin, where it is on permanent display. The Germans conducted
the first major excavations in Turkey so Germany got the antiquities. How ironic that we had to complete our Turkish journey by
returning to Germany.

MODIFIED JEEPS AND THINGS

Lunch was a respite. We pulled into what seemed a cluster of country houses besides the road but the complex was actually a restaurant. The sun filtered through the grape trellis. The food tasted fresh since it was straight from the garden. The tomato tasted like a tomato, not some hard green bud that had been gassed red. The first course was scrambled eggs with tomatoes followed by a salad that included diced tomatoes, cucumbers, onions and greens in vinaigrette. A tasty pizza of egg was next followed by scrambled eggs atop a bread crust. The main course was lamb shishkabob and rice. The dessert consisted of yogurt and fruit. I love food and sunshine moments which always seem to remain firmly in my memory. It is as though sunshine molecules can better access little crevices in my brain that lock them forever in my recollection. The clarity may dim, but the warmth always remains.

Orhan, our tour guide sat down beside us and asked, "Why don't you light up a cigarette after each meal like the rest of the group?"

"Well," my husband replied, "our religion forbids such practice as smoking and drinking alcohol because it is bad for your health."

Another German sitting caty corner from us piped up, "They are the Muslims of the West."

We all chuckled.

Towards sundown the bus had an unscheduled flat tire. We stopped while repairs were made. We walked over to a little square schoolhouse, freshly painted in a bright blue. There were flowers in the window boxes, and a statue of Ataturk commanded the front of the building. In every school in Turkey, a similar statue commemorates this soldier and visionary leader of modern Turkey. Full-grown trees gave us plenty of shade to sit and enjoy some fresh air while we waited.

Two Turkish workmen drove up in a modified jeep. I say modified, because the only things we recognized were the wheels. A flatbed was made of pounded boards, and the steering column was attached to a long pole. The only seat was the driver's chair.

The driver pointed to the flatbed and made a driving motion. My husband tentatively pointed to himself, and then the flatbed. The driver nodded his head up and down in agreement. So my husband climbed on board and took a short circular ride on the pavement. Everyone grinned at our attempts at friendship.

Darkness was already pushing the day to the west when we neared our hotel. The bus driver missed the first turnoff to our seaside resort and couldn't do a U-turn on the narrow, two-lane road, so we kept driving hoping to find the other entrance. In a valley of hills we missed the sunset, but later we saw a full moon send its shimmering light over the waters of the Aegean Sea. The rays were like a heart monitor reading of waving lines printed on the sea.

During the second day we took notice of a lone woman sitting in the front seat. She did not speak German, nor English. We finally discovered that she was Orhan's wife who boarded when we saw Orhan's father-in-law. She seemed a little lonely while her husband was off assisting others in our group, so we made a point of including her. It was not easy since neither of us spoke the other's language. We would smile, or while visiting a site we gestured to have her join us. These were such small things, but apparently appreciated by her and her husband. At the end of the trip, they privately singled out three couples with a small gift of gratitude for making her feel welcome.

PARIS AND HELEN OF TROY

Legends and time have a tendency to exaggerate places and pulling events out of proportion to reality. This is what happened to me at the City of Troy. I had expected the city of Troy to cover a large area. The actual archaeological remains were surprisingly small, at least the excavated portion, covering no more than a standard city block. The early inhabitants built their homes of clay brick, which were leveled to form the base for the next conqueror's home. Since each civilization had built on top of the former, the city became taller and taller in height.

This site was also historically significant because it marked the beginning of modern archeology. Heinrich Schliemann, a German, struck it rich in the California gold rush allowing him to follow his dream--to find the city of Troy. Scholars said the city was imaginary, but Schliemann proved them wrong. He did his research and deduced that the remains would be exactly where he dug. We saw archaeologists still excavating the site. To add to the legend, a tall wooden horse was reconstructed in front of the visitor's shop for tourists to envision the fabled legend of Paris and Helen.

Northward we rode, taking most of the afternoon to cross the Dardanelles Straits, and Gallipoli Peninsula running parallel with the huge Sea of Marmara. A few scattered houses dotted the landscape, but most of the terrain was uninhabited with dry brown grass sparsely growing on barren hills. We saw concrete bunkers leftover from the Battle of Gallipoli in which the British lost to the Turks in 1915. Mel Gibson, the actor, got his start in the film, *Gallipoli*.

British and French troops tried to capture the Ottoman capital of Istanbul because they wanted a secure sea route for the Russians. It was a failed nine-month campaign with heavy casualties on both sides. To this day Australia and New Zealand commemorate the battle. The Turks call it the beginning of the founding of the Turkish Republic.

I was surprised to see signs advertising beer. The Muslim religion demands abstention from alcohol. Perplexed I asked why and was told by one rationalizing worshipper, "In the morning, Allah will forgive all."

ISTANBUL

We approached Istanbul from the west. The moment we paid our toll to enter the city, we hit congested traffic and began inching our way from the outskirts to the center of town. I didn't mind the delay since I loved watching the sun set against the skyline of minarets and skyscrapers. Over 500 mosques in the city create a unique silhouette. The call to prayer could be heard in surround-sound. I could scarcely believe we were here in this legendary city.

I guess being the daughter of a geography professor whetted my appetite for travel. So finally Steve and I were here, and we were both fascinated. Once while watching a television special on Istanbul I passionately stated how much I wanted to visit this exotic city. My husband naively asked, "What is there to see in Istanbul?" I launched off on a professorial discourse--Istanbul was the meeting place between Asian and Europe, between Christianity and Islam, and between modern and old. Afterwards he conceded it would be alluring to visit.

The next day we toured the Blue Mosque, the world's largest which derives its name from the hundreds of indigo tiles that decorated the round domed interiors made in the ceramic capital of Iznik. The dome with six minarets is one of the most prominent landmarks in Istanbul. Every Friday, the Muslim Holy day, the iman, the spiritual leader, climbs the marble pulpit but never to the top to give his sermon. By never climbing to the top, he pays respect to God who occupies the highest rung.

We walked through a garden and toured Hagia Sophia, which was built as a Christian church by Emperor Constantine in 537 when the city was still called Constantinople. For one thousand years it was the largest cathedral in the world. When the Ottoman Turks turned it into a mosque, they plastered over the Christian mosaics, inadvertently preserving the panels. Today the edifice is a massive museum. Considering the age in which they were built, the mosques were engineering marvels. As a matter of fact, they are engineering spectacles even today.

I noticed an Egyptian obelisk standing on a plaza. I took the time to photograph it and fell behind the group. I had to run to catch the group, but not so fast as to pass up a good deal. As I dashed down the street, I spied a vendor cart selling colorful scarves for fewer than five dollars. I whipped out my money, quickly pointed to my scarf of choice, and then resumed running, definitely one of the fastest purchases ever made. The indigo and white scarf is one my favorites.

A short bus ride took us to the renowned Topkapi Palace where the sultans lived with their harems. Rather than being built upward like most European castles, the royal residence sprawled outward over large acreage. Gardens were filled with greenery. The trickling water formed carved rivulets. I soon became disoriented because there were over 400 rooms designed between courtyards and fountains.

On display was the sword that belonged to Mohammed the Prophet as well as the elaborately tiled rooms where the sultans lived. Visiting the costume rooms gave me a greater sense of how much Asia influenced this country. It was as though someone gently took a large squeegee across Asia and blended people, dress, foods, and cultures so they gradually melded into one another yet retained their strong ethnic identities. The only sharp dividing lines were man-made political boundaries.

Next we visited the Grand Bazaar. In ten minutes I was suppose to cover 4,000 booths crammed into a covered mall selling gold, silver, carpets, brass vessels, fezzes, and trinkets. I went crazy with frustration. I whisked into a stall with t-shirts, pointed to the first one with the name Istanbul embroidered on it, paid the bewildered vendor, and ran back to the meeting spot. Few will recognize the great feat accomplished: too many choices, too little time, and yet a purchase.

Our entire group agreed to take a boat ride up the Bosporus Straits, a narrow neck of water connecting the Black Sea and Russia with the Mediterranean. This was the only warm water port for Russia since her other ports froze during the winter. Because of its strategic location many battles have been fought over its control. We cruised along to the second bridge, only recently completed. I looked back at the outline of minarets, mosques, cathedrals, and office buildings. Istanbul truly has one of the most distinctive skylines in the world.

The sun was bright and cast crisp shadows on the shore. The sunrays flitted on the dancing azure waves and the warmth on our backs was countered by the breeze of the boat in our faces. It was as though we could see everyone's blood pressure lower ten degrees. The boat turned back under the bridge, and I silently pleaded, "No, keep going! Don't stop now! We are just beginning! Take us to the Black Sea!" But mine were unspoken words, so I quietly surrendered.

BURSA

Now began our trip south through the interior. We took a ferry, which carried our bus across the Sea of Marmara to Bursa, the old capital of the Ottoman Empire. This area was noted for silk production, replaced today with enormous chain stores and large industrial developments. The ancient village I anticipated was replaced with overcrowded urban sprawl.

We found respite at a sarcophagus of one of Turkey's founders. The tomb was completely covered in small tile. The man's name never crossed my tongue because I could not pronounce it. This visit reinforced my growing awareness of how little I knew about the long and significant history of this part of the world. I had no timeline on which to hang the names and events. Yet to the people here, history was a part of every breath they took. How very cloistered we become. How insulated and narrow we can remain.

I appreciated the fact that we non-Muslims were allowed to enter the mosques in Turkey after cleansing ourselves at the fountains. In many Islamic countries non-believers are not allowed to enter. The open halls were laid end-to-end with Turkish carpets, and the quiet time for reflection left me filled with gratitude toward the tolerant Turkish people.

SHOPPING

Of course, no tour to Turkey was complete without the perfunctory stop at a rug shop. Ours was at an enormous circular building filled with enticing Turkish rugs of every taste and price. The salesmen showed us the silkworm cocoons after they had been boiled, then how they spun and wove the silk threads. After we took tea, the rug show began in earnest. A herd of salesmen appeared from nowhere, all speaking at least one other language besides Turkish—English, German, French, and Japanese. They cordoned off couples and began their sales pitches of quality, beauty, and craftsmanship. A few had moved onto payment for their purchase. Our salesman easily discerned our lack of interest and moved to more promising clients. My favorite rugs were all of silk, in the $18,000 price range. Stephen said that he wouldn't walk on a rug that cost that much, so we patiently watched others make their purchases.

About an hour after the rug shop our bus stopped in Incilik, ceramic capital of Turkey. The craftsmanship was superb and the designs ornate. I had time to decide systematically which items I wanted, nothing like the whistle stop purchases made in Istanbul. The fruit bowl I bought was rainbow colored surrounded by fluted edges. Its design swirled with flowery curls and splashes of bright colors. The ceramic hot plate tiles I chose bore inscriptions in flowing Arabic calligraphy. Finally I bought something noteworthy in Turkey, and made it home without breaking any of them!

YELLOWSTONE OF THE EAST

In the center of Turkey was a hot springs often featured on tourist brochures, Pamukkale, similar to Yellowstone Park in the United States. We walked up a dull looking brown hill and looked over the other side. Bright white calcite terraced pools of iridescent water sparkled below. Early engineers learned how to make cement by studying the calcification of these hot springs. We wound our way down, removed our shoes and balanced barefoot on the paths. I hopped ankle deep into the pools. I had anticipated scalding temperatures but the water was warm. I kept wondering how long it would be before tourists would be banned from overruning the springs.

ANOTHER RENDEZVOUS

With every trip I learn more about this fascinating world of ours. On this expedition, I learned that the Greek civilization extended to both sides of the Aegean Sea; that empires come and go; that Turkey is modernizing at a rapid rate; that some of the finest carpets and ceramic ware in the world are made here; and that all people respond to unspoken kindness.

We had been here a week and seen only the Western half of Turkey. We still wanted to visit the eastern section with the fascinating rock homes in Cappadoccia, and the large historic stone heads of Nemrut Dag. We needed to do more shopping in Istanbul, and see the swirling dervishes!

Mad Dashes Through Germany

November 2000

Knowing this was our last year in Germany, we dashed madly to those spots we had previously left untouched. On long weekends, we piled into the car, grabbed our gas coupons, marked the map, and headed out to explore.

EASTWARD on VETERAN'S DAY 2000

We made a spur-of-the-moment trip on a three-day weekend and headed for Berlin. I was still on crutches recovering from a broken toe, so we did most of our sightseeing from the car. Nonetheless, it was memorable, and illustrated what a diehard traveler we had become.

According to the road map, Berlin was a five-hour drive. In reality, it was about seven hours because of traffic jams at Heilbronn and Leipzig. The main roads in East Germany were new with long divided highways matching those in the west. It was only when we wandered off the main roads that we caught glimpses of the old Eastern Germany. It had been nearly ten years since the unification of Germany, yet the houses were still drab brown and gray with peeling plaster rotting from neglect.

We accepted the neatly painted houses in West Germany as being quaint and pristine. It was only by contrast that we understood the economic disparities that existed between the two divisions. One west German told us how heavily taxed they were to help re-build East Germany, something like 60 percent of their income for several years. I asked him to repeat what he said, because I could not imagine such a hefty tax. It was not bitterness that filled his voice but more resignation and impatience to get on with his normal life.

BERLIN

We were initially intimidated by Berlin's size, and feared driving into the city, but it turned out to be more accommodating than we expected. We immediately entered onto the main thoroughfare that changed its name several times, but was best known as Unter den Linden. This street intersected the Zoo Park, large monumental statues and the Brandenburg Gate, near the Parliamentary area as well as the museum complex.

The Brandenburg Gate was being restored and was under a shroud printed with images (gulp) of the Eiffel Tower and Arc de Triomphe. We chuckled.

The street was suddenly blocked off for a demonstration march. We never did find out what the group was protesting. It was a civilized demonstration by American standards with people quietly walking. We turned off the main thoroughfare trying to make our way through the side streets. In the many narrow and one-way roads, we twisted and turned, and ended up right back on the main thoroughfare—heading straight toward the marchers. We were paralyzed for a moment. What should we do? We gathered our wits in time to exit onto the next street. Wiping our brows, we decided it was a good time to park the car and take in a museum.

THE MUSEUM

The Pergammon Museum was selected because we had recently returned from Turkey. Fortunately, the staff permitted me to ride in a wheelchair since my foot with the broken toe was aching.

The Altar of Zeus and Athena from the ancient city of Pergammon was moved piece by piece from Turkey to Germany. It dates from 180-160 B.C. The bas-relief of gods and men covered the entire front and stretched over the marble steps ascending to the Temple. I debated within myself whether Germany should keep what was discovered in Turkey. Should the British, French and others be allowed to keep Egyptian, Greek, and other artifacts excavated in other countries? It was a complex issue.

The next breathtaking spectacle was the Roman Market Gate from Miletus in its entirety, two stories tall! I was overwhelmed! How did they move the entire façade to Germany? Cost was obviously not a consideration. I imagined Roman voices belonging to toga-wearing senators discussing politics at the entrance with crowds of shoppers milling around. I heard the bustle of vendors hawking their wares, and women carrying baskets inspecting the goods. A wealthy woman beckoned to her maid to load the produce as she collected the change from her shrewd barter. The colors of the fruits and vegetables stood in bright contrast to the brown homespun of the common worker. My nose wrinkled as I thought of the animals wandering through the streets. A man slapped the face of the donkey nibbling on an apple. The marketplace was vividly alive to me.

The third wonder was Nebuchadnezzar's Ishtar Gate and Processional Way from Babylon. This was Biblical in dating, yet the tile was as bright and bold as the day it was fired. I had no idea such monuments existed anywhere, alone in Germany. This spectacular gate from thousands of years ago was real only because it was in front of my eyes. Wasn't Nebuchadnezzar part of the Jewish dispersal at the beginning of our Gregorian calendar? I was stunned that so much history was in one museum!

These were incredible finds! Part of the reason we may not have known much about these museums was because Berlin was in East Germany behind the communist wall, and few people from the west could visit.

THE WALL

Checkpoint Charlie held a special draw since we were children of the Cold War. The little white guard box was moved to the west side of the Wall near the History Museum. A mini billboard of a Russian soldier's picture greeted us. We walked to the other side and there was an American soldier's photograph. What you saw depended entirely on which direction you came from. Many things, I guess, depend on your point of view.

Cemented into the ground were brass markers indicating where the Wall once stood. I had pictured one straight solid line. In reality, the barrier zigzagged between streets. Too much commercialism distracted us from understanding the full impact of how it divided the two Berlins.

CONSTRUCTION

Everywhere we looked in Berlin, there were construction cranes dotting the skyline. The new Parliament building was completed in 1999. Glass and steel were fixed atop ancient pillared buildings. It was as though the people were working to eradicate every evidence of fifty years of communist rule. The old regime was tyrannical, but still a part of their history that I hope they don't totally destroy everything. In the rush to cleanse themselves of a nightmarish chapter, the country may try to eradicate every remnant leaving nothing for future generations to learn and never forget.

WARTENBURG CASTLE

On our way home we toured Eisenach where the castle of Wartenburg stands. This was where Martin Luther translated the Bible into common German, which formed the basis of the modern language. Luther had already tacked the grievances on the door and was in personal danger at this time. The duke sheltered him. I couldn't help but be impressed how during their lives, the duke wielded great power and wealth. Yet, it was the priest without any material goods that we honor today. We scarcely remember the duke's name. The power of an idea can cross centuries of time.

ROTHENBURG OB DER TAUBER

Rothenburg touches the past especially when night falls. The city tour was led by a man dressed in dusty old medieval Night Watchman clothing, carrying a lantern. The city clock depicts the story of its famous mayor who out drank an opponent in a wager to save the city from destruction. By downing a gallon of wine in one swig he won the bet from the invading Imperial forces of Count Tilly.

Rothenburg quickly became one of my favorite spots in Germany, since the city had an allure with half-timbered houses and twisted cobbled streets entirely encircled by a medieval wall. I could see nearly every nook and cranny in a short visit. Many prints of Germany including the one on my wall depicted

Koboldzellersteig and Spittalgasse Streets in Rothenburg with a gate tower surrounded by half-timbered houses.

There was so much of Germany to admire and enjoy. I thought of two places we enjoyed that most tourists never saw.

BERNKASTEL-KUES

No one mentioned Bernkastel-Kues to us, and it was only by accident that we stumbled upon it--one of the most colorful hamlets on the Mosel River. Tall half-timbered buildings dating to the 1600s surrounded the Marktplatz. From a modern road you stepped a few blocks into the center of town and were surrounded by Renaissance buildings six stories tall. A little crooked house standing a half block up the hill was located on a triangular plot. The cottage did not seem livable but from the fresh curtains in the window and the bright red geraniums in the flower boxes, someone resided in this 15th century house. The dark wooden timbers had been recently painted. The plaster filling had been whitewashed. It was two-stories not much taller than my six-foot husband and I think at 5'2" even I would have had to bend over to enter the doorway. It reminded me of Hansel and Gretel's gingerbread house tilting to the right.

HAMMERODE

Once when college friends came, we drove to Hammerode, a tiny farming community near Kassel in the northwest where Wolfgang, one of our friends, was born. He left when he was a child, but had returned often for long summers. He was of northern German heritage, blond hair, light blue eyes, square jaw, and height of 6'4."

Wolfgang's relatives raised over 400 swine. We saw some piglets that were born two days before, their eyes still shut. Descending down the barn ramp, glancing at the piglets and coming back took less than ten minutes, but left us with a smell that clung all night to us. I admired the mistress of the house for her immaculate housekeeping in the face of such a daunting challenge. There was nary a stench in the house although the pig barn was but a few yards away.

We walked to the little local cemetery where Wolfgang's parents' were buried. Even though they had migrated to the States, their wish was to be interred in the land of their birth. We walked through a meadow of gold flowers, Canola, and up a little hill. Wolfgang showed us the cherry trees that his grandfather had planted along the road, a source of income for the villagers. Beneath the trees was a bench dedicated to his ancestor. There was special meaning here because someone we knew personally, had deep roots in this place.

GREAT CARE

We were based in Germany, so we naturally took advantage of learning more about this marvelous country. From the ashes of World War II, the Germans have created a progressive nation based on hard work and planning. I will admit that I am thoroughly addicted to the order, the cleanliness, and charm of Germany!

The fields were edged and neatly cared for. Forests were an excellent mix of pine and larch trees, lending a variation of color throughout the year. Without being told we crossed borders in or out of Germany, I immediately sensed that the landscape changed. The roads, the houses, the fields and vineyards seemed painstakingly organized.

In almost any corner of Germany, we found hundreds of years of history preserved in the architecture. No matter where we turned we found tidy towns and hamlets ready to etch in our memories--each a gem, cut to perfection--breathtaking snow-covered Alps with quaint villages nestled at their base, houses painted with folk tales, preserved medieval half-timbered cottages, meandering cows, and lederhosen-clad men next to a modern and efficient Germany—all radiated sensitive preservation and German personality!

MOROCCO

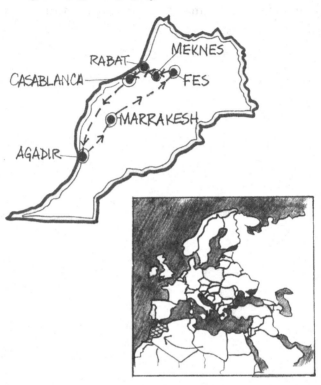

Morocco

November 2000

ON TO AFRICA

Morocco was the first country to recognize the fledgling United States of America after the War of Independence. Being the westernmost country in North Africa and only 8.8 miles or 14 km from Spain, the country enjoyed its juxtaposition of being

African, Arabic and European. The languages spoken are Arabic, French, and limited German and English.

"Sure I'll go if Dad really can't," our son, Scott, agreed. He was visiting us in Germany. My husband had to work at the last minute and was unable to make the planned trip. So mother and son headed off to Morocco. The full German package tour was a no-brainer, since we did not speak Arabic or French.

I had broken my toe in two places from a fall. It had nearly healed, but I did not want to risk my podiatrist ordering me to stay home and cancel the trip. So I said nothing to him. Bug-like antennae stuck out of my big right toe holding the fractured bones in place. I wrapped an elastic bandage over the foot, slipped it into a soft shoe, and hobbled on a wooden cane the entire trip. When we arrived home I inspected the rubber tip of the cane that was more than half worn after the trip.

AGADIR

Scott and I landed in Agadir on the Atlantic Coast, the Miami Beach of Morocco. In two and a half hours, we were transported from the green hamlets of Munich to the sandy beaches of Morocco.

Our first act after tossing our bags into the hotel room was to hail a Petite Taxi, small, red, cheap, and battered, full of character, to transport us to the beach about two miles down the road. The front desk clerk told us it was beach weather 350 days of the year. We strolled along the boardwalk on a Sunday afternoon. An assortment of people basked in the sun. The women were covered from head to toe in bright colors, and scarves. Every imaginable fabric was represented from velveteen to sheer silks in rainbow hues. The pale, flabby Europeans in revealing shorts were a stark contrast to the modestly dressed natives.

We planted ourselves near a nondescript fountain and watched the balloon man do a thriving business. Parents in every

culture have a difficult time denying their children the simple
pleasures of childhood. The nearby café had a four-man ensem-
ble playing an American tune, then a European song, and then a
distinctively Moroccan melody. The band had learned to please
the tourists.

The original city was totally destroyed in an earthquake in the
1960s so, in my opinion, there was not much Moroccan about
Agadir. It was rebuilt with nondescript square plastered buildings. Visitors came for the warm climate and sunshine.

The next morning our tour guide, Ali, picked us up and we
headed north to the four royal cities: Marrakesh, Fes, Meknes,
and Rabat. Each of these cities had once been the capital of the
country under different dynasties.

Ali was a trim man in his forties with a tawny complexion,
a black mustache, and black horn-rimmed glasses. He wore a
black *djellaba,* the name given to the flowing robes. His English
was excellent so we were able to communicate well. There was an
immediate air of gracious concern about him, and fortunately he
did not have an ego to feed. We found him knowledgeable and
solicitous of our needs throughout the trip.

We stopped at an oasis, not the movie variety of swaying
palm trees and lush vegetation, but a commercial strip mall. The
water well and the donkey had to be pointed out to us. At a
restaurant we ordered the national drink of peppermint tea leaves
steeped in hot water with a fistful of sugar, sweet, but refreshing.
We sat outside on the porch, wide enough for a table and chairs,
letting the sun thaw our northern toes. The impression I had of
the inside cafe was plastic—tablecloths, chair seats, salt and pepper shakers and the waitress' demeanor. A couple of young girls
with scarves covering their heads sipped their drinks at a booth,
and discreetly gave us the once-over. I am sure we appeared noisy
and awkward to the locals.

Ali, our guide, told us of the fine agricultural products that
grew in these fertile valleys. The valleys first appeared dry and

barren, but yielded many edibles. I saw for the first time sesame bushes configured like tumbleweeds drying on the roofs of the houses. The houses were squat little square shapes, usually plastered with the occasional smaller second floor attached. All the houses had fences made of adobe. In another time and place, these fences might have passed muster as a Mexican barrier. Both Morocco and Mexico had a Moorish tradition, so the idea is not that farfetched. Haystacks were covered with mud insulating them from the hot drying sun. Labor was still done by hand and donkey.

The spirit of entrepreneurship existed on the road. A rotund barber set up a chair near the pavement, and was neatly cutting his client's hair under an umbrella. Another robed man waited patiently for his turn.

MARRAKESH

Marrakesh lay inland on a flat plain with the soaring snow-capped purple Atlas Mountains forming the background. Exotic palm trees contrasted with every square building. Everywhere we turned houses were painted a rustic ochre color. The avenues were broad, and the city pleasant. This became my favorite refuge in Morocco, for it truly transported me into an exotic world.

Out of the barrenness of the desert, the opulence was a contrast. The Tombs of Saardians, a ruling dynasty, were filled with ornate calligraphy, and rich brocades. Most Moroccan mosques were off limits for tourists, but fortunately these gardens were open filled with shrubs and trees that warded off the relentless sun.

Fortress walls surrounded the city, jutting in and out for almost ten miles. The Koutoubiz Minaret was the city landmark, not much else competing with its height. The minarets in Morocco were not spindly space needles found in many other

Islamic countries, but substantial square towers, like Italian campaniles.

The medina, or shopping area, was a fascinating study of people, smells, objects, and noise. I was impressed by creative workmen fashioning old tires into buckets and useful containers--recycling at its finest. Near the end of the Medina was the Jamaal el Fna, the most famous gathering place in Marrakesh. Dusk began darkening the skies. We clambered up to a third story rooftop restaurant and watched the milling people below, appearing to be worker ants scurrying on the open plaza.

Only on the ground could we fully appreciate the bustle, noise, and smells. A white bearded old man in homespun cloth, a storyteller, held the squatting children spellbound with his tales. Vendors set up stalls selling dates, olives, and every conceivable natural and imported item. Occasionally a pungent whiff of spice tingled your nose. Olives were piled high in green, black, and red mounds. Herbalists dispensed their powdered potions. Dancers leaped into the air. A fire eater strolled through the crowds circling groups. A snake charmer mesmerized live cobras. One gentleman in our group said the snakes were harmless, but I'd read that a lady had once been bitten and died. Fortune tellers squatted in the dark waiting for the next tarot card to reveal their client's future. Water carriers adorned in hats of red, blue, and gold with tassels and colorful garb spent more time posing for tourist photographs than dispensing water.

My son felt a sudden tug on his hand. A girl not more than 10 years old had a vise-like grip and wouldn't let go. She proceeded to apply green henna on the back of his hand, and demanded money in exchange. We had no small change, so my son gave up his four-color pen. He was not happy about being conned or about wearing the artwork on his hand for several days.

No bazaar is complete without food. Four rows of food vendors prepared every remarkable dish. Sheep's heads, pastries piled in pyramids, snails, soups, and sweets were being consumed by mobs of people. Families, young people, and tourists jammed together on the wooden benches surrounding the kerosene stoves.

Mystical and magical were the only words that begin to describe the marketplace. I would have loved nothing better than to sit for a week simply watching the rush of humanity.

We succumbed to dinner at a tourist restaurant on a second floor. As we reached the top of the stairs the most intricate wall carvings of plaster in Arabic calligraphy reflected a yellow light. A drumbeat and a line of dancers welcomed us into the den. We ate a delicious chicken simmered in its own juices in a most distinctive brown earthenware dish with a conical lid called a tagine. Couscous, a national food, was incredibly filling, said to expand the stomach. Experts were able to roll the granules into a ball with one hand, and pop it into their mouths. We were happy to use a spoon.

All evening musicians played oriental music on a flute and drum. After the dessert of fresh fruits, the featured entertainment began in earnest. First, a well-endowed young woman wearing belly dancing garb, entered the room balancing an entire tray of candles on her head. She managed some gymnastic contortions to our polite applause. Next three overweight women who emanated varying degrees of boredom sang and tried to dance with us. We responded in kind to their feeble requests. We were relieved when the male dancer provided much more energy with a long tassel spinning around on his hat. Finally another belly dancer came forward. We were to see similar acts throughout Morocco and I wondered why the only patrons were tourists.

FES

The city of Fes served as a religious and learning center. My son and I found the old town a paradox--ancient square buildings adorned with modern satellite dishes on their roofs.

We learned that the boxy maroon hat with a black tassel was named after this city but was slowly losing its popularity in Morocco. We saw the Fes only worn by elderly gentlemen.

We descended into the Souk or marketplace, a labyrinth of alleys, shops, and worship houses jammed into one square mile. A guide was a must. Blessed with an excellent sense of direction, I was still thoroughly confused by the narrow twisting passageways. We heard the cry of "Balek, Balek!" and felt a hand on our shoulders pushing us out of the way of an oncoming donkey. All goods were brought to the market by this beast of burden, a fact we could smell. And the donkeys were muzzled so they could not eat the produce. The tour hired a local guide for the day. We certainly would have been lost without him.

My son asked Ali if he could purchase a *djellaba,* a native cloak with hood. He did not want a cheap tourist version. He got his wish. Ali located a fine tailor in the middle of many twists and turns. Scott's *djellaba* was black and had three stripes down the side, the latest style. To a Westerner it simply looked black. To a well-trained eye, the details were the important touches. Scott slipped his purchase over his head, and immediately became a Berber.

To prove how convincing his Eurasian appearance was, a native couple came up to him and began asking for directions in Arabic. Scott smiled, shrugged his shoulders and said in English, "I am sorry, but I don't speak Arabic." The couple stood frozen for a moment, perhaps trying to decipher what he had said. Slowly they walked away shaking their heads.

MEKNES

Meknes was a testament to the might of one man, Ismail Moulay, who was born in 1672 and died in 1727 A.D. At the age of twenty-six he ascended the throne when his older brother died in a fall from a horse. He moved the capital from Fes to Meknes and built an extravagant city later destroyed by an earthquake. The ruler was said to have 500 wives and to have sired 900 children. I cannot begin to fathom the logistics in feeding, and clothing such a tribe, let alone keeping them all happy.

The showpiece in Meknes was the horse stables that held 12,000 horses. Only the storage bins large enough to hold several football stadiums have survived the numerous earthquakes. The supporting arches stretched into a repetitious infinity. Another magnificent feat included reservoirs to water his horses that reminded me of a small municipal water supply. Somehow we do not consider that anything made prior to the 20th century could be constructed without oil-eating machinery. Yet, Moulay showed what a determined man could accomplish with manual labor.

We returned to the city center. Across from the Bab Mansour Gate, we entered the souk. A vendor brushed past me as I walked in the crowded market. His squawking chicken did his duty on me shortly before being decapitated. Yuck! Fortunately, I wore drip-dry clothing and a pay bathroom was nearby. I can attest to the freshness of the poultry here!

ON THE ROAD

Morocco had access to water, and its valleys were more fertile than I had expected for North Africa. This was partly because three major mountain ranges were within her borders and captured moisture. Had I read the fact in a textbook, I would easily have forgotten it. Being here in person, I shall forever remember.

A camel herder stopped our tour bus on the open road, and allowed us to take pictures of him and his animals. One camel was as curious about us as we were about him and poked his head into the bus for a closer look. Everyone's camera clicked away.

Men in traditional earthen-colored flowing robes leaned against modern day power poles. Huge bundles with legs were little donkeys carrying bulky burdens. Large vastness of land seemed unoccupied. The sun cast sharp shadows. Everywhere there were scenes to etch in my memory.

We were told that unemployment was remarkably high. One figure was 80 percent without jobs. Poverty was evident particularly in the rural areas. Able-bodied men sat in groups in the middle of the day talking or sipping tea under a shady tree or building overhang. Poverty always leaves me sad. It takes me a while to realize that I cannot help every impoverished person, but the desire to help lingers in my heart, especially if they are very young or very old. The deep weathered lines in faces are not only caused by sun exposure, but because of the hard life they must live.

I feel strongly that Americans, especially children *should* travel. Then they will begin to understand how fortunate they are and perhaps improve some other child's life. For most Americans wealth is like breathing air. You cannot see it, but simply take it for granted. Only when deprived or witness its absence, do we begin to appreciate it.

RABAT

The present capital of Morocco is Rabat. Only the palatial areas seemed to resonate Moroccan character. A rainbow of uniformed personal wearing red, blue and green guarded the king's palace. A man delivering pizzas appeared at the front gate wearing white flowing robes, a red cap, and yellow pointed shoes.

We were surprised to see women directing traffic. The program training women as police officers was only two years old, and was radically new for Morocco. In too many other conservative Islamic countries, women are ciphers.

The founder, Mohammed V, of the new independent Morocco, was buried in a tiled mausoleum at the edge of the sea looking west. A cantor read the Koran all day and night, a great honor. Perhaps it was like our eternal flame concept of forever honoring the deceased. The building had exquisite tile work but was free of any other physical adornments. Watching the sea kiss the shore, I felt I understood the early builders and why it was important to bring the spirit of the sea here. The salt water cleanses not only the body but also the mind—the state of purification and reverence abided here.

CASABLANCA

No visit was complete without a tour of the fabled city of Casablanca, or so I thought. The film of the same name starring Humphrey Bogart and Ingrid Bergman put the city on the world map. I was excited to see ancient arches and souks with their Moroccan personality. Perhaps my expectations were born of too much media stereotypes. Instead I found Casablanca a modern city with a commercial center boasting large skyscrapers.

The second largest mosque in the world, the Hassan II Mosque, was built on a manmade island in this city. Muslims believe the throne of God is located in the sea. We non-Muslims could tour this particular mosque, but we had to pay to enter after removing our shoes. The mosque was made of materials found entirely in Morocco, white/beige stone for the walls and dark polished stone for the floor. The upper floor was essentially an enormous open room three stories high and could accommodate over 20,000 worshippers. A unique feature was the moving roof that could be opened on sunny days allowing sunshine to flood the interior.

THE WESTERN KINGDOM

As we bumped along in our bus heading to Agadir and our return flight home, I tried to recall all we had seen in each capital city--Marrakesh, Fes, Meknes, and Rabat. The cities were weavings of long traditions, culture, and colorful people. I closed my eyes and visualized a desert full of life touched by a living ocean.

We would miss our guide, Ali. His steady, non-intrusive, but constant presence was reassuring to us throughout the trip. He was informative and knowledgeable of facts, yet he did not prattle the entire time, giving us space to absorb his words as well as the scenery. We gave him the polite Arabic kiss, and pressed a *baksheesh* or tip into his hand.

I thought of one of Morocco's distinguished British visitors, Winston Churchill. After the prime minister nobly held his country together during the Nazi bombings in World War II, he came to Marrakesh to recuperate. He continued his visits for over 20 years. I understood why. Morocco was a magical blend of bright clear sun, palm trees, jagged mountains, expansive deserts, grins on weathered faces, noisy chaos, quiet stillness, the tasty, the unusual, the modern, the ancient, and the exotic— all existing side by side. I hope that I, too, will be as fortunate as Churchill in returning to Morocco again and again!

Belgium

Christmas 2000

On our last Christmas in Europe, we didn't want to linger around the house without family. We decided to visit our Congolese friends, Taty, his wife, Bijou, and their twins, Mark and Mariam in Belgium.

GHENT

Ghent was forty minutes north of Brussels, Belgium. The total trip was three and a half hours by car from Landstuhl, Germany. I wished we had visited here more often. I was awed by the scenery in Ghent with twinkling lights reflected in the water and richly decorated Dutch facades, tall, slender buildings with roofs pointing heavenward. Decorative scrolls and plaster-work enhanced the surfaces that were finished with a palette of pastel colors. Medieval buildings with their angular pointed roofs sat facing the water. Canals intersected the city. My recollection of Ghent has always been associated with outstanding medieval architecture.

My first visit to Brussels was in 1999 when I was helping Bijou with the birth of her twins. Vincent, Michelle and Francois' son, had been working in Brussels, and took me to dinner in Ghent. He was the number one graduate of a French school equivalent in age and prestige to Harvard in the United States. We first met when he was an intern in Texas, and stuck entering numbers into a computer. He deemed the clerical task a waste of his time and talent. He approached his supervisor who approached me if I could use him in greeting distinguished guests. We had a great time together. Vincent also visited our home and saw Houston and Dallas. When his sister, Leslie, graduated from high school, we made arrangements for her to stay with various American families across the United States.

BRUGGE

The city of Brugge, thirty minutes away from Ghent, has retained much of its medieval flavor. During the high tourist season, men and women in period costumes stroll the streets. The ornate downtown buildings illustrated the wealth that flooded this town during the thirteenth century. Brugge was a trading center and housed Europe's first stock exchange. French and Flemish occupations wove in and out of the town's history ending with Flemish domination. Traveling during Christmas, we did not compete with the crowds, but we missed the leaves on the trees and the costumed actors wandering the lanes.

Oil painting was invented in Brugge. Jan Van Eyck began the use of this medium, so no visit was complete without a stop at the Groenine Museum. Painted more than 600 years ago, Van Eyck's *Madonna with Canon Van der Paele* showed surprising realism. The painter achieved much of his impact through layered varnish and oil. I had not been a particular fan of medieval art, but in this little museum I gained appreciation for the workmanship of the early Flemish painters, such as Petrus Christus, Han Memling, Hieronymus Bosch, Roger Van der Weyden and Pieter Bruegel.

The Gruuthuse Museum was included in the museum pass, so we stopped by the home of Lodewijk Van Gruuthuse, a powerful nobleman. Large and spacious, the house was built during the fifteenth century. Inside was a small prayer balcony that overlooked the interior of the church next door, the Onze-Lieve-Vrouwekerk, or Church of Our Lady. How amazing to attend church in your own private prayer box without leaving your home!

Drifting around the old city without a time schedule was one of the most delightful things we did. Old buildings leaned into the street, wooden railings were smoothed down from constant use, and cobblestones bumped at our feet.

WATERLOO

"Meeting your Waterloo" or your defeat is a cliché. Folks have nearly forgotten it was a real blood and guts battle between the French and British that took place in 1815 located one half hour southwest of Brussels.

Fortunately the tourist bureau was open on Christmas Eve. Finally we climbed the 226 steps to the Butte du Lion on top of a large hill crowned by a 28-ton lion. From this vantage point we imagined the day of the battle, the terrain little changed from 1815. Napoleon was pressing northward with 72,000 men and 246 cannons, on the offensive. Wellington with 150 cannons, had 68,000 men, mixed Belgian, Dutch, German, and only 24,000 British on the defensive. There were heavy rains during the night of June 17, which hampered the French heavy artillery. In the one-day engagement some 140,000 men fought and 39,000 died. The decisive battle ended Napoleon's bid for power.

The Battle of Waterloo is considered a great turning point in modern history. It ended French domination of the European continent, ushering in drastic changes in political boundaries and the balance of power. Ironically, there were more statues sold in the gift shop of Napoleon who lost the battle, than the British victor, the Duke of Wellington.

BRUSSELS, THE CAPITAL

We arrived at Taty and Bijou's house in Brussels where we spent most of our time playing with the twins, Mark and Miriam. The children were 15 months old and full of energy. We didn't speak French, but somehow the children understood us. We celebrated Christmas Day with the usual feast of turkey and mashed potatoes. In addition we enjoyed fried plantains, a Congolese favorite.

Taty and his wife, Bijou, were married in Belgium away from their villages in Africa. I chuckle that the traditional wedding ceremony was held in the Congo with both families and full festivities while the bride and groom were in *absentia* in Belgium.

I first met Taty while stranded in the Moscow Airport in 1994. I had surrendered the wrong visa and was forced to stay in a secured hotel on the airport grounds. In order to obtain a meal, I had to stand in line for a coupon.

"Is this where I get a meal ticket?" I asked no one in particular.

A young handsome black man leaned against the wall in total resignation and answered. "Yeah, you get the ticket here and go to the restaurant and give the ticket to the girl. She will bring you a dinner of some horrible tasting stuff," Taty answered dully. "I have been here a week."

"A week?" I asked in total disbelief. The look on my face begged for further explanation.

"Yeah, I just walk around and around the airport."

"Well, how come you got stuck here?" I naively asked.

"I was flying from the Congo to Belgium to go to school, and had to route through Moscow. They took my passport away saying my picture did not look like me.'

"Isn't that illegal?"

He shrugged his shoulders. "They say they will force me to fly back to the Congo."

"You have to buy another ticket?" My brain was confused with all this illogical information.

"Excuse my English. It is not very good." Taty apologized.

"No, your English is really good. Where did you learn to speak it? I asked.

"Don't laugh, but I learned it from watching CNN on television."

"Impressive! That's the advantage of being young, I guess, is that your mind absorbs things quickly."

"They won't even return my personal toiletries. I haven't brushed my teeth in a week," Taty moaned.

I rifled through my backpack. I held out my toothbrush and toothpaste knowing I'd be home tomorrow. "I used this, but if you really want it, you can keep it." He took the brush and paste and a faint smile spread across his face.

I finally reached the ticket window and a dour woman handed me a paper coupon, which I took to the cafeteria. After dinner of some dry bread, stout tea, and meat that was heavily laced with garlic, I rode in a two-car shuttle to my hotel. I was the lone passenger. No one spoke to me, probably because they only spoke Russian. My breath formed clouds of steam and I shivered under my long wool coat. For a moment I thought I was going to the Gulags; it was cold enough.

I arrived at a hotel located on the airport grounds where the room was adequate and clean. The shower had hot water, so I warmed myself up. I quickly fell asleep. At five in the morning someone banged on my door. I sleepily opened it and some grandmother spoke to me in Russian pointing to a schedule. I wasn't sure what she wanted, but still I got dressed and showed up in the lobby with my suitcase.

I suspected they had mistaken me for a member of a traveling Japanese group since everyone in the lobby looked Asian, plus it was hours earlier than I had planned. But there was no one to straighten out the situation in English, so I compliantly went along. Sure enough I was the only American passport going through immigration.

At six in the morning I had four hours to kill before my flight took off, so I began window shopping. When I tried to find a seat, I recall people sleeping in every chair in the airport lounge. It gradually dawned on me that nearly everyone was of color, either from Africa or India.

I bumped into Taty again. He pointed out one African wandering about in a catatonic state and told me the man had been camping in the airport for a month. Taty and I spent a pleasant few hours conversing until it was time for my plane to depart. We promised to keep in touch by exchanging addresses. We kept our pledge of friendship through letters and phone calls.

We had a positive impact on his life by helping him find work. After he completed college he would contact a prospective employer over the phone who was eager to have help. Yet, when he showed up with his black face, he was told that all positions were filled. We suggested he put on his resume that he spoke English. He protested saying he didn't speak that well, but we reminded him that we were conversing in English. He listened to us and landed a job with an American company.

While Bijou put the twins down to sleep, Stephen, Taty and I meandered down to the Grand Place, a center that shows off the wealth of the merchant class. The city hall was covered with white twinkling lights. An ice skating rink with skaters filled the center of the Square. Tall narrow medieval buildings gilded with swirls and ornamentation surrounded the plaza. Music filled the night air. I recall the small chocolatier in one corner, brimming with every imaginable mouthwatering morsel.

Brussels was a very large city and not easily navigable. I often got lost. It was a highly diverse, trilingual city of French, Flemish, and English speakers. Now the capital of the European Union with its blatant influx of wealth was expanding in construction and the acquisition of expensive automobiles.

The European Union has three capitals: Brussels where the Council would gather and function; Strasbourg, France, where half the plenary sessions occurred; and Luxembourg which housed the European Court of Justice and European Investment Bank. The thorny challenge of working with independent and fiercely proud nations often leads to unusual compromises.

The issue of two languages has divided Belgium. Flemish or Dutch is spoken in the north and sounds like a cross between German and English. French is spoken in the South among the Walloons. This was the result of small principalities, duchies and counties uniting. Occasionally, however, the prickly issue of creating two separate countries along language lines raises its ugly head.

THE LASTING TASTE

The three stereotypes of antiques, chocolates and lace were very much a part of classical Flanders, but now were reflected against a modern stainless steel Belgium. The country was well worth a tourist's time and attention. Most importantly it was a memorable way to spend Christmas.

Andulusia Spain

February 2001

ANDALUSIA

To what country did the Romans, Arabs, Jews, and gypsies all contribute their culture and history? Spain! My husband loved to practice his Spanish, so we decided to go to Iberia. We landed in Rota, Spain, near Cadiz on the western side of Gibraltar. Our goal was to tour the southern province of Andalusia.

Maneuvering our small car down the narrow streets of Sevilla was a challenge, since the roads were built before autos were invented. The parking garages were minuscule, the size of a large living room in the States. Our attendant did a masterful job of cramming as many vehicles as possible into the tiny lot without a scratch or dent anywhere.

I loved having my own personal Spanish interpreter, my husband Stephen. I had tried learning Spanish on and off for the past few decades, but still spoke verb-less Spanish forming phrases rather than complete sentences. It might have been an illusion but I swear I understood the southern dialect from Andalusia better than those of other regions of the country. Perhaps this was because many immigrants to America originated from this region and brought their regional dialect with them.

SEVILLA

After my first visit with a girlfriend, Linda, the memories of Sevilla stayed with me for many years. It was like the feeling of flamenco music—forceful and haunting. In those days we simply wandered around without a guide or guidebook. This time I saw things from a more studied point of view.

The city boasted many famous citizens. Roman Emperors Trajan and Hadrian were born nearby in Italica. Diego Velazquez spent hours painting portraits of the Spanish royal family, his most famous work being *Las Meninas* (1656). The small golden child in the center of the painting was studied over and over by Picasso. Bartolome Murillo was another famous artist known for his many religious works who painted thirteen canvases for the monastery of St. Francisco el Grande. In every walk of life from the arts to sports, music and politics you can find a Sevillano.

The most prominent landmark is La Giralda, a tall square tower built as a minaret and later made into a belfry. The town of Sevilla is a sister city to my husband's hometown of Kansas City, Missouri. Stephen was tickled to see the genuine Giralda Tower since he had grown up seeing its identical replica in the Midwest.

The Plaza de Espana a large semi-circular building, is the most recognized in Sevilla, the epitome of the Moorish Revival in Spanish architecture. The building is now used for government offices and has served as a popular backdrop for scenes from movies like Star Wars and Lawrence of Arabia. In the center is a large fountain. Scattered around the grounds are 48 benches representing the Spanish provinces each containing a coat of arms and a map.

From my first trip I remembered that the cathedral was massive, one of the largest in the world. Linda wore shorts so she had been denied entrance into the holy sanctuary and I ended up touring the enormous edifice alone. This day my husband and I were able to see it together.

We saw Christopher Columbus' crypt adorned by four sculpted pallbearers, although some speculate that the remains were those of his son, Diego. It's been over five hundred years since Columbus made the voyage to the New World, but he is still remembered and monuments are erected to him. He had a dream and he followed it. He died in poverty, but he opened a whole new hemisphere and left European imprints everywhere. He never could imagine how far reaching his discovery would affect the history of mankind. We never know where our influence begins and ends. We can only pursue our passion. History will sort out the rest.

In a café along the river on my trip with Linda, I introduced fried calamari to her.

"Calamari, por favor!" I ordered.

Linda asked, "What is calamari?"

"Well, why don't you eat one before I tell you. It will be more exciting that way!" I teased.

The plate of golden rings arrived resembling fried onions. Linda bit into one. "Hmmmm, not bad. I'll have another. So, okay, what am I eating?"

"Squid!" I replied expecting a sour expression on her face.

"Really? You know, it doesn't taste that bad, especially if you dip it in ketchup. I think I'll have another." In fact, she took a fancy to the chewy morsels and finished most of the plate.

The best way to see Sevilla is by foot but there simply was so much that by the end of each day I was ready for a foot transplant. I wished I had several pairs of feet that I could exchange whenever one pair wore out. It was a city that we could spend days enjoying--much vitality, manageable in size, and a rich historical tradition. In my opinion, if we saw no other city in Spain, Sevilla alone would convey our concept of the country.

ON TO CORDOBA

After several blissful days in Sevilla we headed east. About thirty minutes down the road I encouraged Stephen to take a turnout at Carmona, a medieval town located on a ridge overlooking the central plain of Andalusia.

A church in the center of town was encircled by narrow cobblestone streets. We saw people slipping into traditional costumes in preparation for a street parade. Five young men in band uniforms, navy blue cloth accented with stripes of red, leaned against the white stucco wall, holding their battered instruments. We guessed it would be a while before the parade began so we didn't wait knowing it might be *"mañana, mañana, mañana!"*

A Roman necropolis, and a Roman burial ground lay nearby and were later occupied by the Moors. Looking from the city through an old Moorish archway, Puerta de Sevilla, onto the breakaway valley below was breathtaking. It may have been the angle of light, or the accumulation of the events we had recently experienced, but the panorama was a painting of the Spain I envisioned. Others would have merely glanced and gone.

As we left, I peered through glass doors into a *parador*, the ingenious Spanish answer to utilizing historic places as hotels, a fascinating way to experience history surrounded by delightful Spanish ambiance. Parador prices are comparable to medium hotel prices.

The drive to Cordoba was through a wide-open range with rolling hills. Villages along the way, called *pueblos blancos* or white towns, were so named because they were whitewashed in the Moorish tradition and positioned on hilltops for protection. The white buildings contrasted sharply with the brown hills, creating an almost surreal atmosphere.

Soon we were running parallel to the Guadalquivir River and reached a simple stone bridge, Puente Romano, built in Roman times. We crossed the five hundred foot span into Cordoba. Directly in front of us was a large square buff-colored building called the Mezquita, a mosque converted into a cathedral. The walls abutted directly onto the street and presented a barren edge.

Stephen and I found a parking space on the street and dashed over to the massive cathedral. Stepping through a doorway into an unlit cavernous room, our eyes adjusted to the darkness. We beheld 850 red and white stone arches, monumental remnants of Moorish occupation. Each arch had alternating white and red colored stones perfectly fitting into the curved space. The pillars were a perfect study in one point perspective, racing hundreds of yards down to ending in one dot.

Steve was in awe of the forest of evenly laid out arches and pillars in what was once the second largest mosque in the world. The double arches consisted of a lower horseshoe arch and an upper semi-circular arch. By the time we were standing under the soaring roof, the structure had been in existence for over 1400 years, being built in 600 AD. The Mezquita is an impressive place.

We walked through the center of town and found statues of catholic saints, lots of tourist shops brimming with typical kitsch, and a lunch of paella. This 10th century city was not laid out in square blocks, but seemed to resemble geometric configurations of trapezoids, parallelograms, and ovals. Each street was unique in shape, and length so we could not assume that one street would eventually intersect another. On one major intersection there was a small statue of the famous Jewish philosopher, Maimonides because he had studied in this city—what a rich cultural heritage of Jews, Moors and Romans!

In Cordoba and throughout Spain the Moors built public baths when the rest of Europe including all good Christians believed that bathing was a diabolical custom to avoid. Moorish monarchs dwelt in sumptuous palaces while the crowned heads in Europe lived in big drafty barns, lacking both windows and chimneys. During the Dark Ages when the barbarians overran Europe, the region lost its tradition of mathematics, literature and science inherited from the Greeks and Romans. The Moors helped preserve many of the traditions, and gave them back to

Europe. Western Europe owes a debt of gratitude to the Moors for inventing and preserving progress made in astronomy, chemistry, physics, mathematics, geography, and philology.

JAEN

We headed eastward on our clockwise journey around Andulusia. In the northeast corner off the beaten tourist path was the province of Jaen. Its name was probably derived from Arabic Jayyan meaning crossroad of caravans. One of the largest producers of olive oil in the world, there is reported to be 150 million olive trees, undulating ribbons of beauty and peace on the placid hillsides.

In so many ways I felt I had been transported back to the Renaissance, the word itself was French, but it flourished in Italy. One particular building reminded me of the Medici home in Florence with varigated windows for each level, surface ornamentation, and a top floor veranda. The cathedral tower gave us a lovely view of the city. When we climbed through the large door, we were greeted by a robed monk who offered to take us to each corner of the building. We happily accepted his offer. We wandered through a building that was hundreds of years old, being led by a man whose order had been in existence nearly as long, momentarily ushering me into a time machine.

GRANADA

We dropped south and stopped at a clean motel north of Granada. I fondly recall arriving in Granada with my friend, Linda, and a widow soliciting boarders at the train station. Her price was modest, and we agreed to stay with her. We soon met her other boarders, two tall handsome men from Sweden, who ended up touring the city with us.

Our main objective was a Moorish architectural treasure, The Alhambra in Granada, one of my favorite places. The Alhambra represents the height of Moorish influence in Europe. The fortress was lost in 1492 to the Christians but remains forever a tribute to its original inhabitants.

Moorish palaces were strategically placed for safety, but were also built to create peace and tranquility. The palace was spread over acres interspersed with courtyards, gardens and fountains to increase air circulation, rather than going upward in layers. Tiles made intricate geometric designs against the walls, while others were perforated screens. Fountains allowed the soul to find trickling refreshment, pools reflected the sky, filigree windows and walls cast lacelike shadows, and plants brought vibrant color.

I was so taken by the edifice that I went again early the next morning to etch indelibly the structure in my mind. Fortunately, there was no crush of tourists in February to distract me. I wanted to contemplate life as it might have been in the 11th century and simply to feel the spirit of the Alhambra. Each line was perfectly proportioned to the other. The series of courtyards were filled with soothing water fountains and narrow channels. Pillars were powerful but softened by delicate openwork. I had never seen such a marvelous structure that spoke so clearly to my senses. The palace was a respite from the outside world achieving its goal of "paradise on earth," and I felt the calm and harmony that was meant to exist.

That evening we took in a Flamenco performance. This famous Spanish dance form was said to have originated in Granada with gypsies as the traditional performers. The clicking heels and castanets of this powerful dance have always mesmerized me. As I listened to the music I could feel the infusion of Moorish origins. The melody could play in the Middle East and easily fit. What I thought was original Spanish tunes were in reality a blend of cultures. I was learning much about the mingling of world influences.

GIBRALTAR

Whoever controlled the Straits of Gibraltar controlled the Mediterranean Sea. Gibraltar is separated from North Africa by eight miles of sea at its closest point, making it one of the most hotly contested pieces of real estate in the world. This large rocky prominence at the tip of the Iberian Peninsula stretches for three miles and rises 1463 feet.

The English have governed the area since 1713 when Spain ceded the territory to England in the Treaty of Utrecht. The Spanish are irked by British control and occasionally assert their authority by closing the border, which occurred from 1967 to 1985. In reality Gibraltar is like a little British island surrounded by a sea of Spaniards.

We expected the Rock to be a solid, immovable mass, but discovered nearly 50 miles of underground tunnels mainly used as ammunition storage and fortification. A steep public highway went right through the rock, which surprised us again since we thought the rock a high security risk area. One famous American had an office in one of the impregnable tunnels. His name was General Dwight Eisenhower.

We parked our car and walked the downtown area, hearing snatches of English, Spanish and Arabic. We poked our heads into the shops and grabbed a sandwich. The most notable difference from Spain was the Bobby, a British policeman with tall rounded hard hats. Their stiff posture seemed a bit staid for the warm climate. We snapped a photo with a policeman and could nary raise a smile.

As we drove back across the border into Spain, we spotted women of all ages in polka-dotted flamenco dresses heading towards Gibraltar. Their tight fitting bodice flared out at the thigh into thousands of ruffles. I was especially tickled by the little toddler in a bright yellow flamenco dress, barely able to hold herself upright trying to balance all the flounces.

ACROSS THE STRAITS

My husband had not been able to make the Thanksgiving trip to Morocco so I insisted we go to Tangiers for a day to catch a glimpse of this exotic country. When I landed in Tangiers on my first trip with Linda we were greeted by pestering little urchins begging for money, and guides shouting to take us through town. Women darted about in long gray robes. We walked across a wooden pier by the old ochre-colored medina, the market. It was a noisy but romantic entrance into my first Arabic speaking land. This time, there was no one to greet us. It was almost too quiet, too sterile. I swear that they also moved the port from the old medina to the business section of town. Most people wore Western clothing, and the city at first sight was not much different than Spain.

We meandered through the business district. We had no Moroccan money thinking we could exchange dollars at a better rate once inside the country. The change booths were closed since it was a weekend, so we stopped at every automatic money machine we could find. No luck. The ATMs would not take our credit cards. Finally we remembered we had some Spanish pesetas so we were able to buy some pastries to eat, staving off our hunger pangs. In a small narrow walkway I peeked into a shop filled with handicrafts. I pointed to a round orange stone box adorned with metal swirls. Stephen agreed that we should purchase it with the remaining coins we had.

It was frustrating to be in an exotic part of the world, knowing we could not buy much, gain admission into an exhibit or purchase any food we wanted. We somehow managed, but have become wiser to exchange small amounts of money beforehand.

Stephen was glad we'd made the effort to go. Now he can say he's been to Morocco calling them Moors rather than Arabs. Visiting the southern part of Spain and now Morocco, he has gained an appreciation of the contributions that this group made to the world.

We ferried back to Spain, and drove late into the night, luckily finding a reasonably priced motel. We presently travelled rather inexpensively. When Spain goes on to the Euro, I fear good bargains will be harder to find.

CADIZ

On our final day we drove to Cadiz along the Atlantic called the Coast of Light or Costa de la Luz. Fishing is still one of its main sources of income. The port of Cadiz was first used by the Phoenicians in 100 B.C. Carthaginians, Romans, Visigoth, and Muslims all touched its shores.

The city seemed very relaxed and unhurried. We leisurely drove around and chose a promising restaurant. We found a parking space in front and walked in through the swinging screen door. Red upholstered benches formed eight booths with tables and chairs in the center of this small family run business. The décor was not stylish but everything was clean. A television on the wall across from the entrance blared the news. An older customer watched television with the owner, and another family of four ate lunch at a booth. It was mid-afternoon.

We sat down. The owner tossed two menus on the table and placed two glasses of water in front of us. We ordered a hearty lamb stew. My husband kept looking at the owner. A gleam formed in his eye and a sly smile curled on his lips and I knew Stephen was going to begin conversing in Spanish. It is curious to me since my spouse is usually reticent in public when English is spoken. The more I've traveled with him, the more I've observed he becomes the talkative partner on our travels. I've even asked him why he likes to talk in Spanish but not in English. He can't pinpoint the reason. I theorize it's because he learned Spanish as a teenager and feels less inhibited.

"Senor, why are there all these pictures of Basque country? Stephen asked.

"Because we are Basque."

"Seriously?" my husband's eyes widened. He had never met a Basque in person.

"Yes, we earn as much money as we can so we can contribute to our cause," replied the owner. He was of medium height, the dark-haired thinning at the top, with a slight paunch. I could not have distinguished him from the thousands of Spaniards we had seen. "We, Basque, are very serious about our cause for independence."

"We were trying to get to Bilbao and see that part of northern Spain. We didn't have enough time to see it all!" Stephen commented as if our desire to go north would win more affection from the owner.

The conversation that ensued was in rapid Spanish and I could not follow. The owner's hand often opened upward or stabbed the air to make a point. Stephen later said they talked about injustices.

Basques? They herd sheep in Nevada and their language is not Indo-European. It is closely related to the Georgian language near the Black Sea. That's what I've known about them. Living mostly at the foot of the Pyrenees Mountains the Basque are a minority people in Spain trying to declare their independence. A radical group, ETA, often resorts to violence by bombings and killings to force the issue, but Spain steadfastly refuses to cede to their demands.

VIVA LA ESPANA!

Our trip was good Spanish language practice for my husband. It was a time of remembrance of my first trip to Spain as well as our discovery of the Jaen area. The food included more than paella and fried fish--a definite improvement from my first visit.

Andalusia, birthplace of the flamenco, is forever the romantic Spain I envision in my mind. Many buildings come to us from the renaissance era and give a timeworn feel. Here the measure of life is little less touched by the rush of modernity. The dry Mediterranean climate and scruffy bushes could pass for the American Southwest yet exudes a *duende*—the soul, the force that inspires flamenco and her people. We learned of the many contributions of the Moors among which was the infusion of Moorish music and song giving us the *cante jondo,* the dark and serious aspects of Flamenco. I could hear the strum of a classical guitar and the roll of rapidly clicking heels evaporating to an *afilla*, the earthy voice of the dance. The spirit of Andalusia will always exist in a tiny corner in my heart. I raise my utterance of approval, of encouragement and recognition of the spirit here-- Jaleo! Jaleo! Jaleo!

Paris In The Spring Time

May 2001

Saying good-bye is never easy. Yet, the time had come for us to prepare to return to the States. For one weekend, I slipped over to Paris to say adieu to friends and to visit the smaller museums on my list. Stephen was in the States at a conference, so I ventured out alone.

MUSEUM AFTER MUSEUM AFTER MUSEUM

Melted watches over barren landscape conjure up the name of Salvador Dali. This eccentric artist's technical competence was superb, so I felt it was worth a visit to his museum. This was the first stop on my ambitious counterclockwise circuit around Paris. I arrived a few minutes before opening, so I stepped into a tourist shop and rummaged through the souvenirs. The cleaning lady mopped furiously without regard to what was in her way including me. She nearly ran me over pushing me out onto the street. So much for doing business there! I simply went next door and bought a red beret.

A renovated two-story house, the Dali Museum was intimate and filled with his work. Seeing a painting is often only half the story. Artists place symbols in their works to convey certain statements. Dali's jointed leg elephant with an amber pyramid represented the future so whenever I spotted this symbol I knew he referred to tomorrow.

By seeing a large body of his work in one place, I gained an appreciation for the man's genius. His art seemed almost mild by today's standards. Yet, I easily understood how radical Dali's artistry was in his day.

Dali was a member of the Spaniard trio of artists living in France along with Picasso and Miro. He was an excellent promoter with the foot long mustache and was said to party furiously for half a year and then cloister himself in seclusion creating the other half. It sounded rather fine to me, since I am gregarious by nature, but still require my solitude.

Art is a lonely endeavor in many regards. There are those successful artists who can afford to hire a staff to produce their ideas. Most artists, though, must struggle to create the idea, then produce the art and market it. In the midst of producing art, the artist must survive the bills for rent, food, and art supplies. It is little wonder that fabulous talent often falls by the wayside. The handful of artists that actually become successful are truly lucky as well as skillful.

As I plotted my next stop, I realized that the cubed arch, La Defense, was nearby. I have been curious about the enormous square arch since the first time I saw it from the Eiffel Tower, so I took an unplanned detour. As I came up to ground level from the metro, I saw crowds of students clustered on the steps in front of La Defense. I wondered if there were a university nearby or if there were a special excursion that day. I walked under the arch and looked up trying to comprehend how a square arch worked. There were elevator rides to the top. As I approached the ticket booth, the weather suddenly became blustery and clouds quickly covered the sky. The visibility from the arch would be hampered, so I walked back down into the subway and on to my next museum.

After a most circuitous route through subways and trains, I made it to the Marmottan Museum. Fortunately, a walking map helped me navigate the crooked streets. Since the L'Orangerie Gallery was closed due to renovations, this little museum housed Monet's water lilies. Finding my way through the classically pillared museum, I found the paintings in the basement. They filled an entire wall. Having visited Monet's home in Giverny made his paintings all the more meaningful.

Monet's wall-sized lilies were honestly more dramatic than the actual fist-sized flowers that grew in the garden. The painted pink water lilies were in perfect contrast to the greens and blues of the water. Nothing was sharply defined, but everything conveyed a liquid movement that enveloped me. Monet had created a visual symphony, a complete masterpiece based on the simple theme of water and flowers. The dominant mood it created was one of peace, with notes of joy and delight. And my soul heard every melodic phrase.

A heavyset middle-aged woman with red hair sat on the divan mesmerized by the paintings. I heard her speaking American English to a guard, so I knew she was a fellow country woman. She simply sat and stared at each work for over 20 minutes drinking in the painting's power. Occasionally she would sigh. I was tempted to ask who she was, but I didn't want to disturb her reverie.

For years I had noted Luxembourg Gardens on the map but always sped by it. This time I stopped. The green park was a welcome break from the asphalt and concrete of the city. It had broad walkways, fountains and open grass, and sculptures both modern and classical lining the walkways. Bright red and yellow tulips enlivened the park. Parisians loitered on the benches reading newspapers or simply watched passersby. Young mothers and nannies surrounded the play areas absent-mindedly watching their charges.

Up a street was the Pantheon a staid structure, but once inside, there were painted murals and a more updated feel than Rome's. A fulcrum pendulum faithfully swung to and fro knocking down wooden pegs every few minutes. A huge crashing sound reverberated through the dome, followed by alarmed guards running. Apparently a plump woman had leaned on a railing and it collapsed under her. The lady was unhurt, but was a bit dazed. She soon regained her composure and dignity. The rest of us uttered sighs of relief.

My next stop was the Picasso Museum. The exhibition was housed in a marvelous old classic mansion, a somewhat incongruous setting for modern art. I was a bit disappointed to find no cassette guide, something that can be a bit tedious but extremely informative. Picasso's full name is Pablo Diego Jose Francisco de Paula Juan Nepomuceno Maria de los Remedios Cipriano de la Santisima Trinidad Martyr Patricio Clito Ruiz y Picasso born in Malaga, Spain in 1881. He was the son of an art professor and showed his artistic talents at an early age. His breadth of styles and the great outpouring of works were impressive. With the perspective of decades, I can truthfully say that I appreciated his creativity. One amazing trait of Picasso's was his evolving art cycles. He was never content to remain locked into one style. Instead he moved through his Blue Period, Rose Period, African-influenced Period, Analytic Cubism and Synthetic Cubism and finally neo-expressionism. He was forever expanding his thinking and his artwork changed accordingly.

One author felt Picasso felt hated women, yet they were intertwined with his life. Picasso's greatest outpourings came when falling in and out of love. He was a prolific artist sometimes producing a canvas a day. Granted Picasso was a child prodigy, but he constantly worked over decades to achieve his artistry. His long exposure to the craft lit a chain reaction of ideas that history often refers to as a genius.

I claimed the last checkout from the museum's cloakroom, and the doors locked behind me as I stepped outside. There were still hours in the day that I could not waste. Even though my feet were thoroughly exhausted, my spirit kept driving me forward. As a diehard tourist, I would not let any opportunity pass.

I gambled that the Pompidou was open at night. I was lucky! People streamed in and out of the building. I rode the escalator to the top floors, grinning, I had made it! I began at the top and worked my way down, asking myself why contemporary art seemed more comfortable this time. Has time legitimatized this form of modern art, or had my own perceptions of what is good and bad art been refined? I can now better understand the strange amorphic shapes on the floors and walls. This does not mean that I like them, but I better appreciated the artist's labor. Too often in history art was relegated to looking nice and pretty. Art whether visual, aural or written, makes a statement about life. That is why it was important for me to learn of these artists so that I might know why they created as they did. Today I was visually fed as if at a grand banquet!

HELLO AND GOOD-BYE TO MICHELLE AND FRANCOIS

Whenever I go to a new locale in Paris or anywhere for that matter I give myself plenty of time to get lost. It was not unusual for me to retrace my steps on the metro or spend time walking up and down streets in search of an address. One of the main reasons for my coming to Paris was to see Michele and Francois, my native French friends. We agreed to meet at Café du Commerce, located only a couple of metro stops away, but I gave myself over an hour time buffer.

We met through their oldest son, Vincent, who my intern in Texas. When Leslie, their youngest of three children and only daughter, graduated from high school, I helped arrange for her trip to Washington, D.C., Utah and Texas. It was an ambitious trip but one that gave Leslie a broad overview of America. When we arrived in Germany we had several occasions to get together since the parents were located an hour and a half from Landstuhl in Metz. They later returned to Versailles. Michele was an excellent correspondent via email, so our friendship flourished.

I arrived with plenty of time to spare so I decided to walk the full length of Commercial Street, stopping to buy a couple bars of lavender soap. A small carnival of clowns marched up and down the pedestrian plaza as I stepped onto the busy street. A portly clown in a white tutu and yellow hair breezed by as well as a half a dozen other white painted faces all dancing to a mambo rhythm blaring off a boom box. The parade made things festive!

I went inside the Cafe fifteen minutes early and quietly claimed a table. I kept checking my watch and when my punctual French friends had not arrived, I decided to check the front door. Michele was waiting outside. We laughed that we were all here but at different spots.

Café du Commerce is well known among Parisians. I tried a typical lamb dish from the Toulouse region, where Francois was born. The meat was cooked for several hours and fell off the bone. Delicious! Shortly before dessert I excused myself to go to the restroom. My friends had the advantage of speaking French, so they always paid the bill. My turn to pay was long past due. I found my waiter and handed him my credit card. I felt rather clever that I was able to make myself understood simply by saying, *l'addition* which was "the check" in French and settled the tab.

We ate desserts of pastries. Delectable paper-thin phyllo dough surrounded tart apples and was topped by a delicately sweetened custard sauce. I am certain there were several hundred decadent calories hidden in the confections, but what did I care. I could eat bread and water any time.

After coffee, Francois kept trying to get the attention of the waiter for the bill. Finally the waiter came over and told him that the meal was paid. My surprised friends looked at me and I just smiled.

We then drove to Versailles where we met Leslie, their daughter. She was tired, but happy. Her college rowing team had just won a crewing championship. The event is usually held on the Seine but since there was too much wind this year the event was moved to Versailles.

Leslie was a wisp of a woman and I could not understand how she could row competitively. I found out that she was the coxswain who provided the motivation and encouragement to the crew as well as making tactical calls. Leslie had also won a first place in marksmanship the year before, shooting with unerring accuracy to win a trip to London. I expressed my surprise at this delicate daughter's athletic accomplishments. Michele confessed they were as surprised as anyone.

Michele had not slept well the night before so she went home to rest, and to prepare dinner. Francois and I went to the Trianon, a smaller palace located on the grounds of Versailles. This is now an official guesthouse, and resembles a dollhouse with everything proportioned accordingly. This was built at the request of Maria Antoinette when she wearied of the intrigue at the court of Versailles.

After the tour we drove to Francois and Michele's apartment. The décor was modern with a brown leather couch in the living room, which sat under a large modern weaving. In Europe they are more into quality than quantity.

Michele's dinner was delightful. She always made at least four courses and served them in order. The salad was a garden green, the soup a clear consommé, the entrée spiced chicken with couscous and the meal topped off with a luscious cake sprinkled with raspberries and cream.

I caught up on the current progress of their three children. The oldest son, Vincent, my intern in Texas, was in the banking business. The second son, Renaud, was involved in scientific research, and Leslie was finishing her degree in business. All the children were educated, accomplished, and doing well.

Each time I was with Francois and Michele, I felt lifted and enlightened to be with gracious, intelligent, and charming company. They had a broad perspective of life having lived in Algeria and South Africa. Good friends help us be better people, and my friends certainly did this for me.

LOST IN THE LOUVRE

My last day in Paris was spent at the Louvre. The admission line went nearly around the entire inner court partly because the museum personnel were on strike and there was no charge. Gratefully I had a museum pass and walked past the snaking column to the entrance.

My goal was to spend time in the lower galleries, which I had never seen. I wandered through the galleys noting one exquisite sculpture by Bertoli, the artist who designed many works in Rome for the Catholic Church. The guard smiled when he saw me walking around and around studying a not-so-well-known piece. The twelve inch sculpture was a marble nude that seemed so lifelike. I have never made a sculpture by removing stone, though I have built up figures with clay. I cannot begin to conceive of having the strength to chisel away the stone while keeping the proportions--requiring skill and strength as well as artistry.

Although my plan of attack on the Louvre seemed straightforward, no one warned me that there were flights of stairs and dead ends between the displays although the maps showed continuous exhibits. I often lost my way. I think I saw the Egyptian collection as well as the Roman, but I couldn't say if I saw it all.

I never realized a fort was under the museum until I stumbled upon it. The castle turret was almost as interesting as the rest of the exhibits. I was probably one of the few that day who didn't see the Mona Lisa. A quick mental calculation of all my visits added up to over a week spent in the Museum--still not enough time to view the centuries of art housed in the Louvre.

RECOLLECTIONS

In New Orleans they speak Creole, a mishmash of corrupted French, Spanish, Portuguese and other languages. One word I particularly liked was *lagniappe,* pronounced *lanny-yap,* meaning "life's little extras" or "something free." If a baker throws in a thirteenth donut when you've ordered a dozen, that's *lagniappe.* If someone shows you an extra kindness that's *lagniappe.* Paris has been a *lagniappe* for me!

Walking back to the hotel, I briefly recalled some of my highlights in Paris. I chuckled at the time my niece, Heather, and nephew, Jonathan, waited in line to buy admission tickets to Disneyland Paris. A dignified Frenchwoman approached us and asked if we wanted three passes to the park for free. With our mouths open in amazement, we quickly accepted her offer. She refused any payment. Unfortunately, none of us spoke enough French to ask further questions. All we could sputter was "Merci! Merci!" This was a marvelous French gift--our *lagniappe.*

I thought of Sacre Coeur in Montmartre district and my husband's Aunt Gwen, whom we affectionately called Galloping Granny. She was the most dedicated traveler I knew. She saved all year working as a librarian, and then took an exotic annual trip. Before she passed away, she had visited every corner of the world. Eighty-five year-old Gwen accompanied her granddaughter on a university music tour to Europe and visited the Sacre Coeur. She was using a wheelchair and cane to get around, and knew she could not get up the mountain to the basilica. She was perplexed not knowing what to do. As if on cue several young college boys traveling with the tour grabbed her wheelchair and ran up the mountain with her. That's what I call diehard traveling and her *lagniappe!*

AU REVOIR

All of life can't be one continuous high, and sometimes we must make transitions which aren't always smooth and easy. I reminded myself to focus on the positive, and be grateful for what I had--three amazing years on an extraordinary European tour! Even with all my rationalizing, it didn't make leaving Paris any easier.

This was also my adieu to my French friends. Little did I know that Michele's cancer, which had been in remission for a decade, would eventually overtake her body. This would be the last time I would see her. So the memories are especially keen.

I remember walking the Montmartre District, my eyes misting over, thinking how fortunate I was to be in Paris, and how I would miss it. I ran my hands over the Art Deco metro arches and tried to etch the beauty into my memory. I patted the vines three times, and entered the metro leaving Paris behind.

SOUDA BAY

IRAKLION

KNOSSOS

ISLAND of CREJE

Souda Bay, Crete

June 2-3, 2001

"Well, I'm not going to sit around all weekend on borrowed furniture, staring at four blank walls!" I complained. Our furnishings had been shipped out to the States and we were camping in our empty apartment with a bed, a dining table, and a sofa. "Besides, it's supposed to rain this weekend." I added.

"And what do you propose to do?" my weary husband asked.

"Go to Souda Bay, Crete!" I replied without hesitation. "Remember Brenda and I tried a month ago and didn't get on the military hop. Fortunately the Homburg flea market saved the day by giving us a reason to buy German antiques."

"But you have to be at the airport at 4:30 in the morning!" my husband protested.

"There's a price to everything. So you lose some sleep. Big deal!" I retorted.

"Okay, okay. You wanna go by yourself?" he meekly proposed.

"Sure, I would, but you'd worry the entire weekend that something might happen to me. We'll just go down on Saturday and come back on Sunday. The weatherman promised us sunshine and 80 degrees!"

Stephen finally surrendered. "Well, I'd better go to bed even if it's only 7:30!"

SPACE A

The next morning we showed up at 4:15 in the morning at Ramstein passenger terminal. We packed a pair of underwear, a toothbrush and an extra shirt. There were 32 open seats. When our call came and few passengers from the lobby moved, we knew we were on board!

In three hours we touched down on Crete, the fifth largest island in the Mediterranean and home of the first European civilization of the Minoans. After a rather lengthy process of signing up for the flight back, renting a car, buying gasoline, and getting directions, we were off! Souda Bay was on the western side of the Island of Crete, and we were headed to the center where Iraklion, the capital, was located.

Although it was only 60 miles on the map, we were never fooled into thinking that it would be a short distance. The roads were not bad, just filled with curves. The scenery was spectacular, though. Bright pink and white blooming oleander bushes edged the sides of the road and the Mediterranean Ocean provided a deep blue background. Winding in and out of bays on the road, rarely passing another car, we often paused to admire the view.

KNOSSOS

Three easy miles from the capital city of Iraklion we pulled into our destination of Knossos, a Minoan ruin. The Minoans, 1200-1450 BC, who lived on Crete, were said to precede the conquering Mycenaean, 1600-1100 BC. Agamemnon was a famous Mycenaean king whose gold mask we saw in Athens. As the Mycenaean group declined, the Greek civilization began to flourish. It was first the Minoan, then Mycenaean and then the Greeks.

Knossos was a great archaeological wonder I remembered from my art history class. We walked by the entrance several times before finding it, since souvenir and tourist shops over-whelmed the entrance sign. Most of us have seen pictures of the famous frescoes of Knossos, but may not have realized they came from the Island of Crete. From this civilization came the fresco of acrobats with long wavy black hair, somersaulting over a bull as it positioned its head to toss. The minotaur, the carnivorous bull-lion in his labyrinth, also began here. And the legend of Icarus flying too close to the sun and melting the wax on his wings originated from this region.

Arthur Evans, a British archaeologist, spent most of his adult life excavating or studying this site. He uncovered a whole civili-zation and the fabulous treasures are now housed in the museum in Iraklion. I was thankful the treasures were close by, rather than in some faraway country. It always amazes me how civilizations are lost to us until someone digs them up. No matter how great or powerful a nation, it can easily disappear under layers of dust.

Bright colors on the walls, ochres, burnt oranges, turquoises, and reds filled the walls. Although the restoration showed no murals, they may have existed in the original palace. The throne room stirred one's imagination of the king holding his court and passing out judgments. The ceiling seemed low making the room dark for a throne room--said to be the oldest in Europe. Even with a detailed query of every corner, it took us only a few hours to wander the grounds. We decided to find lodging for the evening.

UNNAMED TOWN

A shopkeeper directed us to a traditional village for the night. We drove about 10 kilometers from Iraklion, and found a sign that said "rooms for let" or rent. For 6,000 drachma or around $15 we rented a room in the back of a private house. I never saw the owners. There was no hot water, but at least there was running water. Other than the midnight session of killing mosquitoes, it was a great impromptu lodging.

We drove to the tiny village for dinner. A little church with a separate bell tower stood in the center. We studied the street signs for a few Greek alphabet letters we knew, and waited until the restaurants opened at 7:30 p.m., rather tough for my husband who likes to eat at five. Finally we trundled off to the most promising looking restaurant. The clever owner knew that neither of us spoke the other's language. He invited us to the tiny kitchen and showed us several dishes. We pointed to what we wanted to eat, he smiled, nodded, and we returned to our sidewalk table. I am sure we were as much an oddity to the townspeople as they were to us. People stared at us. We stared back.

The Greek salad with tomatoes, cucumbers, olives, onion, and the freshest Feta cheese I have eaten was soon delivered to our table. Olive oil was ladled over the veggies, but we had fortunately acquired a taste for it. Next came our lamb stew, stuffed grape leaves, baked tomato, and bread. Expecting a large portion, Stephen and I decided that one plate for the two of us would be enough--a wise choice.

While we enjoyed our second course, a gentleman and his daughter we had seen at Knossos sat down beside us. We exchanged greetings and learned that they were from the Flemish part of Belgium near Ghent. He was a university professor and his daughter a social worker. They grinned when we complimented them on what a remarkable country Belgium was. We were sincere in our praise.

We had a stimulating conversation discussing a wide range of topics. We found them aware and involved in world issues. Thankfully, our new acquaintances did not ask how long we were staying in Crete. I would have been embarrassed to admit it was for only two days. They would have been shocked, since Europeans take life at a more leisurely pace.

We wandered down the main street past a porch that had earlier been occupied by four older men and one young fellow from the village. The group appeared to be shooting the breeze eyeing every interesting car that passed. Not to disturb the men when I took their photograph, I shot into the rear view mirror of our parked rental. What hard work it was to sit all day and make conversation. When we left town the next morning, the men had already begun their vigil. I chuckled to myself wondering how many of the same jokes had been told over and over.

IRAKLION

The next morning was gratefully free of traffic and we drove a few miles into Iraklion the capital city. We parked the car in a lot that was manned by a crusty old attendant. He spoke lovely English and bragged that his girlfriend was from Japan.

We were happy that the museum opened at eight in the morning so we could meet our flight schedule. The museum was well laid out and contained outstanding pieces. I could not help but be impressed with the Kamares pottery which displayed incredible skill, and a wide variety of designs and colors. These pots were formed on a spinning wheel resulting in a delicate and sometimes egg shell thin walls. The gold work was equally impressive. The rythion, a vessel for drinking, of the bull and the lion's heads were incredibly naturalistic. A little ivory acrobat showed a lyrical motion. The frescoes upstairs, the crowning glory of the museum, portrayed daily life in Knossos, women fetching water, and bull performers. Although the figures were caricatured, they showed a realism unmatched in Europe until the late 8th century. Truly their civilization was advanced. The craftsmanship was amazingly diverse and refined.

Advances in art, literature and culture are made only during times of peace. The Minoan culture flourished for many centuries without wars, and as a result their artistry was unparalleled.

SOUDA BAY

We drove two hours back on the winding road, and ate lunch overlooking Souda Bay. Afterwards we wandered around the piers. It was so peaceful that I hated to leave this sunny isle.

The exchange house refused to convert our drachmas back into dollars, so we bought a few extra souvenirs, a small tablecloth and a couple of aprons with the name "Crete" embroidered on them.

We arrived early at the airport, so we took the grand tour of the naval station located next to the airfield--all five minutes of it. It was one long strip. We asked a young Seabee if there was anything more to see.

He said, "Nope, you've seen it all!"

I casually asked, "How long have you been stationed on Crete?"

"One year, ma'm," he replied and added, "thank goodness."

Our two days in Crete were just what the doctor ordered. Being on this sunny isle certainly was better than sitting in a bare apartment in rainy Germany waiting to return to the States.

Iceland 2003

Coined the Land of Fire and Ice, Iceland was formed by volcanic forces around 20 million years ago. There are over 200 active volcanoes, yet glaciers cover many of the molten mountains. A commonly asked question before we left was "Is Iceland a country?" The answer is "yes"--but only since the middle of the 20th century. Before that Iceland was a territory of Denmark and Norway for years.

Only a quarter of a million Icelanders inhabit the country. Her people are of Viking stock from Scandinavia, and Celtic from the British Isles. They speak English as a second language, and were willing to talk to Americans.

We flew out of Baltimore in the evening and arrived two movies and two meals later. As we completed our six-hour flight over water, our first glimpse of Iceland was totally barren terrain. Because of gale force winds fire trucks formed a circle to break the gusts as we emerged from the plane and walked to the terminal at Keflavik.

The winds were so forceful that we hired a taxicab to drive us across the field to the hotel even though it was only 500 yards away. I am glad we didn't hassle with our bags in the wind. Once in our room we collapsed for several hours. Our rental car was delivered while we were asleep and in a few hours' time a glaze of ice had formed on its windows. That's how quickly the elements work here.

We were anxious to see a bit of Iceland, so we chiseled off the ice on the car window and took a short drive to nearby towns. When we reached the end of the peninsula we saw a large lighthouse at Garour. The gusts were so strong that if we leaned into the wind we didn't fall down. We managed to stagger to the lighthouse. It was a gray, cold day, yet we were happy to be in Iceland.

THERMAL POWER

The next morning we awoke to sunshine. The storm had disappeared. I like to say that nearly every place we visit, we bring solar energy. We toured the Reykjanes Peninsula in the southwest corner of Iceland. We were not certain of distances, but found most places a few minutes' drive if the roads were good. Many major roads, however, were graveled, not paved.

We found Lake Kleifarvatn desolate but lustrous in the rising sunlight. What were curious were the smoke curls rising from the southern end of the lake. We found out they were caused by thermal vents a visual reminder of the volcanic activity of the island. Vents form when tectonic plates slowly spread apart and allow magma to rise to the surface forming mountain ranges in the ocean. As the hot magma combines with the colder seawater, particles form into a chimney-like structure called vents. Icelanders cleverly harness the geothermal heat to warm their homes and buildings—clean efficient energy.

A small sign pointed to a roadside stop--Selfjall, a walkway through bubbling hot water and steam. Mud pots boiled with thin gray ooze. It was amazing to see this volcanic activity right next to the road. Nature, not tourists surrounded us in Iceland.

We followed a gravel road for miles through black curly lava fields. We saw the ocean, sandstone cliffs, and lazy birds buzzing about and even a house that had been overtaken by the slow moving lava. We never saw another car.

We reached the end of the lava field at Grindavik where we enjoyed lunch. We arbitrarily picked a restaurant and were happy that the fish was tasty. We had been warned about the high cost of things so we were prepared to be totally blown away, but the price wasn't too bad.

Just a few miles north of the seaport town we came upon a shiny power plant that converted geothermal springs and steam into energy. The Icelanders cleverly took the runoff water, formed a lake and dubbed it the Blue Lagoon. It has become the number one tourist attraction in Iceland. Everything from swimsuits to towels was available for a goodly rental price, of course. For $12 per person we dipped into the pool and spent an hour and a half wandering around the warm lagoon. The setting was tastefully done with bridges and rocks and included steam rooms and saunas. The white silica mud was purported to have therapeutic value in clearing complexions, so we dabbed the white mud on our faces, looking ready for some native ceremonial dance. It was relaxing and the perfect ending to our first full day in Iceland.

THE NORTHERN MOST CAPITAL

Iceland has the most northerly capital in the world--Reykjavik located an easy 20 minutes north of our airbase in Keflavik. As the only metropolis in Iceland, the capital's atmosphere seemed one of calm, order, and cleanliness. The buildings were modern, reminding me of contemporary boxy German architecture.

Reykjavik was also becoming a new "hot" spot for partygoers. International folks flew in for the weekend reveled in the festivities on Friday night and then returned home.

The older section of town jutted out on a peninsula. We needed coins to park the car at a meter. We drove around looking for a bank to exchange money. After stopping at four banks and finally obtaining change, we pulled into a free parking spot! It was close to the Icelandic House across from Tjorn Lake. We wandered around the old downtown, and poked our heads into several museums.

I was enormously impressed with the city hall, a well-proportioned new building that integrated water, glass, and space well. It was the winner of a competition, but many traditional folks thought it too modern. A lake with white swans gliding on the waters surrounded the building. The basement featured a large relief map of Iceland that helped us understand the terrain of the land better.

Perhaps the best exhibit was at the Culture House Museum that held the parchment manuscripts of the sacred Eddas and Sagas, some of the few surviving early written Icelandic lore. The children's room had real parchment made of calf's skin that felt like paper but sturdier. The Viking display at the top of the museum told of folk life. With poor soil to farm, harsh weather conditions, and short growing seasons it seemed such a subsistent existence for the early people, but somehow they survived.

GEYSIR AND GULLFOSS

The next day we took a long drive northeast of the capital. As we rumbled along the gravel, we noticed a school bus parked on the side of the road. We figured there must be something to see even without tourist signs, so we parked our car. It turned out that a high school class was surveying a natural cave that a family had lived in during the early 1950s. It definitely was a renter's bargain, but probably a bit drafty. A child born in the cave still lives.

It took only one hour from Reykjavik to our first planned stop, the Althing. I remembered hearing about it as a child and for some reason it stuck in my mind. Established in 930 AD it is considered the oldest parliament in the world. Nearly every major historical event in Iceland has taken place here at the Althing on the Thinvellier River. The people decided to convert *en masse* to Christianity in AD 1000. It was also the setting in 1944 when Iceland became an independent nation.

The Althing is located in a rift valley carved out of dark rock, the place where the tectonic plates of Europe and the Atlantic Ocean meet creating a low land between two higher points. Because of the movement of the plates Iceland grows about a centimeter every year. The two ridges ran parallel for miles forming a 50-foot-wide gully. I stood on what is considered the Speaker's Rock.

"Hello! Can you hear me?" I asked in a normal voice.

Stephen was standing in the valley below, a good several hundred feet away, "I hear you just fine!"

"Wow, I am using my normal tone of voice and you can hear me. The acoustics must be something else!" The rocks formed a natural amphitheater.

In the olden days all the tribes in Iceland convened here for two weeks in June to hold their legislature, enact laws, and hopefully do some courting. The main speaker was obligated to recite one-third of all the laws, quite a feat to repeat from memory. Most of this history is contained in the ancient written Sagas.

We followed the road to Geysir where the original word for a "spouting water," gusher or *geyser,* originated. The original geyser doesn't spray often any more, but a smaller one, *Strokkur,* or the Church, shoots up like clockwork about every seven minutes spurting hot water 66 feet into the air. Stephen got very good at predicting when the water would go off. It was lots of fun watching folks ooh and aahhhh as the geyser leaped upward.

Other puddles of boiling water surrounded the area. "Do Not Touch" signs were plastered everywhere. Yet every week curious and disobedient tourists were taken to the hospital for burn treatments.

A few miles down the road was the spectacular Gullfoss Waterfall. *Foss* means falls and *gull* means golden. The large waterfall comprised of two tiers, tumbling 105 feet. A power plant was to be built over the site in 1907, but through the efforts of a farmer's daughter, Sigridur Tomasdottir, the falls were made into a national monument. A small unlearned farm girl stopped a large bureaucracy and preserved the site for generations to come.

We ate our brown bag lunch in the parking lot by the falls. In front of us an enormous glacier hovered over several mountain ranges reminding me of a cake with too much frosting in the middle, spilling over the sides. It was early fall yet the winds began shaking the signs on the telephone poles. We were cocooned in the warmth of our car, but my imagination pictured me as an icicle if exposed to the elements for any length of time.

The route we chose to follow was called the Golden Circle. It took us through wide farm valleys and breathtaking mesas. Moss-covered lava fields with snowcapped mountains faded in the distance. Fields of freshly cut hay lay bundled in white plastic wrap. The sky was clear and the sun filtered softly upon the land. Sometimes the landscape felt familiar and other times it was an alien planet with jagged rocks next to rushing rivers.

In the Biskupstungur Valley I quickly joined a German tour in the Skalholt Church. Steve chose to catnap in the car. The modest white structure was clean but rather plain inside located on a lovely knoll overlooking a pastoral view of the Hvita Rivers. I remember taking deep breaths of unpolluted air and experiencing a tremendous sense of peace. The simple building did not convey its prominence in Icelandic religious history as the ecclesiastical and cultural center for over 700 years. Perhaps I was used to soaring European cathedrals making grand statements.

The quiet reverie hid some of the historic turmoil. One monument was dedicated in 1548 to the last Catholic bishop and his two sons who were beheaded because they opposed the Reformation imposed upon Iceland by King Christian II of Denmark.

VIK

The next day we decided to drive the southern coast. Fog slowly lifted as the day wore on and the sunlight dappled in and out of clouds creating an ethereal subarctic light. We enjoyed three hours of peaceful scenery with cliffs, flying birds, the ocean to our right and sheep farms to our left. The land between ocean and cliffs was often very narrow, barely allowing for the road.

Our destination was Vik, a surprisingly compact town. The road wedged through a narrow opening in the cliffs, and we coasted down to a place of black beaches. At the end of the sand were the sentinel black rocks called the Reynisdrangur—imposing as they stood in the ocean. Legends say that the sea stacks, column-like rocks, are the three solidified trolls caught offshore at dawn and turned into stone for eternity by the sun. If you add a shroud of fog and haze, the rocks could easily be mistaken as superhuman forms.

The sand was even more amazing to me. All the black volcanic stones were laid out from smallest to largest on the beach as though someone had shifted them according to size. Every pebble was smooth and round! I tucked some stones in my pocket for the children in my neighborhood.

On the other side of the cliffs was a beach called Dyrholaey meaning "island with a door," rated by some tour magazines as one of the world's finest. The huge bluffs encased the black polished stones and felt like another world. The jagged monoliths standing in the waves away from the shore added to the spell of long-ago planets. A few of the rocks had arches worn at their base by waves relentlessly pounding against them. We walked along the pebbled beach with not another soul in sight. The sky grew grey and ready to burst so we dashed to our car. The heavens kindly waited until we were snuggled in our auto before dumping bucketsful of water.

As we retraced our steps, the sky cleared and we spotted a powerful waterfall, Skogafoss, from the road. Apparently we had missed it earlier because of the heavy mist. We parked our car, grateful we had our plastic ponchos. As we walked closer and closer to the cascades, the spray totally drenched us, our second bath for the day. We stood there for a moment rooted to the ground, allowing the roar of the spillway to shake every molecule in our bodies.

Water has always fascinated me. It makes up 70-80 percent of our bodies; we can't survive without it. Yet if we take in too much we drown. Lovely droplets of rain kiss the spring flowers but too much can become a gale and destroy everything in its path. Rivers, brooks, rain, floods and tsunamis—some useful, some destructive, and all life itself.

As we left the falls, a small tour bus arrived providing our first encounter all day with other tourists. Summer is high tourist season but we chose to travel off-season because of less competition for sites and hotel rooms. However, weather is more unpredictable as we neared winter. It can change so suddenly and violently that lives could be easily lost if you were away from the major thoroughfares. Within an hour one can experience sunshine, rain, strong winds, ice rain and a snowstorm. That's why anyone traveling Iceland's interior must have a guide. We stuck to the tried and true paths.

As we continued, we caught glimpses through the clouds of the Westmann Islands a small archipelago and home of Surtsey, the newest volcanic island created in 1963. In 1973 an island called Heimaey lost 400 of its 1200 homes to volcanic lava. A video showed a house being moved off its foundations by the slow moving magma dislodging it ten feet and stopping. If there had been a connecting road to the Islands, we would have taken it but the only way to reach the Islands was by boat.

We stopped at Eyjafjallajofoss where we hiked behind the falling waters, fifty feet wide. It was a sight to peer out through the back side of the falls to the green fields and beyond them to the ocean. Each time I see a waterfall, I've always wondered what was behind the cataracts. Falls can represent boundaries we cannot see, sheer curtains separating worlds from each other. I thought of stories where there were empires hidden behind large waterfalls, or where it served as an entrance into other fantasy worlds.

LOOSE ENDS

From all points in the city, the most visible building was the Perlan, a shiny modern geothermal water plant. The creative Icelanders also used this building for other purposes. That day a cardiology conference was being held inside. We walked by the exhibition tables and gathered a few free pens and a t-shirt. We also visited a little wax museum on the history of the Vikings, filled with stories full of blood and quick tempers.

BALM TO THE SOUL

Iceland is a country of pristine beauty, and friendly people. Its citizens are amazingly tenacious subsisting off the thin volcanic soil and ocean. The Gulf Stream keeps the country, whose northern borders touch the Arctic Circle, surprisingly warm in the winter but the skies are often gray.

The word "primordial" fits Iceland. The hot volcanoes glazed with cold snow were living images of how the earth was formed. Fields of knarled and jagged lava lay untouched by human hands. The barren rocks were eroding against the ocean and the rift valley was slowly increasing the land mass a few centimeters a year. All the forces of the earth worked and perhaps played on these grounds. There was something spartan and clean about the land. One could drive for hours without seeing another human. It felt like the primal, the primitive, the beginning—as if the earth had sifted everything away until only the elemental was left. Iceland was a place of beauty in its rawest form.

AZORES

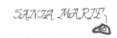

The Azores
Europe's Most Western Point

September 2004

We had seven gloriously sunny days in the little Portuguese archipelago called the Azores. This land was mistakenly named "acores" which means in Portuguese "hawks." The birds were really turkey buzzards

There are nine islands that make up the archipelago directly west of Lisbon, about one-third of the way across the Atlantic on the 39th parallel. They were discovered in 1427 by daring seafarers. King Philip the Navigator recognized their importance in his quest for trade. He knew that these islands could serve as a refueling point and beginning in 1432, he encouraged settlers to develop agricultural pursuits.

Christopher Columbus stopped here on his way home from the 1492 voyage of discovery and the story of Herman Melville's, *Moby Dick*, was said to have taken place near these islands. Today Terceira, the third island in the chain, was a refueling point for the American military.

Everywhere on the islands the Portuguese fly both their national flag and also that of the Azores. Considered part of Portugal, the Azores are self-governing and proud of their independence. Children are taught Portuguese, English and French in school. Most everyone spoke English to us, but it did help to have some knowledge of Portuguese.

Azoreans are descendents of migrants from the Algarve, the southern coast of Portugal, and Flanders in present-day Belgium. They were of mixed European stock so we saw everything from dark swarthy complexions to blue and green-eyed beauties. The younger generation was taller from good diets, but many of the adults were so short I conversed with them eye-to-eye. The people tended to be stockier, too, possibly because of the abundance of excellent cheese and wine.

In doing my research for the trip, it was challenging to find tourist information on the islands. One travel book described details of traveling in Spain and Portugal and threw in northern Morocco, but not the Azores. We knew that this would not be a touristy destination, but then again, there would not be mobs to contend with. We were uncertain about navigation between the islands. We were prepared simply to go with the flow.

HOW TO TRAVEL 18 X 5 MILES

When the morning light broke, we found views of the ocean in every direction and lots of sunshine--setting a great tone for the week. Neat rows of squares fences made of piled volcanic stone were filled with corn or grapes or an occasional dairy cow. Houses were freshly painted in various pastel colors and topped by terra cotta roofs. A unique feature of the houses was a triangular chimney instead of the rectangular ones we were used to seeing. The air was permeated by ocean and cow dung, a bit smelly to my nostrils. From high vantage points, you could see the volcanic cones showing us the origins of the islands. The water was clear, and the ocean was so dark it appeared almost black. As the water crashed upon the jagged rocks, the spray turned into an intense turquoise.

The Island of Terceira, is named as the "third" in the chain to be discovered. It was only 18 miles long and you could probably drive around the entire island in less than two hours.

We decided to pay homage to Angra do Heroismo--a UNESCO World Heritage site that had maintained nearly 80 percent of its renaissance buildings. For three hundred years it served as a strategic port for those crossing the Atlantic. The older two-story homes, usually framed with wrought iron balconies, were squeezed tightly together as if holding each other up. We could easily believe we were in renaissance Europe.

Ancient cities, I have learned, were not built for the automobile. The streets were narrow, barely wide enough for one car to pass and another to park on the curb, and they often ran one-way. We struggled to find our way to the center of the city, since one road does not automatically guarantee a return to the previous street. We were also rather audacious, not having any Euros and hoping on Sunday grace for parking meters. We were lucky on all counts. Stores took dollars when we needed it, but, of course, charged a hefty surcharge of 1.25 Euro per dollar when we could have found a .85 exchange elsewhere. Convenience often overrules frugality when traveling.

The downtown stores were built into the ground floor of the older buildings. One hardware store had not been renovated for at least a hundred years. Open sacks of dried corn and beans sat on the wooden planks that had shrunk with age creating wide gaps in between. The tall ceiling had markings suggesting another floor had once existed. Everything seemed dusted with powder from ceiling to floor.

The most evident landmark in this antique city was the caldera that helped form part of its bay called Monte Brazil. A caldera is usually a large circular depression left at the volcano summit as the magma recedes removing the supporting structure above it, and causing the ground to collapse. We were curious about the mountain top, so we headed over to it. We entered a fortress at the foot of the hill and then followed four kilometers of stone wall up a winding road to a park. We found families having picnics.

AROUND THE ISLAND

In the center of every village was a catholic church and by its side was an Imperio with its eye-catching architecture. Imperios were little one-room chapels always containing a crown, scepter, a white dove and a red banner. Made popular in Terceira by Father

Antonio Vieira during the 17ᵗʰ century, the teaching originated in medieval Germany and was called "Espirito Santo." The local people believe that such conducted ceremonies protected their communities from damage during earthquakes, volcano eruptions, and storms.

We kept driving until we reached the volcano at Santa Barbara, the highest point on the island. We climbed past the 3,000 foot mark above the timber line and found a grassy field and abandoned government observation towers at the summit. High billowy clouds cast cobalt shadows on the ocean. Clouds came running towards us and enveloped us in a heavy binding mist where we could see nothing. Then they broke away allowing us to see the ocean again. Beneath us green fields rolled down to whitewashed villages with red tiled roofs, and then broke at the azure ocean.

Stephen sighted two other islands to the west, St. Jorge and Pico. We even caught a glimpse of Pico, the highest volcano in the chain, peeking out through the indigo clouds. On the top of the hill there were only the two of us with the wind hissing softly in our ears. The quiet was a rare delight to us city dwellers.

A "BEACH" EXPERIENCE

Our first experience with lava "beaches" was in the northern half of the island at "Biscoitos," which means "biscuit" in Portuguese. It earned its name when the lava hardened leaving little mounds that looked like round biscuits. We followed the dirt road to where a dozen people sunbathed on a cement slab, and a few brave ones swam in the frigid water. There was no sand anywhere. Extensive steps and small piers as well as the slab had been molded out of cement, linking several natural pools between the lava rocks. The pounding surf sprayed water over the rocks replenishing the small lagoons. The water was cold, but the lava rocks were warm. I found this "beach" a fascinating adaptation between man and nature.

A BIRTHDAY

Wednesday the twenty-second was Stephen's birthday. Last year we were in Iceland and I almost forgot his birthday until the end of the day! This year I cleverly placed his birthday remembrance in front of him at 4 a.m.! He says he has now reached his prime and it was downhill from now on. I completely disagreed with him.

We decided to drive the southwest part of the island. We found another "beach" called Cinco Riberias, or five Riberias. We dashed down a steep ramp and immediately arrived at the sunbathing rocks. The areas had a lifeguard and a little refreshment bar. We were mere spectators today, not swimmers. The undercurrent seemed too powerful here. As we climbed back to the top of the hill, we heard a friendly "Hello!"

A handsome dark haired man spoke. "Where are you folks from?"

"Washington, DC," we replied. "Where are you from?"

"California, San Joaquin Valley to be exact!"

"What brings you so far?"

"Both my grandparents came from this part of the Azores. My grandmother told me stories about bringing her lunch down to this church by the ocean as a little girl." He pointed to the church behind him. "And now I am here for a month at the home of my ancestors."

"I am curious what route you took," I asked.

"Oh, it was a long trip. First we had to fly to New York then London, then to Lisbon, Portugal and finally to the Azores." He looked fatigued thinking about the trip. "But it was worth it to be here with my cousins."

"So you speak fluent Portuguese?" Stephen asked.

"Yes, I kept up my language so I could talk to my parishioners."

"Oh?" we said in unison.

"Yes, I am a priest in Central California. I work with many of the migrant workers. Did you know that many Azoreans migrated to Central California where they became dairy farmers, because that's what they did here?"

"We probably would have never learned that from a text-book," Stephen exclaimed.

The priest added, "Many Azoreans migrated to Canada and the United States. In fact there are more Azoreans outside of the Azores than the 250,000 living here now."

"It's absolutely wonderful here!" we chimed. He beamed as we shared our opinion of the Islands.

"My relatives like to say that the Azores are the best kept secret and they want to keep it that way!"

"Really?"

"They don't want more development on the island because they know it will change their way of life, and not for the best."

We nodded our heads in agreement. Progress defined as more roads, more stores, and more tourists is not necessarily better. With it comes a host of other challenges like overcrowding, disruption of traditional family patterns, and less peace, the very reasons why people are drawn to the area.

"We hope that you enjoy your month's visit here. It sounds fabulous! *Bom tchau*--goodbye!" We wished him well and climbed back into our car.

NEXT DOOR

On Thursday we visited Prais de Victoria the town next door to Lajes. We walked under cloud cover and over the cobblestone streets. Many black volcanic rock walls were accented by a white stone creating swirling designs. We were surprised to discover a pedestrian center unseen when we drove through town--re-minding us that you miss a lot driving and not slowing down to explore up close on foot. The stores had few souvenir items, a further testament to the locale not being a tourist haunt. In the park older men sat on the plaza bench, contemplating the most recent hemline swishing by.

A RELUCTANT FAREWELL

The Azoreans have a well-guarded secret and want to keep it that way. Commercial flights help it to remain hidden by making it a difficult destination to reach. Our week in the Azores made us privy to her conspiracy, an experience I shall always cherish.

I smile when I think of a funny little incident coming home. When we landed in the States everyone was bustling around reaching for their luggage and fussing with their children. One elderly man reached above his seat to retrieve his baggage. I noticed his bright turquoise shorts. His eyes shifted back and forth quickly looking all around him, and then he abruptly sat down. When he stood up, he was wearing brown trousers and I noticed him adjusting his belt. It dawned on me that his pants had fallen down and he was putting them back on!

More than a farewell to the Azores, this was a farewell to Europe. Our orders had arrived transferring us to Hawaii on the other side of the world, exactly halfway around the globe from Europe. I didn't want to go because I had loved having access to Europe.

"Headquarters sent me new orders," Stephen said.

"Where are we headed to this time?" I asked.

"Hawaii! Isn't that great!" he replied.

"I know it's considered paradise," I said flatly, "but I really don't want to leave!"

Stephen laughed at me. "You know when we left for Germany, you said you didn't want to go! And look at the great adventures you've had!"

"Yeah, you're right. I don't like moving! Maybe I have a hard time leaving places." A new thought was beginning to percolate in my brain, "Hawaii is in the middle of the Pacific Ocean, right? There's all of Asia, Australia and the South Seas. Hmmm, I just *might* like this assignment!"

Afterword

I lived this book! I was there! Yet, I still look back in astonishment that for every month of our three years in Germany I was on the road somewhere. At the time, it became the natural rhythm of things to unpack from one trip and begin planning the next month's adventure.

In Europe we became so used to traveling every holiday to an exotic destination that it got in our blood. When we returned to the States, we stayed home on holidays and puttered around the house, not quite bored, but close to it. It took almost 18 months to decompress from our European "high." I chuckled when my friend, Barbara, who returned a year later went through the same withdrawal that we had experienced returning to the United States.

I will admit traveling to a new place was scary at first. It did take a bit of courage to plunk ourselves into situations where we did not have control, couldn't understand the language, and didn't know what to expect. Yet, we came back richer in memories and friendships.

We learned not to be conspicuous Americans. My husband's greatest pleasure was being mistaken for a native in Finland and Ukraine. It isn't as easy for me as an Asian American to blend in. However muted colors, non-expensive looking travel clothes, and a determined look kept problems at bay. We roughed it a little more than the average, but that simply meant more money for the next trip.

The key was an open attitude. Many American women, away from home for the first time, never ventured further than the grocery store. I rarely saw my neighbor across the way, a senior officer's wife since she locked herself in her house for the first 20 months of their assignment. Radio, television, and newspapers were all in a foreign language. You could find English stations and news, but it did not automatically surround you. It was easy to feel isolated.

Others came with preconceived notions that they would not do certain things. Another neighbor said she would never travel by bus, closing her mind to a very European style of travel and one that often offered some of the best travel deals. I remember wondering how such an intelligent woman could be so narrow in her perspective. She denied herself friends and marvelous opportunities.

On the other hand, I learned much from Jeannie, a visiting scholar's wife. She smiled. She was friendly. She joined in. She didn't speak German, but in a short time was a regular attendee at every social function.

Granted I possess a higher degree of curiosity than most folks. I also had a streak of adventure, and a drive to experience the novel. But our exploits were not so outrageous that I hitch-hiked my way across the Sahara or parachuted the Himalayas. Most every adventure was do-able for anyone willing to go. The difference was our determination.

The outcome of traveling is that we will never again be the same. Oliver Wendell Holmes said: *Man's mind, once stretched by a new idea, never regains its original dimensions.* We learned how interrelated the world is. We realize our home country is not the center of the world and that much of American heritage comes from Europe. Europeans are not antiquated but lead Americans in architecture, culture, and cuisine. Quality of life is richer. Life is definitely slower paced, enjoying more time with family and friends.

Europeans savor a good meal. Now I better understand why my European friend kept insisting on better quality bread while visiting the USA. I kept going to the best bakeries thinking I had finally met his demand for good bread, but each time was disappointed. German bread fills the belly, and has a richer texture.

German cakes are also unparalleled when it comes to variety and taste.

As word got out that we were the consummate travelers, folks asked which place was our favorite. The honest reply was "All of them!" Each locale was fascinating and unique with people warm and friendly everywhere.

I studied an old Roman Empire map and realized that we traveled nearly the entire Empire hugging the Mediterranean Sea. We did not make it to the war-torn Balkan states, Persia, or regions off limits to Americans. Otherwise, we went to nearly every place that was called Roman, the Ancient Empire. Our experiences were but snippets of time. Thus, the title of this book, *Hello, Thank You, Good-bye!*

We learned to say in French, *Bon voyage,* in Spanish, *Buen Viaje,* and in German, *Gute Reiser*—Good Journey!

BENEFITS

So what were the benefits of having seen so much in a relatively short period of time?

We learned about other cultures, their habits, their likes and dislikes, their food, their language, and their geography. The world was made of many different people and it made us stand outside our sequestered American view and realize how much our awareness of others had increased.

Second, would be our increased ability to converse. Nothing was more satisfying than watching the smiles on people's faces as we shared stories of our experiences in their country. People appreciated the fact that we took the time to visit their homeland and learn about their society.

Third, learning how to pack. If we thought we *might* use it, we simply left it home. We brought only what we *knew* we would use. All our clothing was lightweight, easily laundered, wrinkle-free and generally dark in color. Pockets are a must, and the more zippered pockets, the better. The most important thing was comfortable shoes!

We learned to layer to keep warm and to keep in mind that traveling is not a fashion parade—it's okay to wear the same clothes several times. I kept the luggage light because at some point during a trip I knew I'd end up carrying my own bags.

Fourth, we learned how important it was to have a plan but remain flexible. Our plan was not precise, but it was put on paper. Only because we outlined our travel destinations were we able to visit all these countries in a compact amount of time.

There were wistful times when we toured German homes with their elegant views, or saw magnificent antique furniture, or raced around in a BMW, that I momentarily coveted these things, but not enough to give up my traveling

Fifth, we saw relationships on a global scale. Seeing the historical and geographic movement of people and cultures certainly helped us to understand more of why things are the way they are. Stephen's favorite example was the English language. Three major groups influenced English: The Anglo-Saxons from Germany, the Normans from France and the Vikings from Scandinavia. Cognates from all of these places exist today in our language.

Sixth, we realized there was much more to learn. When we toured, we heard names of leaders, sultans, presidents, and heroes who ruled for hundreds and thousands of years, and yet we knew nothing of them. The cliché rang true: *the more you know, the more you need to know.*

Seventh, would be appreciation. Learning about others taught us to see things in a new light, recognizing there were many ways to approach a situation, and enjoying people for what they were. Different doesn't have to mean better or worse. It simply means different.

Eighth, reveling in incredibly dazzling places that tingled the heart, mind, tongue, and spirit. I recall nature's beauty of azure-colored oceans turning into bright turquoise at the shores, the undulating hills of green surrounding a crystal clear lake, and the rolling hills of sand brushed with light blue. I picture man-made monuments that have withstood the march of time from the pyramids to the Eiffel Tower to Hadrian's Wall. These are little snatches of memories bring great joy to my soul.

DO IT AGAIN?

We continued to return to Iceland and the Azores even after we were assigned to Washington, D.C. I took the liberty to include them as part of my European adventure. So I guess we weren't entirely over our European travels.

I quietly laugh to think that this grand adventure began with great reluctance. I truly worried about my aging parents and our son. It took several months to banish those thoughts and swing over to the other extreme of wanting to extend our assignment to do more traveling. Now whenever my husband wants to keep me grinning, he plans a trip.

Would I do it all again? Of course! But next time with even more gusto!

Travel List

Before leaving stop the mail, and newspaper. Arrange for plant care, auto bill payments, and contact your credit card company if travelling international. Unplug electrical products like computers, and set timer lights throughout the house.

Passports
   Visas
   Immunization
Ticket
Money-secure money holder
foreign change/
   Dictionary
Suits-Shirts, Ties, Scarf
Shoes & Socks
   Quick polish touch up
Underwear – quick dry 3
   pairs+
What you wear traveling
Pajamas
Leisure clothes, 3 days +travel
   Tops
   Slacks
   Swimming suit/flipflops
   Small towel
Clothes repair
Sewing kit
   Detergent, sink plug
   Clothes line
Umbrella and/or poncho
Camera/extra batteries/
   recharger
   Lead protector for x ray
Phone and recharger
Calculator
Flashlight/extra batteries/
   headlamp

Alarm clock
Hair dryer – electric adapter
   Steamer for wrinkles
Sundry – small sizes
   Water bottle
   Medication-add extra
   days
      Prescriptions enough
   for a few days after trip
      Vitamins
      Suntan lotion/block
      Insect repellent
      100% deet
      Pepto bismol tables
      Sleeping pills
      Aspirin
      Cold remedies
      Metamucil/laxative
      Toothbrush/toothpaste
Mouthwash
Razor
Soap/Shampoo/rinse/
mousse
Lotion
Talcum power
Personal hygiene/panty
liners
Bandages/Bacitracin
   Nailpolish/remover pads
   Spot remover
   Hairpins

   Safety pins
Plastic bags
Medicine for serious sickness
Reading materials & Eye
   glasses
   Postage stamps &
   addresses
   Guide books
Inflatable pillow/Eyeshades/
   ear plugs
Snacks
   Power bars
   Water heater/cup
Gifts for hostess
Electronics, i.e., ipod, and
   rechargers
BY CAR
   Maps
   Water (12 bottles for 1
   week)
   Music/talks for listening
Food such as powerbars,
   snack tuna, boxed milk,
   spoons/bowls, cold cereal
BY BUS
   Inflatable pillow,
   eyeshades
   Earplugs
   CD for listening
SENSE OF HUMOR

Merci! Danke! Gracias! Thanks!

Writing a book is like giving birth to a baby only it takes eight times longer! Neither is a book an immaculate conception created in a sterile environment, but requires the help of many hands.

The travels would never have happened without my husband whisking me off to Europe and endorsing our grand plans. He was a great travelling companion as we struck a rhythm and helped each other through the challenging spots.

My mother kept prodding me to compile these adventures into one volume. Her bulletin board was plastered with our post-cards and served as a daily reminder that I needed to complete the task.

With his keen sense of story, Scott Hurst reviewed the entire manuscript making insightful suggestions which greatly improved the quality.

Susan Ginsberg did the lion's share of polishing the finished document using her fine editing skills.

Mari Vawn Tinney lent resources, encouragement and her skills throughout the process.

Sharon Furner's myriad of colorful sticky notes and timely suggestions enhanced the finished product.

For my editor, Jade Council, whose prompt responses kept me moving forward to completion.

Each gave in the spirit of true friendship.

And a big hug to the only armchair geographer I know--my father--who inspired me to explore the world!

The Author

When her husband, Stephen, charmed her into marrying him, Aloha Williams never guessed the adventures that awaited her as a military spouse. On their assignment to Europe, she slowly evolved from an occasional tourist into a traveling fanatic. She and her husband presently reside in Hawaii. When she isn't travelling she is a professional educator--a classroom teacher, school principal, and university professor. She calls herself an Arizona State Sun Devil, an Oklahoma Sooner and a BYU Cougar.